OUT OF OUR HEADS

Also by George Case

Silence Descends: The End of the Information Age, 2000–2500
Jimmy Page: Magus, Musician, Man: An Unauthorized Biography
Arcadia Borealis: Childhood and Youth in Northern Ontario

Out of Our Heads

ROCK 'N' ROLL BEFORE THE DRUGS WORE OFF

George Case

Backbeat Books

AN IMPRINT OF HAL LEONARD CORPORATION   •   NEW YORK

Published in 2010 by Backbeat Books
An Imprint of Hal Leonard Corporation
7777 West Bluemound Road
Milwaukee, WI 53213

Trade Book Division Editorial Offices
19 West 21st Street, New York, NY 10010

Printed in the United States of America

Book design by Mark Lerner

Library of Congress Cataloging-in-Publication Data

Case, George, 1967-
  Out of our heads : rock 'n' roll before the drugs wore off / George Case.
    p. cm.
  Includes bibliographical references.
  ISBN 978-0-87930-967-1 (pbk.)
  1. Drugs and popular music. 2. Rock musicians—Drug use. 3. Rock music—1961-1970—History and criticism. 4. Rock music—1971-1980—History and criticism. I. Title.
  ML3534.C343 2010
  781.6609'046—dc22

                    2009047657

www.backbeatbooks.com

The counterculture was less an agent of chaos than a marginal commentary, a passing attempt to propose alternatives to a waning civilization. . . . At their heart, the countercultural revolt against acquisitive selfishness— and, in particular, the hippies' unfashionable perception that we can change the world only by changing ourselves— looks in retrospect like a last gasp of the Western soul.

IAN MACDONALD, *REVOLUTION IN THE HEAD*

From within the light comes the thousand rolling thunders of the natural sound of teaching. The sound is fierce, reverberating, rumbling, stirring, like fierce mantras of intense sound. Don't fear it! Don't flee it! Don't be terrified of it! Recognize it as the exercise of your own awareness, your own perception.

THE TIBETAN BOOK OF THE DEAD

Contents

(Adam Ritchie / Getty Images)

WITH A LITTLE HELP FROM MY FRIENDS
1964-1967

This is *Beatlemania* here!

BOB DYLAN, AUGUST 28, 1964

It was almost a stereotype of clashing national sensibilities: the awkward, deferential Englishmen embarrassed by the easygoing, straightforward Americans until shown how to relax and shed some of their inhibitions. Or it summed up the difference between the guarded, sequestered lives of pop idols and the casual openness of the folk singer, the suit-and-tie quartet throwing caution to the wind at the behest of the irreverent young bohemian. Or perhaps something went the other way that night: the foursome's infectious zest for success and novelty and sensation was caught and retained by the dour protest bard, who went away seeing his own potential in a fresher, suddenly more colorful glow.

On the Beatles' first full-scale tour of North America in the summer of 1964, a meeting between the Fab Four and Bob Dylan was arranged at the Hotel Delmonico in New York City. The Beatles were by then the biggest entertainment phenomenon in the world, riding an unprecedented wave of multimedia exposure: records, radio, film, television, print, and live concerts whose overwhelming effects on teenagers had become a hard news story for bemused and concerned adults. The money was pouring in, though less of it to the Beatles themselves than many supposed. Beatle music and images were everywhere. Bob Dylan, in 1964, was the most visible of a new trend of youthful, idealistic, left-leaning or "topical" singers—an earnest and oddly unvarnished figure whose lyrics were more and more being followed and quoted by students and activists quick to distance themselves from whatever manufactured craze Hollywood, Madison Avenue, or Tin Pan Alley were currently foisting on a pliant bourgeoisie. The Beatles were spectacularly famous and nearly rich, with singles and LPs crowding the top of the sales charts around the globe, while Dylan remained primarily a cult figure in the US, journeying to headline one-nighters and hootenannies around the country.

But the performers, and ultimately their listeners, could still find common ground. They were all in their early twenties (Dylan was born in 1941; the Beatles in 1940, '42, and '43); all ambitious and independent; all capable of writing, playing, and singing their own material; all conscious of their own maturing clout within their industry. Both the Beatles and Dylan had fiercely loyal managers (Brian Epstein and Albert Grossman, respectively) who championed their charges' artistic self-determination, and both the Beatles and Bob Dylan had paid dues in hundreds of near-anonymous engagements in the preceding years. Already wary and weary of intruders but eager for contact with their peers, both parties were ready for each other.

And a party it turned out to be. The Beatles had been listening closely to Dylan's latest record, *The Freewheelin' Bob Dylan*, since its release the previous year. "The day Bob Dylan *really* turned us on was the day we heard his album," George Harrison later avowed, while Paul McCartney added, "We loved him and had done since his first album, which I'd had in

The Beatles began their first full-scale North American tour in August 1964: by the end of the month, their outlook had changed forever. *(John Dominis / Getty Images)*

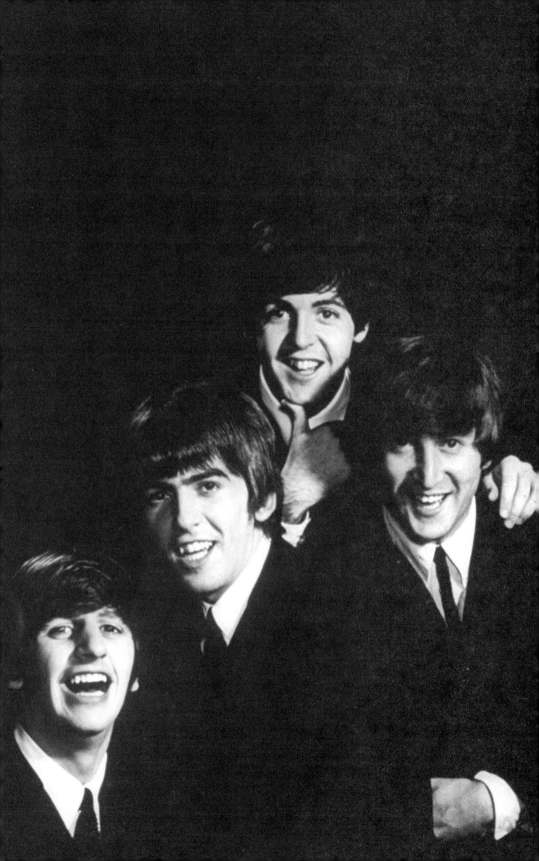

Liverpool." "He was just great, he was this young dude with great songs," said Ringo Starr. Even John Lennon, suspicious of anything he deemed "intellectual," was won over, Dylan's singular, first-person bluntness serving as an alternative to his and McCartney's hitherto "professional" composing method. "Instead of projecting myself into a situation, I would try to express what I felt about myself. . . . I think it was Dylan who helped me realize that," Lennon said. During their US jaunt, the Beatles quietly let it be known that they wanted to see Dylan in person.

The go-between was Al Aronowitz, a New Jersey–based writer and reporter who had covered Dylan, the Beatles, and earlier luminaries like Miles Davis, Frank Sinatra, Jack Kerouac, and Allen Ginsberg, for the middle-class and middlebrow readership of the *Saturday Evening Post*. Older but keen on the artistic and social possibilities evoked by the Beat movement, Aronowitz was now Dylan's leading journalistic champion: "To me, Bob was doing more to change the English language than anybody since Shakespeare." Though Aronowitz and Dylan's then-girlfriend Suze Rotolo (the pair walk arm in arm on the cover of *Freewheelin'*) were impressed with the Beatles upon their arrival in America in February 1964, Dylan was more interested in the Beatles as a rock 'n' roll phenomenon than in their music itself, which he initially thought of as "bubblegum." But he too admitted hearing something unique in the group's sound—rapturous harmonies, unexpected chord shifts, a relentless backbeat—and was at length persuaded, "kicking and screaming," to visit the Beatles.

On Friday, August 28, 1964, Dylan drove from his retreat in Woodstock, New York, with Victor Maymudes to meet Aronowitz, and the

OPPOSITE: Bob Dylan introduced the Beatles to marijuana in 1964, and the rest was history: Everybody Did Get Stoned. *(Express Newspapers / Getty Images)*

trio then took Dylan's blue Ford into Manhattan. Maymudes, also slightly Dylan's elder (he was born in 1935), was the singer's road manager, doing duty as chauffeur, travel companion, and equipment handler in the era before rock tours became the vast enterprises of the later 1960s, run by small armies of technicians, stagehands, and drivers. "When Victor and Bob and I pulled up on Park Avenue in front of the Delmonico," Aronowitz detailed, "I made sure Victor had that baggie full of stash in his pocket," although "Bob was still high on his hill, acting as if he were reluctant to do me a favor and come down and meet the Fab Four." Dylan himself had been introduced to cannabis some time before and was an occasional, though not committed, smoker. "Grass was everywhere in the clubs," he shrugged later. "It was always there in the jazz clubs, and in the folk music clubs . . . and in coffeehouses way back in Minneapolis. That's where I first came into contact with it, I'm sure."

The Delmonico, on Park Avenue at Fifty-ninth Street, was an elegant, expansive lodging besieged by hundreds or thousands of Beatlemaniacs—as all the Beatles' stops were that year—following the band's concert at the Forest Hills Tennis Stadium in Queens. Dylan, Maymudes, and Aronowitz made their way past the girls and security on the sidewalk through the lobby, full of more police and more desperate fans, until Mal Evans, the imposing escort and assistant who was part of the Beatles' inner circle, recognized Aronowitz and cheerfully ushered the guests to an elevator and up to the Beatles' floor. There they found even more cops and a waiting list of hopeful newsmen, photographers, and other visitors, including excitable New York DJ Murray "the K" Kaufman, folk acts Peter, Paul and Mary (who'd had a hit with Dylan's "Blowin' in the Wind"), and the Kingston Trio. These were all kept at bay by Derek Taylor, the Beatles' urbane and very overworked press officer. "I was in the suite next door," Taylor would recount, "running a very courtly, if tense, holding operation with a lot of extremely nice

Greenwich Villagers and suchlike who were eager to hang out with the Beatles, these rough-and-tumble exquisites from over the ocean." "They hadn't had a chance to grow up in the way most people do," noticed Harrison's future wife Pattie Boyd, "and from the moment fame hit, they had been so bombarded by fans and hangers-on, so cocooned by Brian Epstein, that they never knew whom they could trust." In a back room, their small oasis of calm and privacy, were Lennon, McCartney, Harrison, and Starr, dining with Brian Epstein and their other Liverpudlian aide, Neil Aspinall. Mal Evans brought Dylan and his friends over the threshold into the eye of the hurricane.

Some stiff, slightly stilted introductions were made by Aronowitz, and the men sat down. Epstein, always refined, charming, and gay, offered drinks, and Dylan, always eccentric, contrary, and flip, requested his staple: "Cheap wine." Epstein, apologizing that the nearest they had was champagne, ordered Mal Evans out for some Chianti, but Dylan contented himself with the whiskey and Coke that was always kept on hand in the Beatles' hotel rooms. "They couldn't go out of their room," Dylan saw. Like so many others he was struck by the imprisonment the foursome's recognition had wrought. "There used to be people surrounding them, not only in the streets, but in the corridors in the hotel. I should say it was uptight." The Beatles then suggested they share some of their Drinamyl amphetamines, or "purple hearts," but Aronowitz countered that they would prefer pot.

The Beatles blanched. They had never tried marijuana, they said, and were uncertain of its risks. (In fact they had previously encountered it in Liverpool, taking some nervous drags of someone's low-grade herb when drunk, but had gotten nothing out of it and so lost interest.) Dylan and Aronowitz had deliberately brought the weed with them on the assumption that the Englishmen were hip. They misheard and misquoted the lyrics of "I Want to Hold Your Hand" back to the group: "But what about that song of yours—'When I touch you, I get high, I get high . . .'?" John Lennon set them straight, as it were: "It's 'I can't hide, I can't hide.'" Oh. "They wanted to know how the marijuana would make them feel," recalled the journalist, "and we told them it would make them feel good." On Aronowitz's direction, Dylan began to roll a joint from the bag carried by Maymudes, but he was tipsy from drink and an inexperienced roller of what was probably just dried and broken leaves of wild cannabis, as opposed to the highly compressed and cultivated substance usually sold and smoked today. Dylan and Aronowitz warned their hosts about the telltale smell of burning pot, which might attract the attention of so many people (including police) in the adjacent rooms, so the party retreated further into a bedroom and shut the door.

Thus sheltered, Dylan lit the joint and offered it to the Beatles. John Lennon—the aggressive, impetuous founder and leader of the band—was for once cautious, and steered it toward Ringo Starr, the homely, unassuming final recruit. Ringo was his royal taster, Lennon joked. The drummer then began to take a few tentative puffs, and then a few more ("Inhale with a lot of oxygen. . . . Hold it in your lungs for as long as you can," Aronowitz told him), and then a few more. He smoked the entire joint down by himself, like the cigarettes they all drew on incessantly— what did he know? And then he started to smile. "That was the first time that I'd really smoked marijuana," Starr told it decades on. "I laughed, and I laughed, and I laughed."

With Ringo now in a fit of giggling—"The ceiling's coming down on me!"—Maymudes, better with the papers, rolled several expert joints, and before long all ten people were smoking their own. "We all had a puff and for about five minutes we went, 'This isn't doing anything,' so we kept having more," McCartney looked back. Then they were all laughing. "It was the funniest bloody dream going." "We had the biggest laugh all night—forever," remembered John Lennon. "Fantastic. We've got a lot to thank [Dylan] for." "We all got on very well and we all just talked and had a big laugh," summed up George Harrison. That was it—*laughing*. Ever afterward, the Beatles' signal to each other before a smoking session would be, "Let's have a laugh."

They were thinking, too. Derek Taylor put off the outside crush of well-wishers and door-crashers long enough to drop in on the scene. "In the Beatles' lair I was immediately aware of a very unusual atmosphere. In the middle of it, somehow epitomizing it, was the bright-eyed Dylan: very thin, dressed in black, and laughing; a mysterious fragile bird of youth. 'It's as if we're up *there*,' Paul said to me, grabbing my arm and pointing to the ceiling. 'Up there, looking down on us!'" The tortured Brian Epstein broke his veneer of decorous self-denial, pointing to himself in hysterics: "*Jew!*" A few drags later the manager was gasping, "I'm so high, I'm on the *ceiling*. . . . I'm on the *ceiling*!" McCartney had the not-uncommon pothead's experience of the Profound Revelation, grabbing Mal Evans and scrambling to dictate what had dawned on him as the meaning of life. "But of course everyone was so stoned they couldn't produce a pencil, let alone a combination of a paper and pencil. . . ." The next day he found Evans had transcribed, "There are seven levels." "And we pissed ourselves laughing," McCartney reminisced. "I mean, 'What the fuck's that? What the fuck are the seven levels?' But looking back, it's actually a pretty succinct comment; it ties in with a lot of major religions, but we didn't know that then." "It was an amazing night," Harrison said with long perspective, "and I woke up the next day thinking, 'What was that? Something happened last night.' I felt really good. That was a hell of a night." "That was a night!" affirmed Dylan to Derek Taylor in 1986. At the Delmonico, Dylan had set the others off yet again as he would grab one of the constantly ringing phones and answer that the caller had gotten through to Beatlemania. They all had.

It is certainly possible that the ensuing drug revolution in popular culture would have happened without the Beatles, Bob Dylan, or their mutual admiration and shared enjoyment of cannabis. They were hardly the only people in the United States or Europe who had tried it; the stimuli of the escalating Vietnam controversy, African-American self-assertion, and the expanding convenience of jet travel probably would have brought many into contact with illicit and exotic drugs even absent that magical August revel in Manhattan. Indeed, both music and the impulse to alter consciousness have been part of human culture since prehistoric times.

The basic components of rhythm, melody, and harmony, and the mysterious properties of certain plants ingested under certain conditions, were together and separately regarded by primitive societies as channels to supernatural or transcendent experience; in time, song and substances both became prime elements in a diverse range of spiritual traditions around the world. In later centuries, narcotic intake came to be linked with the secular religion of art. For their verses, the poets of the Romantic movement drew on the effects of laudanum (a mixture of alcohol and opium), either as intentional experiments or unwilling addiction to what was then valued as medicine. Samuel Taylor Coleridge's "Kubla Khan" (1816) was claimed by the writer to have been recalled from "a sort of reverie brought on by two grains of opium," while George Gordon (Lord Byron) and Percy Bysshe Shelley also numbered the drug among their numerous other appetites.

In the New World, narcotics, stimulants, and hallucinogens were part of the American underground before there was ever such a thing as pop music. Cannabis grew as a literal weed in the milder climate of the southern and southwestern United States, and its industrial relative, hemp, was cultivated for the manufacture of ships' sails and other practical materials. In an era when alcohol, caffeine, and tobacco were ubiquitous in respectable society, marijuana was largely a pleasure for the poor, the rural, and especially the excluded minorities of Hispanics, Asians, and African Americans. Gradually, however, a range of anti-drug policies became codified in the laws of the US, Canada, Great Britain, and elsewhere. These were, for the most part, inconsistent, ignorant, and born of xenophobic hysteria—an objective scientific understanding of the various effects, benefits, and dangers (if any) of cannabis or opium and their derivatives was badly lacking, and law enforcement still primarily targeted vulnerable groups like blacks, Chinese, and Mexican immigrants.

The most notorious anti-drug crusader of these years was Harry Jacob Anslinger, commissioner of the Federal Bureau of Narcotics from 1930 until his retirement in 1962 (coincidentally, the year both Bob Dylan and the Beatles released their first records). His dire tract "Assassin of Youth" was purported to tell the dark truth about cannabis—"There must be constant enforcement and equally constant education against this enemy, which has a record of murder and terror running through the centuries"—but was full of misinformation and sensationalism, e.g., "In at least two dozen other or comparatively recent cases of murder or degenerate sex attacks, many of them committed by youths, marijuana proved to be a contributing cause." Anslinger did, however, unwittingly identify one of the drug's favored influences:

> Along the Mexican border and in seaport cities it had been known for some time that the musician who desired to get the "hottest" effects from his playing often turned to marijuana for aid. . . . One reason was that marijuana had a strangely exhilarating effect upon musical sensibilities (Indian hemp has long been used as a component of "singing seed" for canary birds). Another reason was that strange quality of marijuana which makes a rubber band out of time,

stretching it to unbelievable lengths. The musician who uses "reefers" finds that the musical beat seemingly comes to him quite slowly, thus allowing him to interpolate any number of improvised notes with comparative ease. While under the influence of marijuana, he does not realize that he is tapping the keys with a furious speed impossible for one in a normal state of mind; marijuana has stretched out the time of the music until a dozen notes may be crowded into the space normally occupied by one.

The good commissioner, alarmed and alarmist though he was, was right about marijuana's infiltration of the American music scene. Jazz, swing, and bebop music were integral components of popular culture in the United States and much of the Western world for almost forty years, and many of the genres' most celebrated composers, soloists, and instrumentalists—not all, but many—were regular, if discreet, devotees of "Mary Jane," "tea," or "gage," and many drifted into harder drugs; some died of them. Louis Armstrong remained a steady marijuana smoker all his adult life, despite a California arrest in 1931 that resulted in a suspended sentence, while other big names in jazz known to use or have tried cannabis included bandleaders Cab Calloway and Count Basie, vibraphonist Lionel Hampton, and drummer Gene Krupa. Armstrong never denied his taste for reefer, and as a beloved show business legend in the 1950s wrote US president Dwight Eisenhower requesting it be legalized; he was, of course, turned down. The illegality of the musicians' private inclinations gave jazz and bebop their attractive hipster auras, making the tunes and their authors seem like a secret connection to an impossibly sophisticated urban milieu: the dim basement nightclubs of Harlem or Paris, the smoky bandstands of Kansas City or Hollywood. "It makes you feel good, man," contended Louis Armstrong. "It relaxes you, makes you forget all the bad things that happen to a Negro. It makes you feel wanted, and when you're with another tea smoker it makes you feel a special kinship."

In the postwar years, an increasing public awareness of drugs arose less from show business than literature. The Beats were a disparate collection of novelists, poets, students, dropouts, and hangers-on who had come of age in the late 1940s and early 1950s. Educated, restless, and alienated from the nascent consumer drive and Cold War paranoia that characterized American society under the administrations of Truman and Eisenhower, they rejected—in their work and in their lives—the suburban martini-sipping standards of their generation and their elders in favor of a quasi-spiritual quest for the epiphany of pure, random experience. In contrast to the thousands of jazz musicians (most anonymous) who came before them, virtually *all* the Beat writers took drugs enthusiastically, and several became household names. William S. Burroughs, author of the surrealistic *Junky* and *Naked Lunch*: heroin, opium, morphine, marijuana, and the South American plant yagé. Allen Ginsberg, creator of the stream-of-consciousness epic poem *Howl*: marijuana, mescaline, codeine, cocaine, opium, amphetamines. Jack Kerouac, chronicler of his and his friends' endless roaming of the American land- and cityscape in search of themselves: marijuana, morphine, amphetamines, heroin, peyote. Kerouac's novel *On the Road* (1957) had several scenes based on his and his buddy Neal Cassady's cannabis bonds: "Victor proceeded to roll the biggest bomber anybody ever saw. He rolled (using brown-bag paper) what amounted to a tremendous Corona cigar of tea. It was huge. Dean stared at it, popeyed. Victor casually lit it and passed it around. . . . Instantly we were all high."

The Beats' United States accommodated this parallel community of outsiders, wastrels, wanderers, and petty criminals, a weirder but no less real and in some ways better nation of truly free spirits whose liberation, they made clear, had been aided through an assortment of widely available (though still illegal) mind-altering pills, powders, and herbs. From the late 1950s on, "Beatniks" were a recognizable caste of US society, propelled by the visibility of Kerouac and by Lawrence Ferlinghetti's 1957 obscenity trial for publishing Ginsberg's *Howl*—". . . angelheaded hipsters burning for the ancient heavenly connection . . . who got busted in their pubic beards returning through Laredo with a belt of marijuana for New York. . . ."

Yet, for all the influence and popularity of both jazz music and the Beats' declarations, to the average citizen drugs remained the amusement, or downfall, of decadent and marginalized social strata. As much as any other factor, public indifference to or ignorance of cannabis and the rest of the alternative pharmacopoeia was due to the size of the potential market. The largest segment of the North American population, and to a lesser extent that of Western Europe, had just begun to enter adolescence. More children were on the way, their parents survivors of the Great Depression and World War II at last prosperous and secure enough to begin families on a vast demographic scale—these millions of toddlers and youngsters were not yet ready for William S. Burroughs or Count Basie. In a few years, though, their ears and minds would be ripe for expansion, abetted by a new species of itinerant poets and musicians who had come of age in their own day. Their forum would not be the backstreet speakeasy or the lonesome highway but the neighborhood record shop, the car radio, and the contemporary family hearth of prime-time television.

Perhaps the most irreplaceable milestone represented by the Delmonico gathering on August 28, then, was its nexus of mass entertainment and underground custom. Bob Dylan and, on a much greater scale, the Beatles were media fixtures and celebrities in the pay of large multinational corporations, but they were also a new class of stars who had begun to dismiss their own stardom, seeing it as more of a happy fluke or a racket that they had wound up on the right side of, instead of a sober responsibility they had the privilege to uphold. They sought to be no one's role models. Just as the four Beatles envied Dylan's being answerable only to himself when they as individuals resented being portrayed as inseparable and indivisible, Dylan was intrigued by the Beatles' amusement at their exalted status, their appreciation of Beatlemania as a ridiculous, fantastic shared joke no one but themselves could understand. "They were so easy to accept, so solid," he recounted. "They offered intimacy and companionship like no other group." Cannabis and its cousins made their intimate, companionable joke even more extraordinary. Together, through the most advanced systems of commerce and communications ever devised, Dylan and the Beatles would let the world in on the surrealism of their own inner and outer realities, and the consequences would be historic.

What drugs were already present in the pop music scene were not really thought of as "drugs" at all. The Beatles, as they indicated to Dylan in their hotel room, were regular users of amphetamines, which they had taken under various trade names since their gigs in Hamburg in 1960. A bronchodilator that opens up breathing passages in the lungs for a rejuvenating blast of oxygen, amphetamine had been developed as early as 1887 but was not widely dispensed for some fifty years. In time, countless musicians, actors, dancers, and comedians had been prescribed speed to meet the fast-paced pressures of their profession, and some, like the tragic Judy Garland, were rendered physical and emotional wrecks over years of overuse; the Beatles' hero Elvis Presley would become the most famous victim of this doctors' dope. Likewise, millions of nameless soldiers, businessmen, and housewives habitually swallowed pills of all brands for weight loss and "pep" while

convinced they were following a perfectly conventional medical therapy. "*A Hard Day's Night* I was on pills," John Lennon said of making
the Beatles' 1964 film. "That's drugs, that's bigger drugs than pot."
Keith Richards, of the Beatles' contemporaries, friends, and rivals the
Rolling Stones explained that he and his bandmates took stimulants
for the same stiff-upper-lip purposes as the aircrews of Britain's RAF
Bomber Command in World War II: "If you've got to bomb Dresden
tomorrow night you get, like, four or five bennies to make the trip
and keep yourself together.... I'm sure it was really good speed those
fuckers got as well."

As Richards suggested, many of World War II's frontline combatants
from both the Allied and Axis sides had been revved on amphetamines
as they were sent into battle; Japanese pilots were given an even stronger,
synthesized version of speed that would later be known as methamphetamine. World leaders of the postwar years, including US president John
F. Kennedy and British prime minister Anthony Eden, were also dosed
with Benzedrine and other forms of amphetamine while deciding on
crucial matters of war and peace. Qualified doctors wrote the prescriptions and made assurances that the pills or injections were helpful and
safe. Suffering from an old war wound and the adrenal disorder Addi-
son's disease, JFK was often supplied with shots and needles to give to
himself by Dr. "Miracle Max" Jacobson, a regular White House visitor
of the Camelot era. "I don't care if it's horse piss," the president said of
his drugs. "It's the only thing that works." That dutiful, patriotic men
in the service of their countries were popping powerful and addictive
drugs undermined the shame and scare tactics that would be leveled
at their peacenik children.

The insight provided to the Beatles by Bob Dylan and his entourage
was that drugs could come in organic, natural forms as well. Marijuana
and hashish originated in colorful, distant lands like India, North Africa,

or the sunny highlands of Mexico, whereas Preludin, Drinamyl, and Dexedrine were mass-produced in soulless first-world factories. "I had swallowed the pothead litany that marijuana grew out of the ground while pills were manufactured," Al Aronowitz wrote. "It didn't seem to have too many side effects like alcohol or some of the other stuff, like pills, which I pretty much kept off," McCartney described marijuana. In 1964 the sedative and anti-nausea chemical thalidomide had only been banned for a couple of years and was still a fresh horror in the public mind, after its catastrophic effects on the unborn fetuses of women around the world had been discovered. The one "manufactured" drug not spurned by the emergent counterculture of the 1960s and '70s was the one with perhaps the biggest impact of all: the female contraceptive pill, first released for sale in the US in 1960.

Inevitably, cannabis, with its earthy, healthy associations, would filter into the songs of rock 'n' roll musicians. Often overlooked in studies of the performers and their output is the fact that they were all very young people signed on to deliver hit records and lucrative concerts at an often inhuman rate. Much of what they drew on for style and subject matter was simply expedient—day-to-day sensations, anecdotes, and thoughts gathered while rushing to meet the next deadline, the next broadcast or live appearance, the next studio session, the next limousine or van or airplane ride. Thus the gradual acknowledgment or promotion of marijuana and, in turn, other drugs by acts like the Beatles and their competitors was sometimes an intentional statement but just as often—in this very early period—an accidental, hurried blurt of truth. "Being a musician means—depending on how far you go—getting to the depths of where you are at," Bob Dylan mused. "So, with music, you tend to look deeper and deeper inside yourself to find the music. That's why grass was around those clubs." "We were going through the changes," said John Lennon, "and all we were saying was, it's raining up here, or there's land or there's sun or we can see a seagull. We were just reporting what was happening to us."

From the latter half of 1964 on a rush of drug influences could be detected in a number of rock 'n' roll hits in Britain and America. Bob Dylan's impression on the Beatles was most obvious at first in the newly personal, downbeat lyrics of Lennon songs like "I'm a Loser," "I Don't Want to Spoil the Party," and "You've Got to Hide Your Love Away," but the band, who had now taken to smoking pot whenever possible, were beginning to experiment with sonic textures achieved in the recording process itself. The warm and lovely "Eight Days a Week" faded *in* rather than out, the pummeling tension of "She's a Woman" made it one of their hardest-sounding tracks to date (the lighting-up euphemism "Turn me on when I get lonely" was also sneaked into one verse), while its A-side, "I Feel Fine," was a waterfall of chiming six- and twelve-string guitar introduced with a drone of feedback—the first time an electronic "accident" had ever been heard in a pop song. Enlightened by marijuana, the Beatles were entering their peak period.

Meanwhile, other acts clambered to get on the bandwagon. California-based folkies Roger McGuinn, David Crosby, Chris Hillman, Gene Clark, and Michael Clarke had been artistically and literally electrified by *A Hard Day's Night*, dropping their acoustic guitars for bright Rickenbackers and Gretsches, calling themselves the Byrds, and cutting rock versions of Dylan's "Mr. Tambourine Man," and Pete Seeger's arrangements of "The Bells of Rhymney" and "Turn! Turn! Turn!" in early 1965. These inaugurated the ephemeral but resonant epoch of "folk rock," where erstwhile purists strove to blend the "relevance" or "poetry" of Dylan with the charm and jangle of the Beatles. For those in the know, hinted drug references jumped out from "Mr. Tambourine Man" ("Take me for a trip upon your magic swirling ship / All my senses have been stripped . . .") and, more obviously, 1966's "Eight Miles High" (". . . and when you touch down / You'll find that it's stranger than known"), while the Byrds' crystalline guitar arpeggios and vocal rounds also had an ear-opening stoner allure. "Of course it was a drug song," said Crosby of "Eight Miles High." "We were stoned when we wrote it."

Further folk rock hits followed: Simon and Garfunkel's "The Sounds of Silence," the Lovin' Spoonful's "Do You Believe in Magic?," the Turtles' Dylan cover "It Ain't Me Babe," English minstrel Donovan's "Catch the Wind," and even confections like Barry McGuire's "Eve of Destruction." None of these specifically addressed drugs, but all drew on the nascent taste for topics beyond boy-meets-girl; these songs required real listening, their boosters enthused. For some years the American music industry had been shifting its center from New York to Los Angeles, and the successes of the Byrds, Barry McGuire, and later Californian soloists and groups confirmed the Golden State as the main source for progressive US pop. Not coincidentally, the West Coast's mild climate and proximity to Mexico and Latin America also made it a hub of the national trade in inexpensive and illegal drugs.

At this point, the trade itself was facilitated by low-level transporters, distributors, and dealers, most bringing in small quantities of cannabis through US-Mexican customs stops at Tijuana, Nogales, Nuevo Laredo, and other junctions into Texas, New Mexico, Arizona, and California. Most of these were amateurs, obtaining their stash from the regions of Chihuahua, Durango, or elsewhere in Mexico, and taking it into the United States for their own use and that of a select circle of acquaintances and associates: classmates, teammates, coworkers, neighbors. Some systems of bribery and coordinated deliveries had been established in Texas among crooked businesspeople with a view to turning a profit, but the economies of scale precluded many from participating. Essentially a harvested crop like wheat or corn, marijuana was simply too bulky to be trucked or shipped in large amounts without seizure (Pacific or

Caribbean seaborne routes were traveled by pleasure craft and other small boats), and although some trafficking in gross was enabled by paid-off customs agents, the majority of grass brought into America in the mid-1960s came in portions of less than twenty kilograms.

Folk rock, whether from lush California or the British Invaders, was a passing fad, but more durable groups also found the Beatles, Bob Dylan, and marijuana to be an irresistible inspiration—and commercial threat. The Beach Boys, led by the erratic Brian Wilson, felt the chart pressure of the British Invasion and the limits of their sun-surf-and-cars thematic formulae, and following his first taste of cannabis Wilson became converted by its impact on his songwriting and arranging: "The catalyst was marijuana. . . . I felt free to explore the boundaries of my creativity, and that meant smoking pot. I thought creatively when high, in ways I'd never done before." The Beach Boys' producer and (with Mike Love) lead singer, he too first tried playing with recording effects and other production techniques to hear where the sounds might lead. The shimmering "Help Me, Rhonda" and "California Girls" (both 1965) and the following year's single "Wouldn't It Be Nice" / "God Only Knows" were his heroic bids to match the Beatles' growing studio sophistication, boasting carefully layered, multitracked harmonies, deceptive fade-ins and fade-outs, and dynamic chord shifts. He wasn't finished yet.

Back in England, still other artists were trying pot and hastening to incorporate its effects into their music. Concerts remained wild scenes of screaming kids and barely audible half-hour sets of pop or R&B numbers, but in the calm of the recording booth musicians were free to try out their latest ideas and push the technology to its limits. The Rolling Stones had moved to the head of the would-be Beatle pack, exploiting the tabloid media's appetite for a surly counterpart to the loveable mop-tops, and as their stock of blues and soul standards to cover depleted they began to compose originals based on their impressionistic views of Swinging London's whirl of sex, class, youth—and drugs. "These songs were really more from experience and then embroidered to make them more interesting," said Mick Jagger, as singer and spokesman the Stones' main point of contention for offended parents. "I think half of starting to take drugs in that early period was to kind of place yourself outside of normal society." They were already vilified as thugs and perverts and so, in contrast with the Beatles, felt less need to censor themselves. "It got to be a state of mind," Keith Richards admitted of the band's impetus. "Every eight weeks, you had to come up with a red-hot song that said it all in about two minutes, thirty seconds."

The Stones had kept going on their earliest British, European, and North American tours with copious amounts of amphetamines and alcohol, but took to the mellower buzz of marijuana in about 1965. A run of 45-rpm outrages proceeded to crackle out of transistor radios around the world: "(I Can't Get No) Satisfaction," "Get Off My Cloud," "19th Nervous Breakdown," "Paint It Black," "Have You Seen Your Mother, Baby, Standing in the Shadow?," and the insightful "Mother's Little Helper," which pointed out that parents' legitimate prescriptions were no less a psychological crutch than their sons' and daughters' illegitimate habits—"And though she's not really ill, there's a little yellow pill. . . ." The quintet's album tracks offered fans more innuendo, with gems like "Connection," "High and Dry," the lustrous "Lady Jane" (as in Mary, it was rumored), and the 1965 album *Out of Our Heads*, and the 1966 compilation *Big Hits (High Tide and Green Grass)*. Cast as bad boys almost from the beginning of their career, the Rolling Stones were getting badder.

Amphetamines—uppers, speed, black beauties, purple hearts, French blues, white crosses—were the specialty of the Who. Troubadours of the English mod subculture that rejected cannabis for the jittery edge of Drinamyl and comparable pills, the Who delivered loud, distorted, and destructive performances that were the perfect accompaniment to gatherings of energized, scooter-racing youth in the seaside resort towns of Britain in the mid-1960s. This was a status thrust upon them by their managers and a receptive media, to the consternation of guitarist and songwriter Pete Townshend, who already preferred marijuana. "I was at art college, had long hair, was smoking pot and going with girls with long red hair and all that. . . . I had to *learn* to be a mod." Their deathless single "My Generation" was taken as a musical evocation of amphetamine overdrive, illustrated by Keith Moon's manic, virtuosic drums, John Entwistle's riled bass breaks, Townshend's clamorous power chords, and Roger Daltrey's stuttering vocals. Other of the Who's early releases, like "Substitute," "Anyway Anyhow Anywhere," and "The Kids Are Alright" were a kind of electronic pop art, approaching the borders of pure noise via free-form guitar solos as Townshend flipped the switches on his guitar for a rapid flurry of on-off crackles and feedback, and the rhythm section of Moon and Entwistle surrounded themselves with a deafening arsenal of drums and amplifiers. "We were complete pill heads," Entwistle stated, and Townshend characterized the band's mental backdrop in those years: "I really thought we were gonna explode. . . . I never ate. It was all dope, dope, dope, and horrible vibes of aggression and bitterness." Wired in the literal and figurative senses, the Who were rock 'n' roll as a clinical study of stimulants and decibels.

By 1966, drug imagery, however coy or coded, was beginning to penetrate the highest reaches of the hit parade. Apart from big-name acts whose personal and aesthetic development was affected by the carnival of money, sex, and intoxicants in which they found themselves, even lesser rockers could exploit the new licentiousness with their (or their managers' or songwriters') own subtle insinuations. A short-lived

Texas act released *The Psychedelic Sounds of the 13th Floor Elevators* that year, and the Association's "Along Comes Mary" (Jane, again?), the Outsiders' "Time Won't Let Me," the Mindbenders' "Groovy Kind of Love," the Count Five's proto-punk "Psychotic Reaction," the Troggs' "Wild Thing," and the Electric Prunes' "I Had Too Much to Dream (Last Night)" all put the language, or at least the dizzy, disoriented *mood* of drug-taking into the Top 40.

More resilient or accessible units also began to capitalize on the incipient spirit. The Mamas and the Papas, led by industry vet and devout libertine John Phillips, had a string of superbly crafted pop tunes like "California Dreamin'" and "Monday, Monday," whose soaring male and female harmonies and indelible hooks described an idyllic, euphoric consciousness that seemed to originate in the gauzy hideaways of Los Angeles's Laurel Canyon. "I volunteered my body as a human test tube for anything I could get my hands on," Phillips owned up. "Mescaline, Black Beauties to keep going, reds to come down, hash and grass for any occasion." In 1967, Phillips also wrote Scott McKenzie's "San Francisco (Be Sure to Wear Some Flowers in Your Hair)," a huge international hit that again seemed to enshrine the ideals of peace, brotherhood, youth— and, by extension, drugs—in mass-marketed entertainment.

Over in Swinging London, the Yardbirds were going beyond their faithful electric blues tributes and pop departures like "For Your Love" and "Heart Full of Soul" to showcase Jeff Beck's squalling guitar heroics in the modest hits "Shapes of Things" and "Over Under Sideways Down," and (with new addition Jimmy Page) free-form misses "Happenings Ten Years Time Ago" and "Psycho Daisies." British Invaders and hard livers the Animals also scored in '66 with "Don't Bring Me Down," as did Donovan with "Mellow Yellow" and "Sunshine Superman." Without explicitly championing anything illegal, there was a definite subversion in all these, whether from flashes in the pan or going concerns: the ecstatic voices, the buzzing guitars, the pulsations of echo, the drone of distortion, and even words or phrases like "13th Floor Elevators," "Mindbenders," "Electric Prunes," "groovy," "psycho," "psychotic," "mellow," "sunshine," "shapes," and "bring me down." At high school dances and in suburban basements around the world, teenagers nudged each other and studied the audio tea leaves for transgression, spreading stories that marijuana grew wild on the roadside in California and that "Mellow Yellow" was really about the hallucinogenic properties of smoked banana skins. Upstairs and outside, their mothers and fathers wondered, what were these longhairs going to sing about next?

LSD. One night over the winter of 1964–65, John Lennon and George Harrison with their respective partners Cynthia and Pattie had dinner at the home of a fashionable London dentist named John Riley. (Other accounts name a Michael Hollingshead as the host.) The Beatles had then reached the elite ranks not just of the music business but of cosmopolitan wealth and glamour, and frequently found themselves approached by sophisticates from other professions to whom pop stars were both trinket and plaything. In what must be seen today as an act of criminal stupidity, Riley slipped the drug into his guests' drinks and said, "I advise you not to leave." "He didn't know what it was," Lennon looked back with justified scorn. "It's all the thing with that sort of . . . middle-class London swingers, or whatever. . . . [T]hey didn't know it was different from pot or pills." The two Beatle couples began to feel the effects and, confused and frightened, left the party. "All the way the car felt smaller and smaller," Pattie Boyd-Harrison related. They managed to drive to their familiar Ad Lib discotheque—"We thought, when we went to the club, it was on fire," said Lennon—and then, after stopping to romp in a field late at night, back to Harrison's residence in Esher. "John and I weren't capable of getting back [home] from there," remembered Cynthia Lennon, "so the four of us sat up for the rest of the night as the walls moved, the plants talked, other people looked like ghouls, and time stood still."

Lysergic acid diethylamide had been developed in Switzerland in the late 1930s and early '40s by chemists Arthur Stoll and Albert Hofmann, in an attempt to synthesize ergot, a fungus infecting grain and grain products and whose beneficial and harmful qualities in human use had been identified for centuries. At work in his laboratory in 1943, Hofmann accidentally absorbed some of the chemical in liquid form and soon experienced deeply mind-altering waves of thought and sensation: "Space and time became more and more disorganized," he documented. "I had the impression of being unable to move from the spot, although my assistants told me later that we had cycled at a good pace. . . . [V]ertigo, visual disturbances—the faces of those around me appeared as grotesque, colored masks. . . . Occasionally I felt I was outside my body. I thought I had died." Originally designated LSD-25 (it being the twenty-fifth formula based around the ergot alkaloids) and at first confined to the sterile practices of psychiatry in the belief that it could be used to understand or treat schizophrenia, by the 1950s LSD began to trickle into more adventurous circles of doctors, intellectuals, and even celebrities like actor Cary Grant and publishing mogul Henry Luce. Government bodies such as the Central Intelligence Agency of the United States administered the drug in researching its potential as a sort of truth serum that might break down the resistance of spies or other enemies of the state. Only in 1966 was LSD made illegal, as officials realized it was being sold and taken outside of the regulated settings of hospitals or clinics; it was now found in posh dining rooms in Belgravia and on the streets of San Francisco. By then the psychiatric establishment had decided it was no longer helpful in mental therapy. "Because of their profound effects, hallucinogens should be restricted to research use exclusively in a hospital setting," stated the *American*

Journal of Psychiatry in 1962. "In our opinion, their use at this time for any other purpose or in any other setting is dangerous." But the genie was already well out of the bottle.

As with marijuana, LSD—or just plain "acid," as it would come to be known—may well have taken hold as a recreational drug among millions of people without a perceived linkage to the Beatles or even rock music. The Beat writers Allen Ginsberg and Ken Kesey had already investigated it and saw it as a way to bring mysticism to the masses, and earlier English writer Aldous Huxley (author of the dystopian classic *Brave New World*) had tried the naturally occurring mescaline, peyote, and psilocybin, as well as LSD, to produce inner visions he elegantly described in his books *The Doors of Perception* and *Heaven and Hell.* Huxley discussed the drugs with psychiatrist Humphrey Osmond, who later coined the word *psychedelic* to categorize LSD and users' reactions to it. But Huxley was not overwhelmed by his psychedelic impressions of music: "I listened with pleasure but experienced nothing comparable to my seen apocalypses of flowers or flannel. Would a naturally gifted musician *hear* the revelations which, for me, had been exclusively visual?"

As also with cannabis, the Beatles and rock music were fixtures of popular culture whose place in the hearts and minds of their audience was immense; any of their or their genre's subjects would fast be transmitted to an entire generation in its own lingua franca of 45s, LPs, TV, and AM radio. The previous generation of deliberate mind-expanders was mostly made up of authors and intellectuals, whose views were shaped by an elitist sense of entitlement, good taste, and moral duty. "[D]o we see respectable psychologists, philosophers, and clergymen boldly descending into those odd and sometimes malodorous wells, at the bottom of which poor Truth is so often condemned to sit? . . . How many philosophers, how many theologians, how many professional educators have had the curiosity to open this Door in the Wall?" asked Aldous Huxley. It never occurred to him that twenty-four-year-old singing sensations might open it instead. "The only thing where it's happening is on radio and records, that's where people hang out," Bob Dylan challenged in 1965. "Music is the only thing that's in tune with what's happening." Nothing a Huxley or Kesey might communicate would have the same instant, electric popularity.

Leaping ahead yet again, the Beatles followed up their uncertain pair of albums *Beatles for Sale* and *Help!* with *Rubber Soul* (1965) and *Revolver* (1966). They had been hilariously, helplessly stoned for the madness of global Beatlemania. Richard Lester, director of the *Help!* movie, looked and smelled the other way while the four stars laughed their way through the photography: "They were high all the time we were shooting. But there was no harm in it then. It was a happy high." "We showed up a bit stoned, smiled a lot, and hoped we'd get through it," Paul McCartney described their acting ability. "We giggled a lot." Though Lennon's claim that they had smoked a reefer in Buckingham Palace before their investiture as Members of the British Empire in October 1965 was later denied, away from the prying eyes of Fleet Street the lads from Liverpool were often buzzed, and for Ringo Starr the joints shared in the Beatles' sanctuaries were the best part of the adventure: "There were good nights and bad nights on the tours, but they were really all the same. The only fun part was the hotels in the evening, smoking pot and that."

During these months the Beatles released the singles "Ticket to Ride," "Day Tripper" / "We Can Work It Out," "Nowhere Man," and "Paperback Writer" / "Rain." "So *Rubber Soul* was the pot album, and *Revolver* was acid," John Lennon distinguished. These records marked the authentic beginning of the psychedelic era. Now their sounds were replete with sitars, strings, sound effects, overdriven amplifiers, jacked-up cymbal, snare, and bass drum punch, and, in "Rain," the first instance of backward vocals ever heard in a pop song by a leading act. This was the result of another accident, Lennon said: "I got home from the studio and I was stoned out of my mind on marijuana and, as I usually do, I listened to what I'd recorded that day. Somehow I got [the tape] on backwards and I sat there, transfixed, with the earphones on, with a big hash joint."

Rubber Soul, as Lennon intimated, was the Beatles album most influenced by cannabis. Lyrically they had moved on from excited songs of juvenile love to adult meditations on independence, estrangement, and brotherhood, like "Think for Yourself," "I'm Looking Through You," and "The Word." "Drive My Car" was a witty, bluesy puncturing of dolly bird vanity, "Norwegian Wood" a novelistic admission of infidelity, "In My Life" both a memoir of home and a farewell to it, and even "Girl" a muted criticism of Christian piety, where the singers' inhalation sounded like a long, relaxed draw on a joint. The record sleeve's gently elongated lettering and photograph—selected by the group when the projection screen on which a slide sample was shown tilted over—captured the Beatles' gently elongated viewpoints.

Revolver was a veritable stash box of drug music and drug lyrics. The soul pastiche "Got to Get You Into My Life" conveyed Paul McCartney's awakening to the bliss of cannabis ("I was alone, I took a ride, I didn't know what I would find there"), "I'm Only Sleeping" featured more reversed tracks (of George Harrison's guitar, this time), and the novelty "Yellow Submarine" encapsulated the childlike, communal surrealism of an LSD trip. "Doctor Robert" was a sly exposé of New York's Doctor Charles Roberts, one of the numerous certified physicians in Britain and America who had profitable sidelines doling out amphetamines and other recreational drugs to a wealthy and famous clientele—while the Beatles did not get their own supplies from this or any other "Doctor

Feelgood," there had always been licensed enablers happy to bend the rules of their profession for certain preferred patients. ("Doctor Robert" has alternately been revealed as another New York pill peddler, Dr. Robert Freymann.) "She Said She Said," a metallic spiral of guitar and drums as aggressive as anything by the Who or the Yardbirds, was John Lennon's veiled remembrance of his second acid experience, this one an intentional trip taken in Los Angeles after the Beatles' second North American tour in the summer of 1965. Surrounded by hordes of female Beatlemaniacs, the group and friends were holed up in a Benedict Canyon retreat on Blue Jay Way with a few guests including Byrds David Crosby and Roger McGuinn, as they tripped out and a heavily dosed Ringo Starr shot pool with the cue backwards. "Wrong end? So what fuckin' difference does it make?" "It was a fabulous day," said the drummer. "The night wasn't so great, because it felt like it was never going to wear off. Twelve hours later and it was, 'Give us a break now, Lord.'" Actor Peter Fonda's claim that he had once been declared medically dead hit Lennon at exactly the wrong lysergic moment, and thus "I know what it's like to be dead . . . And you're making me feel like I've never been born" established the anxious, chaotic mental mood of "She Said She Said." It was almost the most surprising piece the Beatles had yet produced. Almost.

Revolver closed with the extraordinary "Tomorrow Never Knows," another Lennon song inspired by LSD, meant to portray in sound and words the cosmic transport felt by the musician while on acid: the "trip" viscerally rendered in its terrifying, exhilarating actuality. It is less a finished sequence of verses and chorus as a one-chord chant based on lines from the sacred Buddhist text *The Tibetan Book of the Dead*, which had gained currency with the growing Western interest in the metaphysical traditions of east Asia and the Asian subcontinent. George Harrison had already investigated Indian meters and sonorities

on *Revolver*—his "Love You To" and "I Want to Tell You" were each
closer to an authentic raga in mood and instrumentation, and his sitar
playing had already highlighted *Rubber Soul*'s "Norwegian Wood"—but
"Tomorrow Never Knows" considered the Buddhist concepts of self,
thought, spirit, and death through a towering electronic firestorm. Here
all four Beatles and producer George Martin contributed random snippets of backwards tapes they had recorded and overlaid them sped up
and repeatedly cycled over Lennon's singing, while Ringo Starr's repeti-
tive drum pattern (not a tape loop but a human metronome) was itself
run through a wash of echo and compression. Owing to the limitations
of the recording equipment then extant, the effects that spun through
and around "Tomorrow Never Knows" were dubbed on in real time,
meaning the physical manipulation of tape and tape heads in the studio
amounted to a unique and unrepeatable "solo."

The fundamental underlay of Lennon's voice and guitar tone on
"Tomorrow Never Knows" (and the religious and psychological depths
of his message) notwithstanding, it is this improvised, exploratory uti-
lization of technology and craftsmanship that distinguishes the music
of the 1960s and 1970s from that of later years. "I mean, we weren't all
stoned making *Rubber Soul* because in those days we couldn't work on
pot," Lennon noted. "We never *recorded* under acid, or anything like
that." "When we did take too many substances," Starr reiterated, "the
music was shit, absolute shit. . . . It was good to take it the day before—
then you'd have that creative memory—but you couldn't function while
under the influence." The Beatles and others have all commented on
how the sonic vistas they sought during this time were arrived at by
trial and error, with the sympathetic ears of producers like Martin and
willing engineering staffs. "We'd spend hours and hours trying to invent
sounds," George Harrison explained in 1987. "Nowadays it's pretty easy
because there's so many sounds available just by hitting a button—in

fact it's too easy, but it's because of some of those records in the six-ties that they've invented machinery where you just switch on and instantly get an effect which we spent years trying to discover." Between celestial concepts revealed through drugs and old-fashioned tinkering with microphones, wires, and reels, psychedelic music had irrevocably been launched. With "Tomorrow Never Knows" as its climactic track, *Revolver* is widely heard now as the Beatles' finest album.

But while mind-expanding substances had spurred players to toy with instruments and accessories in pursuit of unusual sonic forms, for listeners this could suggest only one component of cannabis or hallucinogenic stimulation. Tripping or being high was not only about responding to physical impressions like pictures or tastes or music, but an initiation into a completely different mode of thinking. As more and more of the audience made second- or firsthand acquaintance with marijuana or LSD, pop records were analyzed for hidden gems of wisdom and reflection beyond merely a puzzling noise or a futuristic guitar tone. This was where Bob Dylan's influence was most acute.

Dylan had taken to the plugged-in arrangements of the Beatles and other British Invaders in his own idiosyncratic way. His *Another Side of Bob Dylan* (1964) retained the acoustic tones of his first discs, but his lyrics were moving away from sociopolitical commentary on injustice or war or poverty toward a more introspective—some said obscure—intricacy. *Bringing It All Back Home* and *Highway 61 Revisited* (both 1965) added electric backing musicians to the mix, among them keyboardist Al Kooper and guitarist Mike Bloomfield, as his songs now delved deeper into private musings and cryptic autobiographical vignettes. His perfor-mance at the Newport Jazz Festival in July of '65, where angry folk fans booed him for taking the stage with the hard-rocking Paul Butterfield Blues Band, became a watershed event in pop history, as mythic a turning point in rock 'n' roll as the Battle of Britain in World War II.

Through all this, Dylan remained detached from the widening drug scene—or so he claimed. "Psychedelics never influenced me," he said. "When psychedelics happened, everything became irrelevant. Because that had nothing to do with making music or writing poems or trying to really find yourself in that day and age." In D. A. Pennebaker's pioneering 1965 documentary *Don't Look Back*, Dylan is quite plainly fired on amphetamines and alcohol more than anything else, but the presence of Allen Ginsberg in the film implies further off-camera indulgence and a limousine conversation with John Lennon edited from the final cut shows Dylan barely coherent—drunk, mumbling, and twenty-four years old. Eventually Dylan declared, "I never got hooked on any drug," although he would also concede, "Who knows what people stick in your drinks or what kind of cigarettes you're smokin'?" Fellow folkie Phil Ochs explicated Dylan as "LSD on stage . . . Dylan is LSD set to music." It was not so much as a user that Dylan's association with drugs became entrenched, but as an inscrutable philosopher to whom users themselves would turn for knowledge, challenge, and enigma.

Between 1964 and 1966, Dylan's music—or, more precisely, the torrential suites of wordplay he set to music—provided intellectual fodder for millions of stoned young people everywhere. The Beatles were playing with your ears, but Dylan played with your mind. Long, rambling confessionals like "Desolation Row," "It's Alright, Ma (I'm Only Bleeding)," "Subterranean Homesick Blues," and "Stuck Inside of Mobile with the Memphis Blues Again" were bottomless sources of insinuation, image, and story line, while the accusatory tirades "Like a Rolling Stone," "Ballad of a Thin Man," "Maggie's Farm," "Positively Fourth Street," and "Just Like a Woman" ("with her fog, her amphetamines, and her pearls") turned a withering eye back on those daring or foolhardy enough to attempt comprehension or, worse, comradeship. Who was Dylan singing to? What did he mean? His public persona was hardly less impenetrable, as he freely gave interviewers contradictory opinions, made up stories of his own life and background, and raised more questions with every answer: "A mistake is to commit a misunderstanding. There could be no such thing, anyway, as this action. Either people understand or they pretend to understand—or else they really don't understand. What you're speaking of here is doing wrong things for selfish reasons. . . ."

Dylan denied any intent to mislead. "Reporters would shoot questions at me and I would tell them repeatedly that I was not a spokesman for anything or anybody and that I was only a musician. They'd look into my eyes as if to find some evidence of bourbon and handfuls of amphetamines." But for a well-educated, information-saturated generation whose mental landscapes were being more broadened still through drugs, Dylan's dazzling linguistic trickery was rightly heard as mind-blowing. He was the master of the head trip. Accompanied by crisp blues-rock performances from talents like Kooper, Bloomfield, and later foundations of the Band Robbie Robertson, Rick Danko, Garth Hudson, and Richard Manuel, and delivered in his own caustic phrasing, Dylan's albums were received as from on high. The performances were flowing out in furies of energy, much of it undoubtedly artificial: the protean "Like a Rolling Stone" was captured in a single take Dylan could never nail before or since. "That was back in the days when we used to do—oh, man, six, eight, ten tunes a session," Dylan remembered. "We used to just go in and come out the next day." Did drugs influence his music directly? "No, not the writing of them, but it did keep me up there to pump 'em out. . . . I was going at a tremendous speed at the time of my *Blonde on Blonde* album. I was going at a *tremendous* speed."

Dylan's most obviously drug-related song is also one of the most obviously drug-promoting statements in all of rock 'n' roll. "Rainy Day Women #12 & 35," from *Blonde on Blonde* (1966), employs one of his simpler literary devices, wherein he puns on the verb for "to be pelted with rocks" with its double meaning when used as an adjective: "They'll stone you when you're trying to go home / And they'll stone you when you're there all alone / But I would not feel so all alone / Everybody must get stoned!"

A rollicking, good-time party song based on blues changes that has since become a cannabis anthem, "Rainy Day Women" is usually identified by its imperative chorus rather than its bizarre numeric title, the words of which are heard nowhere in the lyrics themselves. (In a freaky coincidence, 12 multiplied by 35 equals 420, a latter-day stoner code derived from a prearranged toke time of 4:20 P.M.) By turning the piece into a joke with a complete setup and punch line, and reeling with barrelhouse piano, horns, and background hilarity, Dylan characterized marijuana in the benign, giggle-inducing fashion it warranted—the same funny and enjoyable way he had with the Beatles at the Delmonico Hotel in 1964. Whereas the Beatles would wink at each other to "have a laugh," Dylan, with "Rainy Day Women," let everyone get the humor. "It's not a 'drug song,'" Dylan told interviewers in his deader-than-deadpan way. "I never have and never will write a 'drug song.'" Then what was it *really* about? they pried. "Cripples and Orientals and the world in which they live." Right. "Rainy Day Women #12 & 35" was a Top Ten hit in 1966, and from countless radios and stereos in dorm rooms and rec rooms came the warning that the listeners would all soon be pelted with rocks.

Dorm rooms and rec rooms were where the drug movement was truly being defined. Long-haired musicians were communicating their own rearranged sensibilities, but there were no more than fifty or a hundred of them to be heard at any time; it was anonymous persons in their teens and early twenties who formed the largest cohort of the populations in North America and Europe. These were not only the rock market but the primary drug market. The sheer volume of young people choosing to try cannabis, LSD, and other drugs, either as curious dabblers or eager converts, represented the first wave of a genuine psychedelic society. All of these boys, girls, women, and men were, of course, criminals.

The moral or spiritual dimensions of drug taking were consistently overshadowed by the simple fact that users were breaking the law. Although penalties varied from country to country (and within jurisdictions), cannabis and, after 1966, LSD were contraband, and anyone caught with them faced jail time. Merely to pass a joint between friends constituted "trafficking," as much as smuggling a truckload or boatload of Mexican grass over the border. Suddenly, an entire category of offenders arose out of otherwise law-abiding high school and university students, entry-level employees, and even draftees into the American military: the mainstream *Life* magazine was to call this "the greatest mass flouting of the law since Prohibition." When popular music advised fans that Tomorrow Never Knows, that We've Got a Groovy Kind of Love, or scolded others to Get Off My Cloud because this was My Generation, or invited them to get Eight Miles High with California Girls while California Dreamin', or baffled them with travelogues of Desolation Row as visited by Rainy Day Women, it was participating in a collective crime—and, it was starting to be argued, encouraging it.

For the baby boomers, drugs were a different order of taboo than underage drinking or premarital sex. Under no circumstances were pot and acid sanctioned by church or state; if trying them was a rite of passage, it was probably not one in which one's elders had ever participated. Even long-haired males and unmarried cohabitation, though almost as disturbing to parents and grandparents, were not officially proscribed by law. It was these combined violations of religious, social, and criminal codes that most aroused the ire of what was soon being sneered at as "the Establishment." Cannabis and LSD also stirred a fear in middle-aged legislators, teachers, police, and mothers and fathers, few of whom had tried them for themselves, and who could not comprehend how their children were (or were not) being changed after a toke or a trip. In many families during the 1960s, generational divisions over sex, drugs, and rock 'n' roll were gaps that would never be bridged.

Until the mid-1960s the illegality of marijuana was seen as a marginal issue plaguing slums, ghettoes, and jazz venues. The allure of cocaine and heroin was unfathomable to the man and woman on the street, and something like lysergic acid diethylamide was scarcely conceivable to generations accustomed to the liquor cabinet, the corner bar, the Zippo, and the tobacco shop. By way of introduction, the Beat school had presented vicarious kicks to inquisitive readers and bebop buffs had lamented the junk tragedies of Bird or Lady Day, but with the ascendancy of Bob Dylan and the Beatles and the performers trailing in their wake, the drug "menace" had entered the white middle classes, and rock music evolved from mass, crass entertainment into the clarion call of a potential revolution. It signaled a looming clash between the young and the old, the dove and the hawk, the radical and the traditional, and, increasingly, between the stoned and the straight.

BREAK ON THROUGH
1967–1970

The hippy-marijuana culture expanded at a remarkable and almost exponential rate until it was no longer an American phenomenon. Yet there was one strand that held all the others together and brought millions into the hippy and therefore marijuana sphere. It was rock music.

MARTIN BOOTH, *CANNABIS: A HISTORY*

How exactly do psychotropic drugs affect perception? Why did the sounds of rock 'n' roll become inextricably tied to their use? What does the drugged listener hear or feel that the "normal" audience does not?

Lysergic acid diethylamide slows or stops the function of the brain's serotonin, a neurotransmitter that helps the mind sort and classify the internal or external impulses it is taking in at any one time. By preventing the action of serotonin, LSD loosens the mental gates that maintain order within the cerebral cortex; psilocybin operates in somewhat the same manner, albeit through organic means. Marijuana's active chemical is tetrahydrocannabinol (THC), which has some of the same effects, as well as its own unique actions on receptors in the brain and even a few that parallel the chemical effects of alcohol. Mescaline, from the peyote cactus, contains the operative chemical norepinephrine, which corresponds to stimulants produced within the human body during stress. Mood-altering drugs such as these work not by introducing new elements to the brain but by retarding or increasing the flow of the organ's own compounds that ordinarily kick in as ordinary reactions to outside conditions, "making" the feelings of fear, pain, pleasure, inhibition, and so on.

The principal reaction of those under the influence of cannabis, mescaline, psilocybin, or LSD is one of increased sensitivity to aural and visual stimuli. This does not mean vision or hearing becomes objectively *sharper*; high people who need eyeglasses remain nearsighted and the deaf are no less handicapped. But for the stoned or the tripping, what images or noises are registered become richer in detail and significance. Input through eyes and ears—as well as via tactile and olfactory impressions—is magnified to a point where everyday objects and occurrences are rendered intriguing, amusing, confounding, or overwhelming. Often, the mundane becomes exquisite, and other times the ordinary is transformed into the horrific. "To fathom hell or soar angelic," wrote the lysergic innovator Humphrey Osmond, "just take a pinch of psychedelic."

Music, already a special arrangement of sound and (when sung) language designed to produce emotional results, is to the altered mind a revelation. Scientists have long studied the role music has played in the evolution of ordinary human consciousness, suggesting that a neurological response to tones, beats, repetition, and harmony is no less built into the brain than the capacity for hearing and speaking words. People can "imagine" music they are not hearing (thus catchy songs "stay in the head"), and the almost involuntary physical actions of swaying or tapping feet to rhythms are universal. Mental disorders or brain injuries can change the victim's engagement with music, in ways ranging from a sudden interest or ability where none previously existed to a despairing indifference to or dislike for any tonal variety. So-called idiot savants demonstrate a surprising fluency at the piano or other instrument—repeating complex classical pieces note for note after a single listen—while remaining severely disadvantaged in normal functions. Blindness sometimes seems to have been compensated with a surplus of musical ability, noted in the careers of Stevie Wonder, Ray Charles, Jose Feliciano, Doc Watson, Jeff Healey, and bluesmen like Blind Lemon Jefferson, Blind Willie McTell, and Blind Willie Johnson. When the music itself is altered to correspond to the new sensitivities of a chemically enhanced brain, its results can be immeasurable.

By the mid-1960s, rock 'n' roll had evolved into an art form more sophisticated than its forebears of ten years past could ever have anticipated. While it retained the key elements of a strong beat, an instrumental triumvirate of voice, guitar, and drums, and the bedrock foundation of blues and folk structures, the Beatles had broken the music out of its prescribed three-chord progressions, and Bob Dylan had liberated it from its lyrical clichés. The songs and stage acts of Elvis Presley or Little Richard had carried primitive sexual or racial overtones exciting to fans and disturbing to detractors, but the Rolling Stones, Donovan, the Byrds, and, for that matter, the 13th Floor Elevators implied deeper levels of revolt. Their suggested, and soon enough overt, advocacy of drugs was their most blatant provocation.

Because the musicians themselves were largely unschooled, very young, and contractually obligated to churn out material in a business that had a high rate of attrition and turnover, this advocacy was really just a kind of candor. They were taking drugs and for the most part enjoying them—here was an audio approximation of what they did and heard. By coincidence, the technological advances in sound reproduction and recording that had been made up to that time (advances

devised by engineers and designers who were *not* drug takers) lent
themselves to augmenting the amphetamine, acid, or marijuana reception of music. Multitrack tape decks, for example, allowed players
to perfect and artificially duplicate a single vocal or instrumental performance while leaving finished parts alone: this was a specialty of the
Beach Boys' Brian Wilson, who, inspired by the early '60s productions
of Phil Spector, had taken to endlessly embellishing his songs over fundamental rhythmic bases (which were often provided not by the other
group members but Los Angeles studio pros). "My real intention was to
redraw the entire map of pop music," Wilson said. Stereo gave a volume
and fullness to tunes that were intended to be played live and loud with
widely spaced electronic speakers, and reverb or echo brought a depth
and presence to soloists or small combos that could hitherto only have
been achieved with big bands or orchestras. Without such technology,
the drug visions of "Eight Miles High," "Like a Rolling Stone," "Rain,"
"19th Nervous Breakdown," and "God Only Knows" might have sounded
merely flimsy—with them, they had a powerful auditory impact.

The most vivid shapers of cannabis- or acid-based compositions
were the outboard signal-altering devices invented for electric guitar-
ists. The onomatopoetic wah-wah pedal and the distortion, or "fuzz,"
box translated single notes into nuanced densities of noise. Just as
marijuana smokers found an intensity of meaning in the clink of an
ashtray or the sibilance of their own inhalation, so the wah-wah and
the fuzz took regular guitar tones to unimagined heights of magnitude.
Distortion, whether made through a foot pedal or directly through an
overheated tube amplifier, blurred the conventional bright twang of
six-strings into a thick, snarling darkness; soon after its debut its most
audible deployments were on the Beatles' "Day Tripper" and "Paperback Writer" and the indelible intro to the Rolling Stones' "Satisfaction," arguably the most identifiable five notes in popular music. The

wah-wah let the player rapidly adjust from treble to bass in the same chord or lick, giving progressions or solos a speechlike quality; it first came to prominence at the feet of ex-Yardbird Eric Clapton when he formed Cream with drummer Ginger Baker and bassist Jack Bruce in 1966 ("Acid was conducive to exploring music," Clapton reported). The Leslie cabinet, a speaker that physically revolved to generate a bubbly, churning effect when recorded, was also heard on numerous Beatles vocal and guitar lines, while compression electronically dampened drum tracks to give them a tauter, more physical attack. Here too, effects that might have been only taken as jokes or science-fiction novelties to an older generation acquired an extra character for their toking and tripping children.

For some, psychedelia's preoccupation with modified noises for their own sake, or the muddy streams of consciousness transcribed by Dylan and his imitators, were precisely how rock 'n' roll lost its earlier verve. Gone was the economy of technique that had made the great two-minute hits of, say, Roy Orbison or Chuck Berry; gone were the gorgeous melodicism of the Beatles' "She Loves You" or the political bite of Dylan's "Masters of War." After drugs were introduced into the pop music milieu, it is said, pretension and self-indulgence followed, in the form of purposefully obscure lyrics barely intelligible even to the songwriter, and long instrumental breaks that absorbed the musicians but alienated the listeners—or those brave (or clearheaded) enough to admit their boredom. Commentator Thomas Frank has written that "the relics of the counterculture reek of affectation and phoniness, the leisure dreams of white suburban children," while rock critic Lester Bangs contrasted the goofy innocence of the pre-pot British Invaders with their later incarnations: "In the fatuity of their enthusiasm lay their very charm. . . . 'Good Day Sunshine' was wonderful at the time but responsible for 'Feelin' Groovy' and a whole generation of ersatz good vibey airhead salutations (well, okay, the Lovin' Spoonful hadda share some blame)." Author and musician Mike Edison has gone so far as to say that "the day Bob Dylan got [the Beatles] stoned for the first time was one of the blackest days in history."

Yet it is difficult to imagine how rock 'n' roll could not have been changed by the climate of sexual and chemical permissiveness that swept through the 1960s and '70s. For all the dead ends and missteps taken by popular musicians in these decades, they were reflecting the community that enveloped them with an accuracy and an immediacy that would never be achieved again. The commercialism of the music derived not only from the records themselves but from the audience's identification with the artists and vice versa, the feeling that they were living parallel lives and making simultaneous forays into forbidden realms of thought and action. If the results were sometimes awkward, embarrassing, or quickly dated—or incriminating—that was the price to be paid. Had rock never undergone a psychedelic phase, it would never have grown successful enough to merit an anti-drug, anti-pretension, anti-indulgence backlash.

Indeed, in 1967 rock 'n' roll hits and twenty-something Americans and Britons may have celebrated psychedelics obliquely, but at the same time, a widely heard clique of middle-aged academics and writers was touting them as nothing less than a panacea for a society that had lost its moral and political bearings. The foremost of these was Timothy Leary. Like Humphrey Osmond an accredited medical man, Leary had been fired from Harvard University in 1963 for his personal and haphazard research into psilocybin ("magic mushrooms"), in the course of which he shared the drug with Allen Ginsberg as well as painter Willem de Kooning, jazz pianist Thelonius Monk, and poet Robert Lowell, among

OPPOSITE: The Beatles in 1967, the year they released *Sgt. Pepper* and launched the psychedelic era. *(MGM / Photofest)*

other notables. After this, he embarked on his own crusade to spread the word of psilocybin's and, in turn, LSD's benefits for mankind. "It seemed clear," wrote counterculture historian Theodore Roszak, "that the research laboratories of Western society . . . had presented the world with a substitute for the age-old spiritual disciplines of the East. Instead of a lifetime of structured contemplation, a few drops of homebrewed acid on a vitamin pill would do the trick." Leary's immortal mantra "Tune in, turn on, and drop out" called for a wave of individual psychic liberation across national and generational lines that would amount to nothing less than a worldwide spiritual awakening: "The instruments of systematic religion are chemicals," he was to write. "Drugs are the religion of the twenty-first century."

Leary, with another ex-Harvard researcher, Richard Alpert, plus Ginsberg and acid-versed novelist Ken Kesey, became the leading non-musical spokesmen for LSD consciousness, lending a façade of scholarly or mainstream credibility to the trend for psychedelic experimentation. Mind-expanding drugs, they claimed, were the means by which a sexually repressed, violence- and death-obsessed Western culture could finally redeem itself into something peaceful, life-affirming, and cooperative; Leary had even upheld the Beatles as "evolutionary agents sent by God with a mysterious power to create a new species—a young race of laughing freemen." At his most persuasive, Timothy Leary was a celebrity of some stature through press coverage and condemnation, conferring a gurulike status for himself on behalf of the hippie sects and earning President Richard Nixon's denunciation as "the most dangerous man in America."

In the end, Leary's proselytizing, though sincere, would be discredited as irresponsible. The notion that religious transformation could be dispensed via tabs of LSD was at odds with the rigorously ascetic demands of Christianity, Islam, or Buddhism, which held that visionary states could only be attained through prayer, fasting, and meditation—an acid trip's proximity to the netherworlds charted in *The Tibetan Book of the Dead*, which had fired John Lennon's imagination to create "Tomorrow Never Knows," was superficial at best. Leary, like Aldous Huxley, was an educated adult better equipped to frame and articulate the LSD voyage to himself and others than the thousands of teenage truants who heeded his advice. Finally, lysergic acid diethylamide was and is a powerful chemical with unpredictable effects from user to user (especially when the drug itself is produced in a range of clandestine "labs" with little clinical supervision) and whose long-term effects after occasional or sustained ingestion were still unknown in the 1960s. "Since approximately the fall of 1965 the incidence of adverse LSD reactions throughout the country has mushroomed," discerned the *American Journal of Psychiatry* in 1968 (making an unintentional pun). But if Timothy Leary himself was eventually seen as something of a flake and a publicity hound, a vulgarized, abbreviated version of his ideas remained in circulation through the medium of rock music.

And whereas Leary was a huckster and Ken Kesey a self-described Merry Prankster, rock fans could look to artists and authors from decades past for a more substantial validation. Endorsement by contemporary lecturers or novelists was no match for the historic tradition of drug use witnessed in the lives and work of long-dead literary personages studied at university: that great books, plays, poems, and paintings had been made by people who were no less high than present-day rock groups and their disciples was a thrilling and subversive realization. Thus young record buyers could compare the black-and-white sleeve of *Revolver* to the line drawings of controversial Edwardian illustrator Aubrey Beardsley; could compare the fish-eye portrait on the Byrds' album *Mr. Tambourine Man* to the warped dreamscapes of Salvador Dalí; could hear the Zen surrealism of Dylan's "Subterranean Homesick

Blues" anticipated by Hermann Hesse's *Siddhartha* or the symbolism of Charles-Pierre Baudelaire, Arthur Rimbaud, Paul Verlaine, all
members of the Parisian *Club des Hachichins* (Hashish Eaters' Club)
in the nineteenth century. The imaginary worlds of J. R. R. Tolkien and
H. P. Lovecraft, and memoirs like Thomas de Quincey's *Confessions of
an English Opium Eater* and Mezz Mezzrow's *Really the Blues* were
rediscovered by the rock generation who now read them with a colorful, freshly enhanced perspective.

Nowhere was this continuity with the avant-gardes of yesteryear
emphasized more than on the cover of the next Beatles album, *Sgt.
Pepper's Lonely Hearts Club Band.* Released to international fanfare
and acclaim in June 1967, even before the vinyl was removed from the
sleeve it boasted surrealist credentials with its gallery of cover subjects,
numbering among others Aubrey Beardsley, Edgar Allan Poe, Oscar
Wilde, late comedian Lenny Bruce (dead of a heroin overdose in 1966),
Beat writers William S. Burroughs (*Junky*) and Terry Southern (the sex
farce *Candy*), English occultist Aleister Crowley (*Diary of a Drug Fiend*),
hallucinatory children's storyteller Lewis Carroll (*Alice in Wonderland* and *Through the Looking Glass*), Bob Dylan, a T-shirt welcoming
the Rolling Stones, and Aldous Huxley. *Sgt. Pepper* was hailed as the
Beatles'—and rock 'n' roll's—masterpiece from its first spins, the first
of a new line of "concept albums" comprised not of unrelated pop dit-
ties but organic movements of sound, music, and words around single
themes. According to Paul McCartney, the concept of *Sgt. Pepper* was
"[d]rugs, basically . . . [They] colored our perceptions. I think we started
to realize there weren't as many frontiers as we'd thought there were.
And we realized we could break barriers."

Pepper was preceded by the Beatles' double-A-sided 45 "Strawberry
Fields Forever / Penny Lane" a few months previously, which, like the
subsequent album, marked the band's mastery of studio effects and

orchestration in depicting the mental patterns contoured by LSD and marijuana. "Strawberry Fields Forever" was a kind of audio montage of John Lennon's haunted boyhood recollections, built up from multiple takes played at different speeds and tones and augmented with celli, a mellotron, and an Indian string instrument called a swarmandal. McCartney's "Penny Lane" likewise examined the innocence and wonder of childhood through a grown man's rapturous drug haze—which would become a common motif in rock—with summery flashes of Liverpool citizens and locales conjured up over an effervescent backing of piano and horns. Though the Beatles definitely took cannabis, speed, and even cocaine during breaks at their Abbey Road workplace, they seldom incapacitated themselves ("I used to have a bit of coke and then smoke some grass to balance it out," said McCartney), and the time and effort they lavished on devising the aural settings of "Strawberry Fields" and "Penny Lane" were not wasted. "They'd come back and it would be obvious," remembered producer George Martin of their occasional joints smoked over long days and nights at Abbey Road, "but it seemed to help and they had an enormous enthusiasm for recording in those days. They worked very hard."

Hard work also went into *Sgt. Pepper*. Several of its songs, namely "Fixing a Hole," "Getting Better," "Lovely Rita," "Being for the Benefit of Mr. Kite," and "When I'm Sixty-four," are actually less than the group's best or most memorable compositions, but the record's seamless production and instrumentation elevate them all, and the title track, its segue into "With a Little Help from My Friends," plus "Lucy in the Sky with Diamonds," "She's Leaving Home," "Within You Without You," and the shattering close of "A Day in the Life" are some of the Beatles' uncontested landmarks. All of these were heard as drug-based material, and many (though not all) were intended to be. The "LSD" initials of "Lucy" were a coincidence (the song was based on a school picture by

Lennon's five-year-old son Julian), although its pictures of *newspaper taxis* and *kaleidoscope eyes* were nothing if not acidic, while "With a Little Help" did blithely acknowledge getting high and the symphonic rush of "A Day in the Life" was meant to be what McCartney called "a real turn-on song." A gabble of rumor to the contrary, "Fixing a Hole" and "Mr. Kite"'s "Henry the Horse" did not refer to heroin, although given the overall mood of the disc, they may as well have.

It was not the music alone that seemed to extol the virtues of lysergic acid and cannabis, but the variety of sonic ornamentation—sound effects, echo, compression, distortion, *musique concrète*. Though more quickly dated than earlier and later Beatles efforts, *Pepper* was the perfect artifact for the short summer in which it appeared. "If such a thing as a cultural 'contact high' is possible," assessed musicologist Ian MacDonald in 1994, "it happened here." Bob Dylan's sometime collaborator Al Kooper praised *Sgt. Pepper* as "incredibly well done—sociological opera for its time"; Donovan remarked that "if you could only dig it when you were high, then it wouldn't have been so popular because not everybody was getting high, but if you *were* sitting smoking something there was definitely an opening up"; and Allen Ginsberg concluded: "After the apocalypse of Hitler and the apocalypse of the Bomb, there was here an exclamation of joy, the rediscovery of joy and what it is to be alive." The last vocal line on *Sgt. Pepper's Lonely Hearts Club Band* is "I'd love to turn you on."

After *Pepper* there could be no doubt that the drug revolution in pop music was well under way. Nineteen sixty-seven was the climactic year of LSD's influence in the record business and the record market, and though other drugs would pervade rock 'n' roll and its successors for years to come, there never was a comparable discography of psychedelic sounds as were recorded and issued over those months.

Not every hit song alluded to drugs, of course: this was also the era of Engelbert Humperdinck's "Release Me," Frank and Nancy Sinatra's "Somethin' Stupid," and Aretha Franklin's declaratory "Respect." But the top reaches of the sales charts were also dominated by Scott McKenzie's "San Francisco," the Young Rascals' "Groovin'," the Grass Roots' "Let's Live for Today," "Incense & Peppermints" by the trippily named Strawberry Alarm Clock, and Procol Harum's majestic reverie "A Whiter Shade of Pale."

Other top talents recovering from the Beatles' inventiveness were bound to compete. Overworked and overstimulated, Bob Dylan had been badly injured in a motorcycle accident in 1966 and was out of commission but gave oblique approval: "Acid tests were in full swing, acid was giving people the right attitude. The new worldview was changing society and everything was moving fast—lickety-split. Strobes, black lights—freakouts, the wave of the future." The Rolling Stones put out *Their Satanic Majesties Request* in late '67 to critical carps that they had made a clumsy imitation of *Sgt. Pepper*, complete with a costumed band cover (visible in a 3-D effect, no less) and a vivid gatefold collage, but *Majesties* did contain the excellent stoner hymnals "2000 Light Years from Home," "2000 Man," and "She's a Rainbow," and the troubled quintet had come up with their own blissful single, "We Love You" / "Dandelion" a few months before. "I think we were just taking too much acid," Mick Jagger apologized. "We were on acid doing the cover picture." "I was never hot on psychedelic music," Keith Richards conceded later, although this was hardly the last of the Stones' drug-infused records. The Who's "I Can See for Miles" demonstrated that act's evolution out of its speedy mod beginnings into the more ambitious attempts by Pete Townshend to combine the electric urgency of rock with the grandiosity and pomp of opera. And Brian Wilson, now suffering the mental strain of the Beach Boys' leadership (he had withdrawn from live performance in 1965), his determination to match and best the Beatles' latest musical innovations from *Rubber Soul* and *Revolver*, and his own fascination with cannabis and LSD, had been moved to create his final great track for the group in late 1966, the incandescent "Good Vibrations."

"Good Vibrations," co-written by Wilson and Tony Asher, was the product of a six-week series of recording sessions that cost almost $75,000 in studio time. The fast-deteriorating Wilson planned the cut as "the summation of my musical vision, a harmonic convergence of imagination and talent, production values and craft, songwriting and spirituality," but the difficulty in assembling its disparate parts and the other Beach Boys' doubts about its appeal took their toll. "Between the pot I smoked, the pills I popped, and the lack of support I got from the guys, I began losing faith ever so slightly in my judgment," Wilson looked back. Ultimately, "Good Vibrations" became another world-wide success and revered as no less a masterwork than "Strawberry Fields Forever" or "Penny Lane"—an ebullient Pacific symphony of cello, harp, clarinet, and the electronic warble of a theremin which, from Wilson brother Carl's own rhapsodic vocal introduction to its serene fadeout may well be the most remarkable three minutes and thirty-nine seconds of pop music ever made. Ever since, picking up "vibrations" and "vibes" have denoted the spiritual receptiveness accorded by psychedelic drugs.

Despite the unqualified triumphs of the Beatles and the last gasps, forgivable fumbles, and new directions of Brian Wilson, the Stones, and the Who, however, the most intoxicating musical breakthroughs of 1967 came from a roster of untried bands. At least two of them came out of the city John Phillips and Scott McKenzie had serenaded: the American West Coast had always been a terminal for unconventional, uninhibited souls, from author-adventurer Jack London to Beats Jack Kerouac and Lawrence Ferlinghetti, and in contrast to the smoggy hustle of Los Angeles, the City by the Bay had long nurtured a tranquil, tolerant social outlook. Temperate in climate, home to the liberal Stanford University and University of California at Berkeley, and a melting pot of Asian, Hispanic, and Native and African-American populations, no other US metropolis but San Francisco could have produced the Airplane and the Dead.

The Jefferson Airplane, the Grateful Dead, Moby Grape, Quicksilver Messenger Service, Big Brother and the Holding Company, the Charlatans, and other San Franciscan rock groups, like their predecessors the Byrds, were essentially electrified folk ensembles whose relative lack of training in the disciplines of rock 'n' roll and rhythm 'n' blues allowed them to improvise their songs around fewer and simpler chord changes, leaving more space for instrumental passages and voyages into pure sound. Less skilled as musicians than many rock performers out of LA or Britain, they made up for their technical shortcomings by embracing them as a testament of authenticity and proof of identification with their own audiences. Virtuosity was never the point; it was all about community. In this the San Francisco Sound was helped by the ubiquitous presence of acid, at house parties, at rehearsals, and especially at gigs. In San Francisco, LSD trips were taken on both sides of the stage.

The West Coast shows where "acid rock" developed in 1965 and 1966 were initially little more than public jam sessions of good-natured amateurs attended by their classmates, housemates, friends, and neighbors. Blues covers, folk chestnuts, and jug ballads were played through amplifiers while someone drummed, and meanwhile peyote, mescaline, and acid were handed out to all comers. Unsuccessful as the Warlocks, Jerry Garcia, Ron "Pigpen" McKernan, Bob Weir, Phil Lesh, and Bill Kreutzmann morphed into the Grateful Dead as the musical accompaniment to the Acid Tests of Merry Prankster Ken Kesey, where the chemical entertainment was provided by Augustus Stanley Owsley.

Kesey was already a popular writer through his 1962 novel *One Flew Over the Cuckoo's Nest* and had driven with Leary, Neal Cassady, and a gang of partiers on a fabulously colored bus throughout the US between 1964 and 1966, all taking acid and warming to the notion of LSD's place in festive gatherings, not simply one-on-one psychoanalysis. Settling back in northern California with the rest of the Pranksters, Kesey began to conduct his Acid Tests with an eclectic mix of invitees; the presence of the Grateful Dead and Stanley Owsley was at first incidental. The older Pranksters and the young rock 'n' rollers originally saw each other as convenient foils more than comrades, as Jerry Garcia related. "One day the idea was there—'Why don't we all have a big party and you guys bring your instruments and play, and us Pranksters'll set up all our tape recorders and bullshit, and we'll all get stoned?'" This was the ad hoc, see-what-happens impetus New Journalist Tom Wolfe investigated for his own best seller, *The Electric Kool-Aid Acid Test.* "They both, Kesey and Garcia, had been heading into the pudding, from different directions," Wolfe gauged. "For Kesey—they could just play, do their thing." The Grateful Dead were in fact some of the more proficient musicians in San Francisco rock and after a while grew too big to play second fiddle to Kesey's "Can you pass the Acid Test?" directives. "Why should we blow our hard-earned scenes for Kesey?" they thought.

Owsley, a young, scientifically inclined drifter from a prominent military and political family, began concocting and selling methedrine (injected liquid amphetamine) and LSD when it was still legal, and his earnings helped finance the Dead's growing payload of instruments, state-of-the-art amplification, and futuristic lighting. "The sound went down so many microphones and hooked through so many mixers and variable lags and blew up in so many amplifiers and roiled around in so many speakers and fed back down so many microphones, it came on like a chemical refinery," Tom Wolfe's readers learned. Owsley had trained

and worked in the discipline of sound engineering, and built a succession of custom-crafted stage rigs for the group, incorporating stereo
and delay innovations that would only be taken up by other acts years
later. "Everything is designed to envelop and overwhelm," the Dead's
manager and friend Rock Scully wrote of an Acid Test. "There's a Moog
synthesizer with sound coming out of sixteen phased speakers so the
sound rushes 360 degrees around the hall like a sonic demon. There
are ices spiked with LSD. A gigantic speaker painted in spectacular
Day-Glo colors is set up on the edge of the stage. . . ."

"By this time," Phil Lesh said of the Dead's collective state of mind
in 1966, "everyone in the band, except for Pigpen, had been taking acid
at least once a week for more than six months. It's safe to say that in
the ninety days or so that the Acid Tests existed, our band took more
and longer strides into another musical consciousness, not to mention
pure awareness, than ever before or since." "We'd met Owsley at the
Acid Test and he got fixated on us—'With this rock band, I can rule
the world,'" affirmed Jerry Garcia. "So we ended up living with Owsley
while he was tabbing the acid in the place we lived . . . [a]nd we were
just musicians in this house, and we were guinea-pigging more or less
continually. Tripping frequently if not constantly." Why? Garcia: "To get
high is to forget yourself. And to forget yourself is to see everything else.
And to see everything else is to become an understanding molecule in
an evolution, a conscious tool of the universe." Whoa. "LSD turned up
the volume," recalled Dead co-drummer Mickey Hart, enlisted after an
acid jam, "and all those things the conscious mind edits out as useless
noise—spiritual epiphanies, paranoid fantasies, imaginative leaps of
connection—suddenly come blaring through, loud and clear." Between
their association with Ken Kesey and their support from Stanley Owsley,
the Grateful Dead were the most genuinely drug-oriented rock 'n' rollers yet to appear. With bigger names, cannabis and LSD were only the

players' offstage predilections or their lyrical subtexts; with the Dead, they were the essential premise of the organization.

At the Acid Tests and Be-Ins, Garcia and Company remained home-town heroes, but it was the Jefferson Airplane who put San Francisco on the psychedelic map. Following the recruitment of Great Society singer Grace Slick, their albums *Surrealistic Pillow* and *After Bathing at Baxter's* were national smashes in 1967, featuring the ragalike drones of "Somebody to Love" and the *Alice in Wonderland* imagery of "White Rabbit." Like the Dead, Slick and the other members of the Airplane all lived, toured, and created the same warped existence they sang about, merrily sampling pot, acid, and nearly anything else with enthusiasm—or by accident. Backstage at one concert the performers bent for a quick hit from a plate of recreational substances proffered by their road manager. "One section held vitamins, while others held, respectively, a nasal decongestant, crystal methedrine, cocaine, LSD, and some popular headache remedy," recalled Grace Slick. "We thought we were each taking a couple of snorts of cocaine, but due to the lack of lighting, the entire band made the mistake of honking up enough acid to make the whole night a complete joke." Sometimes the joke was someone else's prank. "Since acid was tasteless, colorless, and effective in very small quantities, it was easy to slip someone a hit without their knowledge," Slick noted. "[I]f one of the guys set down his 7-Up bottle in the dressing room, the doser, usually a member of another band, might put a little acid on the bottle's lip. The next thing the thirst quencher knew, the walls were dripping green slime, he thought he was Napoleon, and it was time to go onstage." Even forty years on, the drugged bolero

OPPOSITE: **With their LSD-inspired hits "White Rabbit" and "Somebody to Love," Grace Slick and the Jefferson Airplane brought the psychedelic sounds of San Francisco to national prominence.** *(Robert Altman / Michael Ochs Archives / Getty Images)*

of "White Rabbit" is the standard cue for latter-day cinematic depictions of the '60s, California, and the phantasms made manifest with LSD.

San Francisco was also the center of a psychedelic spin-off of rock music that represented the drug scene in a visual format: poster art. A gallery of unique and beautiful handbills and advertisements for concerts at the city's Avalon, Fillmore, and Winterland ballrooms were designed and exhibited daily for several years, and they were copied and adapted for hundreds of other recitals around the world. Drawing on artistic influences as eclectic as the ravishing Art Nouveau of Henri de Toulouse-Lautrec and Alphonse Mucha, the vivid Technicolor hijinks of old Walt Disney or Warner Brothers cartoons, elaborately worded medicine show posters of the Old West, and Native American iconography, proclamations for shows by the Jefferson Airplane, the Grateful Dead, and virtually every other act promoted by San Francisco impresario Bill Graham became almost as mind-blowing as the gigs themselves. The designers—among them Stanley Mouse, Alton Kelley, and the mesmerizing Rick Griffin—rarely crafted their work while *on* psychedelics ("I wouldn't even think about trying to do a poster under the influence of acid," said Kelley), but the posters were certainly illustrated and lettered with a stoned or tripping readership in mind. "I knew Bill would make some comment, because he always did," remembered artist Wes Wilson of Graham's reaction to his latest picture. "He just looked at the poster, looked at me, and said, 'Well, it's nice, but I can't read it.' And I said, 'Yeah, and that's why people are gonna stop and look at it.'" Looping, nearly indecipherable text (hand-drawn in a method contemporary computer programs still cannot replicate) and absurdist visuals of anything but the performers being announced did for the eyes what distortion and wah-wah pedals did for the ears. They were the pictorial analogs of the San Francisco Sound. "What you had in San Francisco was the right combination of people walking around in the streets and timing," said Alton Kelley. "Everything that was happening in the culture came together—at least for a while."

For a while. San Francisco's status as a mecca of drugs and psychedelic music elapsed nearly as soon as it had begun. Even in 1967, press overexposure could ruin a natural, unplanned confluence of youth, art, style, and politics such as had occurred among the Be-Ins and Love-Ins of Golden Gate Park; that year journalists from across the US and abroad descended on San Francisco to inform Mr. and Mrs. Middle America of the bizarre subculture of young people in the shops and streets and dilapidated Victorian homes of the old Haight-Ashbury district (the Grateful Dead and their circle shared a place at 710 Ashbury Street). A local bus company even began offering guided tours of the neighborhood, like some sort of human wildlife refuge. Police had taken notice as well, and antagonism toward stoned "freaks" from square "pigs" was rising. And already the casualties of overindulgence were starting to appear in alleyways and emergency rooms. These were the people who had uncritically embraced the teachings of Timothy Leary and Allen Ginsberg and heedlessly partaken of the latest batches of Stanley Owsley. They were all rock fans, of course.

Paul McCartney had visited San Francisco in April 1967 and thought, "I can't see this lasting because the media are going to get here and pretty soon it will turn into Rip Off Street." "When the summer came," the Dead's bassist Phil Lesh looked back, "tens of thousands of young people thronged the streets of the Haight . . . coming from all over the country to seek whatever it was the media had told them to expect— free love, enlightenment, like-minded companionship, the freedom to just be themselves—and instead finding hard drugs, rip-offs, rapes, and murders." On August 8, George Harrison, with his wife Pattie and Beatles associate Derek Taylor, toured Haight-Ashbury, all three on LSD. Venturing from a limousine while strumming a guitar to the Beatles' fresh "Baby, You're a Rich Man" (from their upcoming *Magical Mystery Tour* album), Harrison was dismayed to find himself surrounded by "horrible spotty dropout kids on drugs . . . It certainly showed me what was happening in the drug culture. It wasn't what I'd thought— spiritual awakenings and being artistic—it was like alcoholism, like any addiction." "Everybody looked stoned—even mothers and babies," Pattie noticed. Spinning from his own acid trip and pressed by dozens of surly teenagers offering him drugs of all varieties, Harrison fled, accompanied by the other English visitors. It was not the last time rock 'n' roll stardom and banned chemicals combined for bad vibes.

Down in Los Angeles, home of America's "professional" music industry, other psychedelic bands were being signed and debuted to gradual or instant popularity. In 1967, Arthur Lee's Love had released a second LP, the folk gem *Forever Changes*, which has since become a classic, but it was Love's Elektra labelmates the Doors who hit very big with their self-titled first album in January, with its leadoff singles "Break On Through" and then, in April, "Light My Fire." Nothing before "Light My Fire" could be more construed as an inducement to ignite a joint and have sex then and there. The Doors had taken their very name from Aldous Huxley's *The Doors of Perception*, in whose title Huxley in turn quoted the Romantic poet William Blake's *The Marriage of Heaven and Hell*: "If the doors of perception were cleansed every thing would appear to man as it is, infinite." Huxley felt that "to be shown for a few timeless hours the outer and inner world, not as they appear to an animal obsessed with survival or to a human being obsessed with words and notions, but as they are apprehended, directly and unconditionally, by Mind at Large—this is an experience of inestimable value to everyone

OPPOSITE: **Jim Morrison, aka Mr. Mojo Risin', aka the Lizard King—one of the most celebrated hedonists in all of pop music.** *(Michael Ochs Archives / Getty Images)*

and especially to the intellectual." The writer had also complained that
"[f]or unrestricted use the West has permitted only alcohol and tobacco.
All the other chemical Doors in the Wall are labeled Dope, and their
unauthorized takers as fiends." All four Doors smoked marijuana and
took organic and chemical hallucinogens—guitarist Robby Krieger and
drummer John Densmore's prior band had been named the Psychedelic
Rangers—but it was the vocalist Jim Morrison who was the boldest,
most open Door of the group and who became one of the most celebrated hedonists in all of popular music.

An intelligent, well-bred youth from a military family, Morrison was
a twenty-two-year-old film student at the University of California at
Los Angeles when he joined the Doors with Krieger, Densmore, and
keyboardist Ray Manzarek. Cinema and poetry were Morrison's real
interests; he had never considered himself a musician, much less front
man for a rock 'n' roll act. But drugs and alcohol, both of which he took
in quantity, allowed him to see his role in the Doors as that of a kind
of shamanistic performance artist, a brazen preacher of transgression
leading his audience into higher realms of mental and spiritual awareness. "On the outside," Densmore would look back, "Jim seemed to be a
relatively normal college student. . . . After a few hours with him when
he'd been chain-smoking dope and rapping philosophy, however, another
side emerged. Sometimes I was frightened. I'd ask myself, Goddamn, how
far down does this guy go?" Morrison had soon come to understand that
experimental film and free verse did not offer the same platform for his
messages as rock, and his personal articulacy, smoldering good looks,
and hypnotically sexual stage presence made him the Doors' automatic
center of attention, despite the fact that "Light My Fire" was mostly
composed by Krieger. Doors cuts like "People Are Strange," "Riders on
the Storm," "Not to Touch the Earth," "Break On Through" ("We chased
our pleasures here, dug our treasures there"), and "The Crystal Ship"

("Before you slip into unconsciousness, I'd like to have another kiss . . .") were freighted with the stratospheric metaphors of the drug lexicon. And like the members of the San Francisco bands, Jim Morrison honestly believed in the freedom made possible through altered consciousness. In the recording booth and on stage—and most of all in his daily life—he could be drunk, tripping on LSD or mescaline, stoned on marijuana or hash, or blasted on cocaine or amyl nitrate (a powerful heart stimulant). He was determined to scrub his own perception clean.

Yet Morrison was not the quintessential hippie dropout of the type that had scared off George Harrison in Haight-Ashbury. He was educated, skeptical, dismissive of panhandlers and welfare cases, and, over the course of the Doors' short career, more and more suspicious of his own following. "I suddenly realized in a way that I was just a puppet of a lot of forces I only vaguely understood," he admitted after watching a film of one of his own riotous performances. After his infamous 1969 Miami arrest following a gig where he exposed himself, Morrison explained to an interviewer, "I think I was just fed up with the image that had been created around me, which I sometimes consciously, most of the time unconsciously, cooperated with. . . . I guess what it boiled down to was that I told the audience that they were a bunch of fucking idiots to be members of an audience." Though Morrison's lyrics for the Doors could be a derivative shambles of Romantic and Symbolist influence, and Morrison himself was a chronic and unmanageable drunk, he played his part with conviction and expected listeners to be correspondingly serious. He was not content to be a mere rock star and not satisfied with mere partying. "Everybody smokes grass. I guess you don't consider that a drug anymore. . . . I think the highest and lowest points are the important ones. All the points in between are, well, in between. I want freedom to try everything—I guess to experience everything at least once."

Exploding at nearly the same time as the Doors was a trio led by Morrison's only equal in the pantheon of stoned and doomed rock stardom, Jimi Hendrix. In 1966 and '67, Hendrix was a veteran sideman and bandleader who had developed a spectacular reputation as a performer and, of course, as the most accomplished and innovative electric guitarist ever to plug in for a rock 'n' roll set. Steeped in soul and blues music and fascinated by the mystique of Dylan, Hendrix ran his guitar chops through convulsions of sustain, reverberation, distortion, and feedback to achieve with one instrument on stage what others had needed an entire band, multiple recording tracks, and a fully equipped studio to do; Hendrix is debatably one of the few musical geniuses to be heard in classic rock. He also smoked cannabis heavily and took frequent LSD trips.

This druggy element in his life and work was what many listeners heard more than anything else he was trying to play. His colorful clothes, acidic album covers for *Are You Experienced* and *Axis: Bold as Love*, and endearingly wasted conversational ramblings were psychedelia personified. Songs like "Are You Experienced," "Stone Free," "Up from the Skies," "Room Full of Mirrors," "Third Stone from the Sun," "You Got Me Floating," and the ineradicable "Purple Haze" (Stanley Owsley named a batch of LSD after the title and brewed it specifically for Hendrix himself) seemed no less invitations to toking or tripping than "Light My Fire," "Rainy Day Women #12 & 35," or "White Rabbit." "Are You Experienced" alone—the climactic track on his 1967 debut album—is spun with backwards guitars and drums, and the singer's slurry affirmation, "Have you ever been experienced? Well, I have. . . ." On one live take of the Beatles' "Day Tripper," heard on a BBC Radio spot, Hendrix called out, "Ah, Owsley, can you hear me now?" during a solo, and of a 1967 concert in West Germany his bassist Noel Redding said, "Jimi was so stoned that I had to tune his guitar for him." His gem

"51st Anniversary" contains the sound of what can only be Hendrix having a toke midverse: "You must be losin' your [rapid inhale, pinched breath] sweet little mind. . . ." Even more so than with other music and musicians of the era, separating the career and compositions of Jimi Hendrix from the sway of marijuana, lysergic acid, and miscellaneous chemical and sexual debauchery is impossible.

But Hendrix was a contradictory figure. An ex-paratrooper who wore *Sgt. Pepper*–like soldier's uniforms out of an abiding respect for the military ("The Americans are fighting in Vietnam for the complete free world," he felt) and an ambitious, self-taught musician who aspired to play with Miles Davis, he grew tired of the psychedelic label and spent the last years of his fleeting trajectory trying to break out of the artistic and theatrical pigeonhole in which his management and audience had placed him. He differed from many contemporary rock 'n' rollers in that drugs for him were more a means to calm or dull the restlessness he felt offstage, as opposed to the songwriting enhancer they had been for the Beatles or Brian Wilson, or the jamming component on which the Grateful Dead relied. Like Jim Morrison, there is a sense with Hendrix that he was struggling to advance a philosophy of personal freedom and inner wisdom more reasoned than just an endorsement of getting high; and far more than Morrison there is the tragedy that he would never realize the full measure of his talent. With both, however, there is the lasting fact that they embodied for millions the charisma and Romantic decadence of rock at its most self-indulgent and most self-destructive.

The Jimi Hendrix Experience, his group with Englishmen Redding and drummer Mitch Mitchell, was launched in the US at the Monterey Pop Festival, south of San Francisco, in June 1967—presented by the Stones' Brian Jones, Hendrix was flying on Purple Haze LSD while he tore through the Troggs' "Wild Thing," B. B. King's "Rock Me Baby," and Dylan's "Like a Rolling Stone" before setting his Stratocaster alight. Monterey was the first of the great rock extravaganzas, organized in part by confirmed psychedelic rangers John Phillips and Derek Taylor and bringing to international prominence Hendrix, Janis Joplin, the Who, Simon and Garfunkel, the Jefferson Airplane, the Steve Miller Band, the Grateful Dead, Otis Redding, and George Harrison's sitar mentor, Ravi Shankar. The Airplane's guitarist Paul Kantner was not alone in his revulsion toward the predatory LA industry sharks sniffing around Monterey for marketable talent, but did allow that "everybody was there very positively to enjoy themselves, to meet other people, to find new friends, old friends, old drugs, new drugs." The concerts were successful and the crowds peaceable, either in spite or because of the massive amounts of dope taken by players and fans alike. STP, a new potion from the busy laboratory of Stanley Owsley that combined the trip of acid with the energy of amphetamine, was also given a major introduction at Monterey. Owsley obtained the formula for this from an ex-staffer at the Dow Chemical firm. "He had this stuff, and we thought it might be good. . . . It turned out that it wasn't." Hendrix titled one composition "The Stars That Play with Laughing Sam's Dice," its evident acronym STP / LSD. The drug was properly known as DOM or dimethoxyamphetamine: the name STP was sometimes said to stand for "Serenity, Tranquility, Peace," but was also a reference to the high-potency fuel additive pumped into racing cars.

Monterey, along with the synchronous emergence of Love, Hendrix, the Doors, the Jefferson Airplane, Haight-Ashbury, and *Sgt. Pepper's Lonely Hearts Club Band* all through the warm sunshiny months of 1967, signified rock 'n' roll's rise from teenybopper fad to the soundtrack of a worldwide political groundswell among the young—so it was feared and so it was hoped. By then the eyes and ears of authority were trained on rock shows and rock records, and any gathering or demonstration by hippies, students and other protesters was taken by those on either side of the barricades as a first skirmish of a fomenting insurrection. "The combination of a joint, the right company, and the right long-playing record seemed to have redeemed the traditional Romantic promise," recalled activist Todd Gitlin, allowing the sharers "to see and feel truly the grain of the world, the steady miracle ordinarily muffled by busyness but still lurking in the interstices, a revelation of your astonishing existence in an electric universe."

What neither side realized at the time was that because the use of illegal drugs was the most immediate gesture of generational "resistance" it was also the most enervating. No society could ever be really overthrown when the forces of overthrow were too sapped by marijuana or acid to collect themselves into a meaningful campaign. "Stoned consciousness darted, flowed, went where it wanted to go, freed of rectilinear purpose and instruction," Gitlin discovered. "Routine talk seemed laughable; weird juxtapositions made perfect sense; sense made no sense at all." For all the hundreds of thousands of people marching on campus or on Washington on behalf of free speech, free love, racial integration, or an end to the US war in Vietnam, the biggest social change in which drugs and rock music played a part was the increasing prominence of drugs and rock music.

Vietnam was both condemned in songs by drug users and fought by drug users listening to the same songs. "Is it true there's a marijuana problem in Vietnam?" kidded Armed Forces Radio disc jockey Adrian Cronauer. "No, it's not a problem—everybody has it." In 1967 more US servicemen were charged or reprimanded for smoking pot than for any other offense. The American firefights in Indochina were largely conducted by young draftees sprung from the same slums, farms, and suburbs inhabited by their brothers and sisters back home, and an inevitable crosscurrent of contraband transpired from war zones on either side of the Pacific—from the jungle to the ghetto to the college square, in the same continuum of violence and disorientation Jimi Hendrix lamented in his desperate "Machine Gun." "I'd like to dedicate this one to all the soldiers fightin' in Berkeley—you know what soldiers I'm talkin' about," Hendrix would say. "And oh yeah, and all the soldiers fightin' in Vietnam." GIs smuggled powerful Asian strains of cannabis and opiates back from their tours of duty while being shipped the latest product of the Rolling Stones or the Jefferson Airplane, entrenching the ties between activism, drug use, and subversive music. Whether or not real reversals of policy were accomplished by the protest movement, what mattered was that officialdom felt itself under attack and, in 1967, had begun to lash out.

The first musician of the classic rock era arrested under a drug law was the mild English folk singer Donovan, fined £250 (about $1,200) for possession of marijuana in July 1966 after what a London newspaper described as "a reefer smoking party in his flat." Donovan's bucolic ditties like "Wear Your Love Like Heaven," "Jennifer Juniper," "Hurdy Gurdy Man," and the ethereal "Lalena" went with his shorthand characterization as the British Dylan (he was seen on the sidelines of *Don't Look Back*), but he was no psychedelic rabble-rouser. "[H]aving experiences on visionary drugs like marijuana and LSD didn't make me *write* songs," he clarified. "But the amazing experience of 'parting the veil,' of actually seeing into the paradise, of experiencing what Aldous Huxley called bypassing the valve which prevents us from seeing the workings of the universe—that *was* extraordinary. . . . So I wanted to sing about these things, not to encourage drug-taking, but to encourage awareness." Donovan was a soft target.

On February 12, 1967, a weekend house affair at Keith Richards' Sussex home of Redlands was interrupted by a squad of nineteen police who found amphetamines in the pocket of a jacket Mick Jagger claimed was his (it was actually his girlfriend Marianne Faithfull's) and cannabis residue on the premises; a friend, art dealer Robert Fraser, was also discovered with heroin. Jagger had the misfortune to be coming down from his first acid experience when the raid occurred. "They [the police] were awfully big and fat and rosy-cheeked, and we were all so small and thin and *different*," Faithfull observed. "They were one genus and we were another, like the two races in H. G. Wells's *The Time Machine*." "We were just gliding off from a twelve-hour trip," said Richards. "You know how that freaks people out when they walk in on you. . . . As [the police] went, as they started going out the door, somebody put on 'Rainy Day Women' really loud—*'Everybody must get stoned.'*"

Though today it seems amusing to credit the knighted and enshrined Rolling Stones as a danger to the Establishment, in 1967 their reputation among friends and foes was no joke. The Redlands bust has since been viewed as a conspiratorial sting operation by the law and the media who each had reason to catch wealthy and shameless high-profile pop musicians with illegal drugs: the sneering, shaggy-haired quintet who sang "Get Off My Cloud" and "Mother's Little Helper" were prime suspects well before the arrests took place. The Stones certainly were guilty of drug offenses, but the circumstances of the apprehension, coming soon after a breathless run of tabloid headlines on rock 'n' rollers' disgraceful proclivities—and the presence at Redlands of a shadowy acid kingpin named David Schneidermann plying his wares and who somehow escaped the country a free man—suggested a frame-up.

In May, on the same day Jagger, Richards, and Fraser were formally charged in court and pleaded not guilty, Brian Jones was likewise arrested at his home and found with hashish and cocaine. Again, the criminalizing of professional entertainers loved by the young but notorious among their elders appeared highly suspicious. Jones was apart from the rest of his group with a friend and vehemently denied the white powder was his. "Yes, it is hash," he said to the intruders. "But not the cocaine, man. That is not my scene." Already beginning an estrangement from the Rolling Stones, Jones was shaken up anew by the solitary and shady bust. "He was very talented," Mick Jagger said of him, "but he had a very paranoid personality and [was] not at all suited to be in show business."

Jagger, Richards, and Fraser were tried in late June of '67, during the same tumultuous summer of Monterey, Hendrix, "Light My Fire," and *Sgt. Pepper*. It was amid the circuslike atmosphere of the proceedings that the London *Times* published the editorial "Who Breaks a Butterfly on a Wheel?," the title quoting Alexander Pope's eighteenth-century poem *Dunciad*. "If we are going to make any case a symbol of the conflict between the sound traditional values of Britain and the new hedonism," ran the essay, "then we must be sure that the sound traditional values include tolerance and equity." The implication was that Jagger had received harsher treatment as a controversial celebrity "than would have been thought proper for any purely anonymous young man." Only Jagger and his pocket of pep pills were being discussed—no concerns were raised over the cannabis and heroin infractions of Richards and Fraser. Both Stones were briefly jailed but released on appeal, with Jagger receiving a conditional discharge and Richards' conviction overturned. Robert Fraser did four months in prison, and Brian Jones ended up with a fine and probation. The publicity surrounding the Redlands raid and the postures of the defendants as they denied the charges against them became a legendary instance of rock's martyrdom on behalf of drug libertarianism, although they had frankly lied about the acid and hash they had enjoyed in the Sussex cottage. "Did you have any idea that anyone in your house was smoking cannabis that weekend?" the defense counsel asked Richards. "No, sir." "Would you have allowed such a thing to happen?" "No, sir."

On October 2, 1967, the Grateful Dead's pad in Haight-Ashbury was subject to the same treatment—a sleazy setup, several arrests for marijuana possession, and a resultant media fanfare with insouciant guitar players put under a different spotlight than the ones to which they were accustomed. The Dead, though, made no attempt to evade the accusations against them. They denied nothing and said they had nothing to apologize for. "We're a nation of outlaws," asserted Jerry Garcia (who had eluded the bust). "A good outlaw makes a new law, makes it okay to do what he's doing." Executed without a search warrant, the charges were dropped, but not before the band and management prepared a press release that avowed that "almost everyone who has ever studied marijuana seriously and objectively has agreed that, physically and psychologically, marijuana is the least harmful chemical used for pleasure and life-enhancement." Here was another gang of rock 'n' rollers sacrificed on the altar of what to their followers and supporters looked like a hypocritical, outdated, and senseless legal restriction.

The final years of the decade abounded with drug songs, drug albums, and a general evocation of the drug experience in pop music. The Beatles dealt the stoned wit of "Get Back," which had an Arizonan transvestite named Jojo on a quest for Californian cannabis, in addition to John Lennon's befuddling "Come Together" and "I Am the Walrus" (Lennon: "The first line was written on one acid trip one weekend, the second line on another acid trip the next weekend") and their animated film *Yellow Submarine*, where the happy Pepperland was saved from the allegorical Blue Meanies in a psychotropic cartoon dreamscape. English mods the Small Faces, who had put out the sublime marijuana paean "Itchycoo Park" in 1967, had a hit with 1968's *Ogden's Nut Gone Flake*, an album whose foldout packaging imitated that of a can of an esoteric weed, complete with rolling papers. Creedence Clearwater Revival's "Bootleg" made a telling comment on how drugs' illegality made them all the more alluring: "Give you a glass of water, make it against the law / See how good the water tastes, when you can't have any at all." Pete Townshend and the Who's heroic rock opera, *Tommy*, had a solo turn from the sinister "Acid Queen," and they had also solicited passengers for their freaky "Magic Bus." Folk scion Arlo Guthrie recorded the pot smuggler's worry "Comin' into Los Angeles," while the Amboy Dukes, featuring a maniacal guitar slinger named Ted Nugent, in '68 offered a "Journey to the Center of Your Mind," the same year the proto-metallic Steppenwolf maintained they liked "smokin' lightnin'" in "Born to be Wild," and that they would take you on a "Magic Carpet Ride" to an unmistakable destination. In 1969, Steppenwolf's cover of Hoyt Axton's searing "The Pusher" (an angry and open distinction between drug vendors and drug inducers) was heard in the breakthrough movie *Easy Rider*, along with Jimi Hendrix' great "If 6 Was 9" and the Fraternity of Man's splendidly lighthearted (and light-headed) "Don't Bogart That Joint." Erstwhile bubblegum acts like Tommy James and the Shondells went to number one in '69 with the mystical "Crimson and Clover," keeping company with the Zombies' slow-burning "Time of the Season" and the Lemon Pipers' wavy "Green Tambourine."

African-American pop was adapting as well. Groups on Detroit's Motown label, which had steered clear of some of the more excessive drug sounds emanating from LA or the UK, took on more relevance with the Temptations' "Cloud Nine" and "Runaway Child, Running Wild," and the Supremes' doleful "Love Child"—more messages of urban unrest were to follow the next year, with the Supremes singing of "Stoned Love" and the Tempts heading for the "Psychedelic Shack." The Chambers Brothers had already told of how their souls had been psychedelicized in "Time Has Come Today," and AM-friendly songsters the Fifth Dimension scored big with covers of Laura Nyro's "Stoned Soul

Picnic" and a medley from the hippie musical *Hair*, "Aquarius / Let the Sunshine In." In San Francisco, a former DJ and record producer named Sylvester Stewart changed his name to Sly Stone, and with his familial band made a flurry of dazzling 45s and LPs where the propulsive funk of James Brown was painted with a Haight-Ashbury utopianism: "Everyday People," "I Want to Take You Higher," and "Dance to the Music" were psychedelic soul for an audience as multihued as Sky's integrated band of blacks, whites, men, and women.

But as the drug songs kept coming, so did the drug busts. The Rolling Stones' Brian Jones was nabbed with hashish in his residence in May of 1968. "Why do you always have to pick on me?" pleaded the despairing Jones, who had been subject to a prior arrest twelve months past. John Lennon and Yoko Ono were found with cannabis resin at a London flat, formerly home to Jimi Hendrix, in October. The Beatle claimed the dope had been planted and that the arrest was another frame, pointing to the dozens of police participating in the raid on two individuals and the number of newspaper cameramen waiting outside. The home of George Harrison and his wife Pattie was invaded in 1969 by a team led again by Detective Norman Pilcher, the same fervent anti-drug and anti–rock star zealot (the "semolina pilchard" lampooned in "I Am the Walrus") who had apprehended Jones and Lennon and once attempted to catch Eric Clapton; Pilcher smugly produced a huge brick of hash from one of Harrison's shoes. Jones, Lennon, and Harrison all were convicted, fined, and freed, although the legal ramifications of their criminal records would affect their careers. Pilcher himself was eventually imprisoned for his role in later drug seizures, in which he was shown to have planted evidence and otherwise conspired to arrest supposed drug users, confirming the sense of victimization felt by Beatles, Stones, and thousands of ordinary stoners.

Entering Canada from the US in 1969, customs officials found heroin in Jimi Hendrix's luggage—Hendrix took a lot of illegal drugs, but heroin was not normally among them, and he argued in court that it had been left in his personal effects by a hanger-on or other acquaintance of the kind who were constantly donating soft, hard, and intermediate drugs to him (to the extent of secretly spiking his drinks or cigarettes). The guitarist was acquitted, but this was an early example of the hazards faced by young jet-setting, border-hopping musicians. "All of that is the Establishment fighting back," Hendrix believed of his harassment. "Eventually they will swallow themselves up. But I don't want them to swallow too many kids up as they go along." It was not exactly bad publicity for Hendrix's fan base (the way it might have been for a Charlie Parker or Gene Krupa), but the case demonstrated yet again that rock stars were prize trophies for police and, as celebrities whose work left little uncertainty as to their recreational tastes, uniquely vulnerable within their own entourages.

The decade closed with the Manichean rock festivals of Woodstock in August 1969 and Altamont in December. Pot, mushrooms, and acid were rampant at both, but one is remembered as Three Days of Peace and Music and the other as the Death of the '60s. In reality, other large-scale rock 'n' roll events in '69—outdoor shows in Palm Springs and Newport, California, and Denver—had ended with injuries, arrests, and management chaos, and the line between celebration and riot at such scenes was at the time difficult to perceive (a *New York Times* editorial described Woodstock as a "Nightmare in the Catskills"). Both Woodstock and Altamont were plagued by the nebulous "bad acid": inferior or bootleg LSD that either had no effect or all too much, although

OPPOSITE: Their provocative music and images made rock stars easy targets and prize trophies for law enforcement. Jimi Hendrix was arrested for drug possession in 1969. *(Michael Ochs Archives / Getty Images)*

different breeds of cannabis were more widely circulated at every rock concert and there were no emergencies ascribed to "bad weed." "There was so much grass being smoked last night that you could get stoned just sitting there breathing," claimed a Woodstock camper, and when Ten Years After's Alvin Lee requested some smokes from a stagehand, only cannabis was found: "He came back with twenty joints. Nobody had any cigarettes." "[W]hat they thought was an alternative society was basically a field full of six-foot-deep mud laced with LSD," grumbled Pete Townshend, onstage with the Who. "If that was the world they wanted to live in, fuck the lot of them."

Both Woodstock and Altamont were poorly organized, too, but Woodstock took place in the warm summer of upstate New York, where numerous top-level acts were spread out across the schedule, while Altamont was held in the chill Californian autumn as the very stoned Jagger, Richards, and company were at their most languorous in showing up long after the crowd had grown tired of Santana and the Flying Burrito Brothers. Thorazine, a commercial brand of the sedative chlorpromazine typically administered to people suffering from acid good or bad, was in short supply at Altamont, and the vicious Hells Angels and their aspirants charged with maintaining order were stricken with acid themselves. Viewers of the documentary *Gimme Shelter* beheld a terrifying shot of an Altamont Angel just offstage as Jagger sings "Under My Thumb," the biker spasmodically wallowing in some dreadful lysergic firestorm. Drugs were neither the salvation of Woodstock nor the downfall of Altamont, but they magnified the happy or unhappy circumstances of each.

Likewise, drugs and rock music were not the sole determinants of the Manson murders in Los Angeles in August 1969, but popular memory has conflated them into a single abattoir of Beatles, LSD, and butchery. It was not until the next year, following the apprehension of Charles

Manson and members of his family and their trial for the savage killings of the Tate-LaBianca households, that the murders were revealed
to have been motivated in part by a hideous misinterpretation of lyrics
from the double album *The Beatles*, along with Manson's acidic methods
of persuasion. In the first days after the killings of Sharon Tate and her
houseguests—Hollywood beautiful people with ties to the jet-set drug
scene—speculation was that it had been a ritual slaughter with occult
overtones; Tate lived at the former home of LA insider and sybarite
Terry Melcher, which further added to the weirdness. "We know what's
behind these murders," an LA detective told some fellow cops as the
autopsies commenced. "They're part of a big dope transaction." In fact,
Charles Manson was simply a manipulative ex-con with a conceit of
musical potential, who had attempted to cultivate Melcher and Beach
Boy Dennis Wilson as tickets to fame and fortune, and when his goals
failed to materialize he recalled Melcher's address when dispatching his
lost and very impressionable minions. Public opinion of flower children,
hirsute musicians, and drugs dropped sharply in the wake of the trauma,
but Manson's "Helter Skelter" was born as much of his semi-literate
jailhouse racial fantasies as of the records he played to his disciples and
the hallucinogens they all took together. Lots of people got high, tripped
out, listened to the Beatles, and daydreamed with each other about a
coming new age—99 percent of them never killed anyone.

The far more common, not to say stereotyped, response to drugs and
pop music in the late '60s was one of synesthesia, the phenomenon of
seeing colors as sounds and vice versa, hence the psychedelic vogue
for a palette of tinted visuals: "A Whiter Shade of Pale," "Purple Haze,"
"She's a Rainbow," "My Green Tambourine," "Mellow Yellow," "White
Rabbit," Cream's "White Room," and then the trend for incongruous
group names like the Jefferson Airplane, Electric Flag, Moby Grape, the
Strawberry Alarm Clock, Vanilla Fudge, Iron Butterfly, Led Zeppelin,

and Pink Floyd. The last of these had formed in London in 1967 and built their loud and stroboscopic performances around their audience's chemically opened eyes and ears, much as the Grateful Dead did at the Acid Tests, although Floyd's space expeditions were unlike the Dead's cosmic bluegrass. The currency of synesthesia, the clouds of Mexican or Lebanese smoke billowing up over hordes of attendees at gigs by Sly Stone or the Stones or Pink Floyd, and the range of amplified and distorted blues, boogie, funk, and folk lumped under the all-inclusive term "acid rock" suggested that drugs were now so central to pop songs, the record industry, and youth culture as to have together become a total way of life. In the next few years the convergence would sometimes become a way of death.

HARVEST
1970-1973

Why does rock music appeal to someone who's stoned?
Because the good stuff is full, rich, exciting music. . . .
Rock music is written by and for heads. It's a rather well-known
fact that almost all rock groups are heads, and most of the
writing and composing is done while they're stoned.

JACK S. MARGOLIS AND RICHARD CLORFENE,
A CHILD'S GARDEN OF GRASS

At the turn of the 1970s, young people's preference for soft drugs such
as marijuana was less of a political act than, in the new argot of the
day, a "lifestyle" whose social acceptability in appropriate settings was
assumed. Some of this derived from the very nature of a cannabis high—
unlike with alcohol, after a joint or two most tokers could walk down
the street, go to class or work, or engage in other common activities
without anyone noticing obvious impairment. Pot, magic mushrooms,
and even the nearer reaches of an LSD outing afforded a pleasantly
dreamlike engagement with the world that remained the dreamer's
private insights rather than an outward episode of dementia. Countless
numbers of these sly stones were sneaked by parents, teachers, bosses,
and police everywhere. The US National Commission on Marijuana and

Drug Abuse, which began its work in 1970, estimated that twenty-five million Americans had by then tried marijuana at least once, counting fully 40 percent of citizens between ages eighteen and twenty-five as onetime, occasional, or regular users. The figures in Britain, Canada, Western Europe, Australia, and New Zealand were comparable.

Among rock musicians, roadies, managers, producers, talent scouts, and promoters, marijuana and other drugs were almost ubiquitous. Little distinction was made between taking a few hits off a joint, a couple of lines from a mirror, or a quick taste of a tab; because straight society had pronounced all of them equally bad the artistic community that could afford and accept them had contended that they were all equally good. "We all knew—because it was common, accepted knowledge— that cocaine was not addictive," David Crosby was to recount. "The authorities screwed it up by overdoing it. Remember, they told us that if we took acid we would burn out our eyes looking at the sun. . . . And because they lied to us first, we thought everything they said was bullshit." In the folk clubs and pop studios of Los Angeles in the late '60s and early '70s, it was difficult to tell where the partying ended and the music making began. The scene was a jumbled network of rising stars, hopefuls, hustlers, wannabes, and no-hopers all writing, jamming, planning, and sleeping with each other, and music and drugs were the twin threads that united them all. "[N]ever once . . . did I ever record, perform, or do anything any way except stoned," ex-Byrd and LA rock pillar Crosby said. "I did it all stoned."

Woodstock had seen the third public showing of one of the first so-called supergroups, Crosby, Stills, Nash, and Young, assembled in the City of Angels from the shards of three moderately successful acts: Crosby's Byrds, Steven Stills and Neil Young's Buffalo Springfield, and Graham Nash's Hollies. Early tryouts of Crosby and Stills together had been dubbed "the Frozen Noses," after the numbed nasal passages left by

cocaine. By then, manager-agents like David Geffen and Elliot Roberts
had entered the picture, as young, hip entrepreneurs who championed
the integrity of their clients while accommodating their every whim.
These were not paternal overseers, as the Beatles' Brian Epstein or the
Stones' Andrew Loog Oldham had tried to be, chaperones who might
rein in the players' most damaging (or most visible) tendencies. They
were deal makers who won the most lucrative contracts and gave the
performers a license to do what they pleased, as long as marketable
product kept coming. The instant popularity of CSN and sometimes
Y—represented by Geffen and Roberts and signed by an enthusiastic
Atlantic Records, the band saw its first records all shoot to the Top Ten
in '69, '70, and '71—took them to heights of artistic and chemical self-
indulgence rarely seen in the industry up to that time.

Personal, romantic, and creative rivalry fragmented CSNY soon
enough, but all four were able to maintain professional momentum.
Of the quartet, it was Neil Young who became the most recognized
as a soloist and who unintentionally was to encapsulate the reflective,
rustic ideals of the drug culture with his two albums *After the Gold Rush*
(1970) and *Harvest* (1972). The Canadian Young had come down from
the north after a brief collaboration with future Super Freak Rick James
in Toronto ("We used to pop amyl nitrates before going on stage") and
was a veteran pothead (subject to a 1968 arrest with other members
of the Springfield and a strip-searched Eric Clapton), although he was
leery of the heavier drugs filtering in via Crosby, Stills, and members
of his own group, Crazy Horse: "Anything that killed people, I didn't
want to have." His earlier efforts, a self-titled debut and *Everybody
Knows This Is Nowhere* (1969), conveyed the atmosphere of a smoky
jam session where the only element not exhausted was the bottomless
bag of weed. The title track from *After the Gold Rush* made an offhand
mention that the singer "felt like getting high," while *Harvest* took a

stand against "The Needle and the Damage Done," Young's haunted take on the heroin addiction of Crazy Horse guitarist Danny Whitten: "I hit the city and I lost my band / I watched the needle take another man . . ." Both discs cemented Young's persona as a rugged independent who was content to leave the Hollywood elite for the simple, acoustic satisfactions of the country; Young's blue jeans and boots, quiet, reedy voice, and deceptively plain chordal arrangements characterized him as a laid-back, rural strummer tending his own patch of homegrown while composing verses about love ("Don't Let It Bring You Down," "Birds"), politics ("Southern Man" and "Alabama"), and solitude ("Heart of Gold" and "Old Man").

This was only one facet of Neil Young's life and music, but the image stuck. "[H]ow would I have kept this together for so long if I was on drugs?" he later explained. "I smoked a lot of grass in the sixties, continued to smoke grass into the seventies, and dabbled around in other drugs. . . . I experimented, but I think I'm basically a survivor." Aside from the spiraling Whitten, Young was also in the ambit of CSNY roadie Bruce Berry, himself a heroin user, and recorded with producer and arranger Jack Nitzsche, another Los Angeles industry player with his own substance issues. Like Terry Melcher and John Phillips, Nitzsche was the kind of rock insider who knew everybody and whose skills as a musical fixer could make or break artists—he had helped create Phil Spector's Wall of Sound techniques and salvaged Mick Jagger's musical contributions to the drug-sodden 1970 film *Performance*—but who also lived the rock stars' decadent existence without the compensations of unlimited cash and public adulation. Young and Nitzsche worked together fitfully over several of Young's records. "We've been friends for so many years off and on," Nitzsche said. "We've been enemies too." "I'm one of the lucky ones who was able to do that and able to stop," Young described his intakes with hindsight. "But it wasn't easy to stop that lifestyle. I had to spend some time." Deserved or not, his reputation as the ultimately mellow toker who meant no harm to himself or anyone else sheltered marijuana in the audience's categorization of soft drugs, well removed from the fatal highs in which his compatriots were trapped.

Out of the same social, commercial, and regional mix as Young came the Eagles, also signed by the energetic David Geffen, who formed around wandering LA minstrels and certified druggies Don Henley and Glenn Frey, in coalition with bassist Randy Meisner, multi-instrumentalist Bernie Leadon, and contributing songwriter J. D. Souther. The Eagles took the introspectiveness and folk-rock stylings of the other Laurel Canyon singer-songwriters and gave them a more jaded, morning-after feel—critics would soon label their sound "cocaine 'n' cowboys." "We used to go camp out in the desert and do peyote rituals," Henley recalled. "The photo of us on our first album [*The Eagles*, 1972] is one when we were ripped on peyote." Like Neil Young, for whom they sometimes opened concerts, the Eagles seemed to take their own and others' drug use for granted, harmonizing about the trials of the denim-clad, post-Woodstock generation thumbing their way across the American Southwest in "Take It Easy," stubbornly burning out in "Desperado," driven mad by a silver spoon in "Witchy Woman," or attempting to "Take It to the Limit" ("But the dreams I've seen lately / Keep on turning out, and burning out . . ."). Their songs had none of the blatant psychedelia associated with Jimi Hendrix or the Jefferson Airplane, but acid and revolution had grown stale as subject matter, and the characters of the Eagles' little novellas were really living out in their day-to-day experience the models established by the class of '67. Anonymous young heads' quiet quests for an emotional or geographic promised land were the Eagles' domain, from which they would perfect a singular portrayal of time, place, and partying.

Meanwhile, drugs had begun to color a completely different sphere of pop music. Rock 'n' roll had been flirting with country as a form for a few years before country responded to rock 'n' roll as an idea. In 1969 country performer Merle Haggard achieved a massive hit with his outspoken "Okie from Muskogee," which declared, "We don't smoke marijuana, We don't take our trips on LSD," and that the decent people of the eponymous Oklahoma burg didn't defy conventional dress, patriotism, and morality "like the hippies out in San Francisco do." Haggard, in truth, was a reformed criminal and no prude, and "Okie from Muskogee" was sung with his tongue partly in cheek, but just as political conservatives embraced his bold resistance to cultural fashion, marijuana- and LSD-taking hippies couldn't help but admire it. "I'd been in prison and I felt very, very happy with the freedom that I had here in this America," Haggard reflected on the song's inspiration. "I felt the kids who were bitching about things didn't know any more about it than I did. . . . But that's the way I felt in 1969." Haggard was one of a wave of artists who had rejected—or been rejected by—the strictures of Nashville and the Grand Old Opry and distanced themselves from the implicitly Republican values of the older country market. The wave would be dubbed "Outlaw Country" and tolerance of drugs among its practitioners and fans would be one of its signatures.

As with other genres, country music had always harbored a drug element, but it was mostly limited to amphetamines; the rural and white working-class staple of alcohol was always more prevalent. Hank Williams had died from a combination of booze and pills at age twenty-nine, and Johnny Cash battled a speed addiction and a 1966 arrest for pot along with playing "Cocaine Blues," but it was not until country-tinged

OPPOSITE: Outlaws Waylon Jennings and Willie Nelson helped make the drug culture palatable for the country music audience—and country music palatable for the drug culture. (*Alan L. Mayor / Getty Images*)

rockers like the Byrds, Buffalo Springfield, and CSNY started drawing away the younger segment of the demographic that cannabis and other contraband began to be acknowledged in the scene. Bob Dylan's 1969 album *Nashville Skyline* was recorded with Cash and numerous Nashville session players to codify the intersection of country tones (acoustic and pedal-steel guitars, honky-tonk piano) with rock 'n' roll attitude (autonomous, intimate, liberal, world-weary), and Cash's later "Man in Black" stood up for "the reckless ones whose bad trip left them cold." Thereafter, outlaw country and its corresponding vices had a niche.

The mainstay of the outlaws was Willie Nelson, a gifted songwriter ("Crazy" for Patsy Cline; "Night Life" for Ray Price) and longtime though prudent pot smoker, who walked away from Nashville back to Austin, Texas, in the late '60s and took careful notice of the freaks and dopers both flocking to rock shows and giving them. "I saw a lot of people with long hair," he said. "People in jeans, T-shirts, sneakers, basically what I grew up wearing. I remember thinking, 'Fuck coats and ties! Let's get comfortable.'" Deliberately adopting the scruffy clothes and tonsure of the Woodstock nation and crossing it with a Lone Star cussedness, Nelson found his identity and his fortune. With "Whiskey River," "I Gotta Get Drunk," and "Bloody Mary Morning," he sang unashamedly of drinking, but other hits like "Me and Paul" ("Almost busted in Laredo / For reasons that I'd rather not disclose") and a duet with Waylon Jennings, "I Can Get Off on You," made no secret of his other pleasures. "I can roll a joint faster than any living person," Willie later boasted. "[Marijuana] is still the best natural medicine in the world. . . . I don't smoke weed to get high; I smoke it to take the edge off, so I'm not out there like a turkey sticking his head into everything." Other Outlaws included Haggard, Jennings ("One of My Bad Habits"), Kris Kristofferson ("Sunday Morning Coming Down"), and Hank Williams Jr. ("O.D.'d in Denver," "In the Arms of Cocaine"). Outlaw music was made by and for a rowdier, looser strain of country folk than the groomed polyester influences of Tammy Wynette or Chet Atkins, reinvesting the tunes with the streak of ain't-nobody's-business independence that had been smothered in Nashville—and along the way, it proved that drugs were now seen by almost everyone outside the justice system as no more than a personal recreation among consenting adults, like liquor, cigarettes, and sex. The outlaws made country cool and marijuana even cooler.

Yet not everyone had jumped on the bandwagon. Even in the first years of the 1970s, there were isolated cases of diehard rock 'n' rollers who were nonetheless diehard opponents of drug use. For some it was simply a matter of not wanting their musicianship compromised by intoxication; for others getting high interfered with the deeper satisfaction of getting laid; for a few it was a career decision to avoid hassles from police and exploitation by promoters and record companies. For Ted Nugent it was all of the above, plus an authentic belief in the benefits of self-sufficiency and healthy outdoor activity. "In the sixties, I was ridiculed and outcast by some of the people that I had great respect for in music. They made fun of me then because I wouldn't smoke their dope, and because I carried a gun and went hunting. They thought it was dangerous to carry a gun but cool to get high. Now they're dead, and I'm still Ted. I never needed their kind of danger." Never mind that the former Amboy Duke had hair cascading down his back, played at eardrum-perforating volume ("I'm surprised I still have a head left"), and performed songs like the libertarian "Stormtroopin'"—the Motor City Madman made no secret his distaste for drugs of all kinds. "That's the essence of a full life—using your gifts in an intellectual, spirited, and humorous fashion, and not letting those gifts be confused by destroyed signals from alcohol, tobacco, and fast food," he proclaimed. Nugent's stance eventually became a kind of shtick, but in his own genre of loud and macho arena rock, he was esteemed for his unapologetic opposition to the counterculture ethos. Before a Nashville recital of his sex maniac "Wang Dang Sweet Poontang," Nugent warned the crowd: "Anybody who wants to get 'mellow,' you can turn around and get the fuck outta here! Do you hear me?"

Alice Cooper was another abstainer, at least from drugs. Starting out in the same Los Angeles as the Doors and the Eagles, former minister's son Vincent Furnier had dabbled with marijuana and acid but contented himself with oceans of beer and whiskey as the theatrical gimmickry of his stage act took shape between 1969 and 1971. Cooper liked the idea of rock as a big spectacle—costumed, garish, nightmarish—that didn't need the distraction of being high to appreciate. "No stoned-out shoe-gazers in this band," Cooper said of his act's first appearances. "We looked right into the eyes of our audience with arrogance about who and what we were." The grotesque trappings of the Alice Cooper image, featuring guillotines, nooses, boa constrictors, and necrophiliac boogie like "Is It My Body" and "Under My Wheels," were a calculated ploy to generate publicity and break with the mellow orthodoxies of the hippie years: "We are the group who drove a stake through the heart of the Love Generation," he would tell scandal-hungry journalists. Unlike Nugent, Cooper never preached the virtues of staying clean, and didn't recoil from the drugs taken by his friends and band members; he merely preferred drink. "I wasn't shooting heroin and I wasn't snorting cocaine—none of that evil stuff," he recalled. "It was just beer. Except nobody noticed that I was drinking more than a couple of six-packs every day." A textbook functional alcoholic who could daily put away a case of beer and a quart of whiskey while continuing to perform and record, the

OPPOSITE: **Shock rocker Alice Cooper (background, between curtains) was personally down on drugs but still emblematic of rock 'n' roll depravity. Here, he and his band relax between gigs.** *(Jorgen Angel / Getty Images)*

singer ground on for much of the '70s while his health steadily declined. He was later institutionalized and resumed his career sober.

Even more emphasis on comic-book showmanship was placed by Kiss, to even greater success. Kiss had formed in the early 1970s around Stanley Eisen and Gene Klein, ambitious and canny New Yorkers who, like Cooper, disdained the carelessness and self-indulgence of their competition in the industry. Knowing that rock 'n' roll was always a business unforgiving of inattentive or unprofessional talent, Eisen and Klein changed their names to Paul Stanley and Gene Simmons, respectively; recruited guitarist Paul "Ace" Frehley and drummer Peter Criss, née Criscuola; and kitted themselves in makeup and a parade of superhero regalia to stand out from the crowd. Although Frehley and Criss were happy drinkers and stoners, Stanley and Simmons had both hands on the Kiss wheel and had little time for drugs. "I never went for drugs or booze," said Simmons. "Someone told me your dick stays limp when you're drunk. I thought, 'What a horrible thing!' Power, fame, wealth, women—that appealed to me. . . . People avoid the fact that even if you're a heroin addict with a guitar, you're just as much of a businessman as a guy sitting behind a desk with a suit and tie." To them, the Kiss brand was what made the gig work; they knew the infectious but rarely inspired music itself might not have succeeded otherwise. As with Alice Cooper, Kiss didn't risk alienating their fans by celebrating their leaders' drug-free status (the protagonist of their vehicular wipeout "Detroit Rock City" announced, "First I drink, then I smoke," before his fatal concert road trip), but behind the scenes they made it known that they were not addled and gullible kids who would trust anyone, play anywhere, and sign anything.

More elevated but equally uninterested in the cannabis outlook was another East Coast rocker who made his first records in the first years of the 1970s: Bruce Springsteen. Almost uniquely in pop music at the time, Springsteen's songs drew on a pre-Beatles, pre-psychedelic influence, reflecting instead the soulful urgency of an older wave of rock 'n' roll and R&B: Elvis Presley, Chuck Berry, and the two-minute teenage anthems of Motown and the Brill Building. His background as an introverted and isolated youngster who'd only wanted to listen to the radio and practice his guitar kept him removed from the surging drug culture. "I never did any drugs," he flatly stated. "When I was at that age when it was popular, I wasn't really in a social scene a whole lot. . . . Plus, I was very concerned with being in control at the time." Springsteen's detachment gave him an unusual perspective on the changes occurring around him and made him a voice of a working-class, Rust Belt cohort that had similarly missed out on Monterey and Haight-Ashbury. "I was totally involved in what I was doing, and I had no need for anything else, or for anybody," he said. His "Meeting Across the River," from his breakthrough album *Born to Run* (1975), is one of the very few great rock titles to address not the wild sensation of drug taking but the petty and squalid life of drug dealing ("Well Cherry says she's gonna walk 'cause she found out I took her radio and hocked it / But Eddie man, she doesn't understand that two grand's practically sittin' here in my pocket"), and Springsteen's heroic live shows offered convincing proof that being stoned was not a prerequisite for making passionate, powerful rock 'n' roll.

The most voluble critic of drugs in rock music and the lives of rock musicians was Frank Zappa. "I don't understand why anybody should devote their lives to a cause like dope," he complained. "It's the most boring pastime I can think of." Zappa had formally trained as a composer and excelled at orchestration, production, and the subtleties of jazz, and by the mid-1960s he had turned his acerbic eye and ear on the pretensions marijuana and LSD had encouraged in untutored, starstruck amateurs. Always an instinctive satirist (and among the first to spot the appeal of the creepy Alice Cooper band), he saw most of rock as just another type of conformity dressed up as rebellion. "'Freaking Out' should presuppose an active freedom," he declared in 1966, "freedom meaning a liberation from the control of some other person or persons. . . . Do we really listen? And if we really listen, do we really think? Freedom of thought, conversely, brings an active responsibility. Looking and acting eccentric is NOT ENOUGH." He famously dismissed the rock intelligentsia thus: "Rock journalism is people who can't write, interviewing people who can't talk, for people who can't read." Because much of his material took on twisted sexual and scatological themes ("Don't Eat the Yellow Snow," "I Promise Not to Come in Your Mouth," "Titties and Beer," "Why Does it Hurt When I Pee," etc.), he had run into trouble with the law and didn't want the presence of drugs in his circle to expose him further. "If you're traveling around with a band that says in their lyrics some of the things that I say, it would be best if you didn't give a government agency the opportunity to take you away for potential infringement of some particular regulation," he explained. As much as anything, Zappa was a conscientious artist who demanded high levels of chops from the players in his act and fired anyone who showed up under the influence. "[O]nce they're on the tour or in rehearsal or in recording, they have to be on top of it," he decreed. Though Zappa was never more than a beloved cult figure for those who could get his stinging jokes and his inventive arrangements, his refusal to bow before rock's sacred cows—e.g., the righteous splendors of dope—earned him grudging respect from those who did.

All of these, however, were a minority. The explosion of cannabis, acid, and harder substances that had reverberated throughout rock 'n' roll since 1964 had a few years later started to rack up its first roster of casualties. Some were still active as earners of royalties and as concert attractions, but had retarded their creative growth or even their mental capacity under concentrated doses of drugs sustained in what today seems a brevity of time literally mind-numbing. Coupled with the already dislocating effects of fame, constant work and travel, the vagaries of income and management, and their own immaturity and truncated formal educations, the blizzard of drugs many performers had endured made for a psychically devastating experience from which none would emerge unscathed. Those least cushioned by lenient record labels or supportive attendants were left high and dry, like the 13th Floor Elevators' Roky Erickson, whose lysergic abandon landed him in a mental institution in 1968 and subject to shock treatments. He later made a notarized avowal to his captors: "I, Roger (Roky) Erickson do hereby declare that I am not a member of the human race (not an earthling) and am in fact an alien from a planet other than earth."

More secure performers were left veering from imperial vanity to bemused humility, unsure whether to believe the exegeses of their most fawning admirers or to dismiss the whole thing as a sequence of flukes, misadventures, and misinterpretations. Often they would recollect the epoch with amazement, and there are repeated claims that rock stardom amounted to a species of premature aging: "Although [the Beatles] only toured for two years, it seemed like a lifetime," George Harrison said. "I remember wandering between my house, John's house, and Ringo's house and sitting in gardens looking at trees for years and years. That year [1967] really did take about fifty years to complete." "I'm not denying that I've had a good time these past three or four years," Jim Morrison echoed in 1970. "I've met a lot of interesting people and seen things in a short space of time that I probably wouldn't have run into in twenty years of living."

One of the earliest to succumb to the combined pressures of drugs and celebrity was Brian Wilson of the Beach Boys. He had suffered a nervous breakdown as far back as 1964 while embarking on a tour, and had given up stage appearances with the band in order to devote his time to songwriting and production. But even this proved too much for him. Smoking pot nightly, trying LSD, and devouring junk food all the time, he saw his weight balloon, and the Beach Boys' chart fortunes began to decline after the album *Pet Sounds* (1966) and the unreleased *Smile.* The other group members chided Wilson to return to making hit records, but he was sinking into paranoia, depression, and a growing cocaine habit. "Here's the money, give me the coke," he would say. "Every day and night the same. Snort more coke . . . I was schizophrenic and didn't know it. Life began to resemble the distorted images of funhouse mirrors." Brother Dennis Wilson's brief association with the Charles Manson Family did nothing for his insecurity—"The idea of this Wizard filling my house and studio with bad vibrations freaked me out"—and the leader, creator, and presiding genius of the Beach Boys sat out the 1960s and most of the next two decades withdrawn in obesity, addiction, and mental illness.

Eric Clapton was also in trouble. A living legend since his mid-'60s work with the Yardbirds and John Mayall's Bluesbreakers, he had triumphed with the pioneering heavy rock of Cream and slipped with the supergroup collaboration of Steve Winwood, Ginger Baker, and Rick Grech in Blind Faith. But the expectations placed on him by a worshipful rock audience, his then-unrequited love for George Harrison's wife Pattie, and a substantial appetite for cocaine and alcohol were wearing him down. He retreated to a studio in Miami, Florida, with a new ensemble of partiers, including slide guitar virtuoso Duane Allman, and recorded the classic double album *Layla and Other Assorted Love Songs* (1970) under the pseudonym Derek and the Dominos. An aching document of emotional distress articulated by the six-string phrasings of Clapton and Allman on "Bell Bottom Blues," "I Looked Away," the cover of Jimi Hendrix's "Little Wing," and the deathless title track, *Layla* was made while Clapton doused his sorrows in the old jazz and blues consolation of heroin. "The album was the culmination of about a year of hippie living," he said in retrospect. "We were staying in a funky little hotel on Miami Beach where you could score hard drugs in the gift shop by the front reception desk. You just placed your order with the girl who worked there, and you'd come back the next day and she'd hand it over to you in a brown paper bag." As a blues player, Clapton seemed to feel that heroin was the necessary ticket to artistic validity: "I still feel that to be a junkie is to be part of a very elite club. . . . I enjoyed the mythology surrounding the lives of the great jazz musicians like Charlie Parker and Ray Charles, and bluesmen like Robert Johnson."

But *Layla* was not an instant success, and the dejected and addicted guitarist spent the subsequent three years in his home, spending an estimated £1,000 a week on his fix. "The concerns of others meant nothing to me because I was feeling great, and I would continue to feel great as long as I had the powder." Heroin's dangers were spotted soon after it was first developed from morphine (itself an opium product) in the nineteenth century, and it had been banned in the US since 1924 and legally available in the UK only with a doctors' prescription; it was a cruel joke on Eric Clapton and other guitar heroes that the German drug firm Bayer had first named it for its "heroic" effects. He did not get fully clean until well into the next decade.

Other English bluesmen were on the same path. The Animals' vocalist Eric Burdon was a regular LSD traveler, and as that act disintegrated in the later '60s he became fixated with the life and music of Jimi Hendrix, made the hallucinatory albeit divine "San Franciscan Nights," and fell into a series of bizarre delusions around Christ, Buddha, and his prospective new profession as an actor and filmmaker. He was involved with the funk-rock band War for a short while, recording the dopers' delight "Spill the Wine" (the later pot party favorite "Low

Rider" was made by War minus Burdon) before almost abandoning the music business altogether and not returning to perform until 1977 with a revamped assembly of Animals.

Peter Green, meanwhile, had propelled the raunchy Fleetwood Mac to fame on the strength of his blistering lead guitar turns of "Oh Well" and the original "Black Magic Woman," but the introverted and spiritual musician was undone by the strains of Mac's touring and recording schedules; he showed up to perform wearing long robes, grew his hair and beard to biblical extents, and insisted that the group donate its earnings to charity. He also took a lot of acid. Playing in Germany in 1970, recalled drummer and leader Mick Fleetwood, Green got involved with "a bunch of rich German hippie brats. . . . They had a commune in a big old house with a lot of LSD floating around. During our stay in Munich, Pete was whisked out there and spent all his time getting stoned. . . . Peter Green was never the same after that." Green served out his remaining gigs with Fleetwood Mac and then retired into a self-imposed exile for several years. "If I ever meet those bastards . . ." Mac bassist John McVie reflected on Green's German housemates, "because what they did to him was unforgivable." The Mac's Jeremy Spencer also took a plentitude of drugs and joined a religious sect in 1971, and Danny Kirwan gradually went insane following a backstage blowup with the rest of the band.

Drugs had changed Motown's Marvin Gaye, too, though at first it seemed for the better. His classic album *What's Going On* (1971) made him one of the first and biggest of the label's stars to turn to the candid, socially conscious artistry of his white counterparts, after his romantic hits like "Ain't Nothing Like the Real Thing," "Ain't No Mountain High

OPPOSITE: Guitar hero Eric Clapton's most memorable work came while he was a serious drug abuser. "I still feel that to be a junkie is to be part of a very elite club," he reflected. *(Michael Putland / Getty Images)*

Enough" (both with Tammi Terrell), and "Can I Get a Witness" and "I Heard It Through the Grapevine." Cannabis made the difference. *What's Going On* was an intensely emotional portrait of African-American reality conceived by Gaye as a way of reintroducing his brother Frankie, returned from service in Vietnam, to the stateside scene at the turn of the decade, highlighted by the snare-tense "Inner City Blues (Make Me Wanna Holler)," an environmentalist "Mercy Mercy Me (the Ecology)," and the drug seduction "Flying High (In the Friendly Sky)," where the soul singer soars "without ever leaving the ground . . . I go crazy when I can't find it . . . I'm hooked my friend . . ." A deeply conflicted man torn between the sacred indoctrinations of his upbringing and the profane pleasures of his sex-symbol stardom, Gaye was high on cannabis and, increasingly, cocaine, all of his waking hours. "Reefer is an interesting thing," he surmised. "I respect reefer. If you're an artist, you'll recognize its creative possibilities. . . . Slowly you see the world through this fascinating filter, and slowly you decide you'd rather live your life stoned than straight. You know it's not good for you . . . but it's too late. You're a pothead."

Even some rock 'n' rollers who remained relatively lucid came out of the 1960s bearing the mental baggage of the wealth, sex, drugs, and sheer surrealism of what they had been through and what they were supposed to have stood for. Bob Dylan, though never a dangerously heavy drug user, reinvented himself numerous times after the amphetamine-pumped blast of records that preceded his motorcycle accident; he went through a difficult divorce, which was described on the cathartic albums *Blood on the Tracks* (1975) and *Desire* (1976), and then was identified with evangelical Christianity and Orthodox Judaism. Throughout, he carried the unfathomable burden of signifying the ideals of the entire rock generation: "I'd also seen that I was representing all these things that I didn't know anything about—like I was supposed to be on acid. . . . This was just about the time of that Woodstock festival, which was the sum total of all this bullshit." Bike crash or not, he didn't know what had hit him.

John Lennon suffered a brief heroin dependency as the Beatles slowly broke up (his hard-hitting solo cut "Cold Turkey" describes his withdrawal), but he had also taken what he guessed to be "thousands" of LSD trips, to a degree that between 1966 and 1968 he was said to have been almost continuously wired. "I was reading that stupid book of Leary's [*The Psychedelic Experience*] and all that shit," he said in his *Rolling Stone* interview of 1970. "We were going through a game that everybody went through, and I destroyed myself. . . . And I destroyed my ego and I didn't believe I could do anything, and I let people do what they wanted and say—let them all just do what they wanted, and I just was nothing, I was shit." For the remainder of his life, even while he was reasonably healthy and coherent, Lennon's view of the world was warped by his acid years. "I've had bad trips and other people have had bad trips, but I've had a bad trip in real life. I've had a bad trip on a joint. I can get paranoid just sitting in a restaurant."

The most renowned drug victim to have staggered out of the 1960s alive was Syd Barrett of Pink Floyd. Floyd had been a London sensation during the English Summer of Love, giving spacey light and sound exhibitions at the Middle Earth or Unlimited Freak Out (UFO) clubs where Barrett's guitar, Roger Waters' bass, Rick Wright's keyboards, and Nick Mason's drums did not so much play songs as provide sonic accompaniment to a visual evocation of LSD. Yet Barrett, who had founded the group, was a clever composer and a unique if inexpert guitarist who led Pink Floyd to their first commercial successes with the 45s "Arnold Layne" and "See Emily Play," and the debut album *The Piper at the Gates of Dawn*, its title taken from a chapter in the children's novel *The Wind in the Willows.* Under Barrett's guidance, Pink

Floyd had defined the childlike fascination with reality that drug users
sought in 1967, no less than Floyd's EMI labelmates the Beatles had
with "Strawberry Fields Forever" and "Penny Lane."

But Barrett took an extreme quantity of acid during this period, and
by the end of 1967 he was reduced to an incommunicative shell of a
human being, unable or unwilling to engage with his fellow musicians,
their followers, or people in general. "There was so much dope and acid
around in those days that I don't think anyone can remember anything
about anything," said Waters, who nonetheless remembered more than
the guitar player. Onstage Barrett refused to sing, play his instrument,
or even mouth the lyrics of his songs during TV appearances. An unhappy booking in Los Angeles had Pink Floyd sharing a bill with the
Alice Cooper band, and Cooper testified of sharing a crash pad with the
group: "He used to sit silently in the kitchen, wearing his pink crushed-
velvet pants. I'd wake up and there would be a box of cornflakes sitting
on the table, and Syd would be watching the box of cereal, transfixed,
the same way most of us would watch television. He was that gone early
on." As he slipped further and further into the recesses of his own mind,
the other members of Floyd elected to replace him with their mutual
school friend, guitarist David Gilmour.

With Pink Floyd a massive record draw and concert attraction in
the 1970s, a dedicated cult of Barrett developed, fans contending he
was not a victim but a sort of pioneer who had only reached a higher
or deeper level of awareness than those around him. He released two
post-Floyd solo albums, *Barrett* and *The Madcap Laughs* (both finished
under the sympathetic oversight of Gilmour) and withdrew to his home
in Cambridge, whose quintessential Englishness had so colored his
and therefore the Pink Floyd aesthetic. There he lived quietly with his
parents for many years, earning royalties from his share of Floyd but
otherwise unreachable. "Syd's story is romanticized by people who

don't know it," Gilmour maintained. "Syd was one of the great rock 'n' roll tragedies." It is possible that Barrett's deterioration was sparked by an inherent mental illness that would have taken hold in any case, but there is little dispute that his heavy LSD consumption contributed to it, and psychologists insist that hallucinogens do carry the risk of instigating permanent psychoses in the vulnerable. Syd Barrett was undeniably one of them.

At least he was alive. The celebratory mood of the 1960s was forever darkened by the pall cast over an exactly twenty-four-month span in which four famous rock performers died, all of them in the proximity of drugs: Brian Jones, Janis Joplin, Jimi Hendrix, and Jim Morrison. Other than their *J* initials, there was an almost premonitory link between them. Joplin and Hendrix had made it big after their Monterey spots, where Jones had introduced the Jimi Hendrix Experience and shared a loose jam with Joplin and the guitarist offstage; Hendrix and Joplin were also rumored to have had a hurried dressing room liaison at a San Francisco gig and had been on the same bill at Woodstock. Jones and Hendrix were on friendly terms and had partied and informally played together, including on a preliminary take of "All Along the Watchtower." Jim Morrison and Janis Joplin had had an inebriated, unsatisfying sexual encounter of their own, and had each made records produced by Paul Rothchild. A very drunken Morrison had twice approached Hendrix during club shows but was turned away, on one occasion when Joplin smashed a bottle on his head. After Jones died Morrison wrote a poem, "Ode to LA While Thinking of Brian Jones, Deceased"—"That porky satyr's / leer / has leaped upward / into the loam." After Hendrix died Morrison asked acquaintances, "Anyone believe in omens?" After Joplin died he told them, "You're drinking with number three."

Brian Jones drowned in his swimming pool on July 3, 1969, after being ejected from the Rolling Stones for chronic intoxication and a history of drug busts that would have complicated his accompanying the band on overseas tours. A talented but unpredictable multi-instrumentalist who, like Syd Barrett, had originated and named his group, Jones had been gradually sidelined in the Stones by his inability to write songs of his own and his fraught personal issues with drink, drugs, women, and the Jagger-Richards partnership. His last major contributions to the Stones were heard on 1968's *Beggar's Banquet*; after that the others would often unplug his guitar in the studio and leave him off wangling alone. "Brian was a very infuriating guy," said Keith Richards. "Firing him was hard for Mick and me, but he could hardly play, hardly stand up, hardly breathe. That was one of the things we'd gone on to Brian about—he'd drink and take barbiturates on top of his respiratory problems. . . . You'd see him choking in a corner many times, pumping his inhaler into his mouth." "He ended up the kind of guy that you'd dread he'd come on the phone," his friend John Lennon recalled. The asthmatic Jones was drinking and swallowing barbiturates ("downers") when he went for his late-night swim, although longstanding rumor has held that his death was no accident but murder at the hands of a resentful contractor who was working on his Sussex home. He was the first major artist of the classic rock era to die young—he was twenty-six—and with a record of illegal drug use.

Jimi Hendrix was next to go, found dead in a girlfriend's London apartment on September 18, 1970. Buffeted by contractual problems, uneven live gigs with a confusion of backup players, and years of road work and heavy drinking and drugging, he took some Vesperax sleeping pills on top of wine and cannabis and went to sleep. He never woke up. "Jimi was a waste, I thought," remarked Bob Dylan, whose songs "Like a Rolling Stone" and "All Along the Watchtower" had been dazzlingly transformed by Hendrix. "I saw Jimi . . . [O]h man, that was sad when I saw him. He was in the backseat of a limousine on Bleecker Street, just . . . I couldn't even tell then whether he was dead or alive." Age at death: twenty-seven.

Blues mistress Janis Joplin followed a few weeks later. Joplin had become an overnight star following her appearance at the Monterey Pop Festival in 1967, and her subsequent career had highs with the raw emotionalism of "Down on Me," "Piece of My Heart," and "Try (Just a Little Bit Harder)," and lows with Joplin's own difficulty finding a worthy group to back her up, on top of her romantic disappointments and ongoing taste for liquor and heroin. Posthumously she was a legend; between 1968 and 1970 she was just a sometimes compelling singer whose managerial and backstage woes kept her from rising to her full potential. Friends tried to steer her toward the domesticity she may have secretly wanted, but she rebuffed them: "I don't want to live that way. I want to burn. I want to smolder. I don't want to go through all that crap." Alone and drunk in her room at the Landmark Hotel in Los Angeles on October 4, she shot herself up with heroin of a higher purity than her customary dose, fell over, and smashed her head on the bedside table. Age at death: twenty-seven.

Jim Morrison was found deceased in Paris two years to the day since Brian Jones went under. Mystery has surrounded his expiry, attributed variously to a heroin overdose, a cocaine overdose, a heart attack aggravated by his terminal alcoholism, or even a hoax, instigated by Morrison himself as a means to finally escape the prison of the Doors and rock 'n' roll notoriety in which the self-styled poet felt himself trapped. Few were surprised by the news, however—one way or another, in the not quite four years of his time as charismatic vocalist for a popular rock group, Jim Morrison had run out of options and run himself into the ground. "But is this really what it all came down to in the end, is this *it*?" mourned his legal wife, Patricia Kennealy. "All the leather pants and Lizard Kingdoms and busts and boozing and gold records and silver noses—all that merely sufficed to buy him earth enough in this city to lie in forever. . . ." Age at death: twenty-seven.

Around this era came a rash of lesser-known but still discouraging rock fatalities. Al Wilson of the down 'n' dirty blues act Canned Heat OD'd on downers on September 3, 1970, at age twenty-seven. Gram Parsons—of latter-day Byrds and the Flying Burrito Brothers, later a solo performer—became pals with Keith Richards, and the two shared both a love for traditional country music and a heedless inclination for drugs. Parsons took a shot of heroin and cocaine in a California hotel and died on September 18, 1973, soon to be lauded as a lost genius of country rock. "I'm aware of those rumblings," admitted Richards later. "'Oh, Gram would still be around if it wasn't for Keith Richards.' But I would honestly say that his attitude . . . reminded me of what was going on everywhere." Parsons was twenty-seven. Cass Elliot, formerly of the Mamas and the Papas, a user of heroin and barbiturates and battling longtime weight issues, had a heart attack in London on July 29, 1974, at age thirty-two.

Guitarist Danny Whitten of Neil Young's Crazy Horse was in a steep decline—drinking, hooked on heroin, stealing friends' guitars to support his habit, and utterly incapable of playing despite Young's unrealistic hopes for a recovery. The disheartened Young was forced to fire Whitten on November 18, 1972, after which Whitten went back to Los Angeles and took a lethal amount of alcohol and the sedative Valium. Age at death: twenty-nine. Bruce Berry, a likeable on-and-off roadie for CSNY, had been turned on to heroin by Whitten and followed the same trail into hard-core addiction, ripping instruments off acquaintances and employers and falling out with nearly everyone who knew him. "He

OPPOSITE: **Impassioned blues vocalist Janis Joplin was among the first wave of famous rock drug casualties. She OD'd on October 4, 1970.** *(Photofest)*

was always like a light, and now there was a shade over that light," said his friend Richard O'Connell. Berry overdosed on heroin and cocaine in Los Angeles on June 7, 1973, in his midtwenties. Neil Young eulogized Whitten, Berry, and the accumulating morgue of drug deaths in his great, groggy songs "Tired Eyes" ("So, was he a heavy doper? . . .") and "Tonight's the Night." "This is much more of a dope generation that we're in now," Young asserted to an interviewer in 1973. "[T]hey don't expect to live any more than thirty years and they don't care." In the liner notes he scribbled for an eventual compilation album, *Decade*, Young wrote of his funereal "The Needle and the Damage Done": "I am not a preacher but drugs killed a lot of great men."

Young's assessment of the new culture was accurate. Marijuana was a staple high for millions, and now was sold in a colorful range of varieties and prices, often named, like fine wine, for its regional origins: Acapulco Gold, Kona Gold, Maui Wowie, Panama Red, Oaxacan, Michoacan, Colombian, Jamaican, Thai stick, and so on. An ounce of weed might retail for between $10 and $20 in early '70s American currency, and kilograms, or "keys," were priced anywhere from $90 to over $200 across the United States. LSD was a known quantity (usually purveyed at between $1 and $5 per tab or hit), but now a plethora of more exotic chemicals had entered the universe of rock musicians, their attendants, and their audiences. In addition to the furies of STP and amyl nitrate there came the synthesized hallucinogen DMT (dimethyltryptamine), a manufactured version of the substances found in some South American plants that could induce mania along with a frantic heart rate; there was PCP (phencyclidine hydrochloride, phenyl cyclohexyl piperidine, or angel dust), employed as an anesthetic in human and veterinary medicine, taken up as another hallucinogen by the hippie society, and in heavy doses known to cause delirium, convulsions, and insensitivity to pain; there was MDMA (methylenedioxymethamphetamine), a powerful mood-altering pill that was later nicknamed Ecstasy for the giddy, euphoric reactions of its users. More downers came in the form of Quaaludes and Mandrax, comparable hypnotics or sedatives categorized under the title methaqualone, and often taken in combination with alcohol or other drugs for a "leveling" effect, and the painkiller Dilaudid. Quaaludes were supposedly named to convey the comfort of a "quiet interlude," the name's double *a* syllable borrowed from the manufacturer's successful Maalox stomach remedies. Valium (diazepam) was another sleeping pill widely ingested as a lifestyle drug. Not every rock 'n' roll maker or listener took any or all of these, of course, but all were easily procured by the initiated and their presence backstage, in the studio, or in the concert bleachers would have raised few eyebrows.

Above all, however, there was cocaine. The chewed leaves of the South American coca plant (*Erythroxylon coca*) had first been identified by European explorers as an invigorating asset to native populations' activity in mountain ranges, where their use was later dated back to 2500 B.C. In the nineteenth century various recipes of processed coca trickled into the more dubious corners of Western medical and psychological treatments (Sigmund Freud endorsed it as making him feel "strong as a lion, gay and cheerful"), and in the United States were even sold as over-the-counter remedies for hay fever and used as an ingredient in the original bottles of the wonderful "nerve tonic" Coca-Cola. But cocaine's habit-forming qualities were detected early on, and its use was more and more regulated out of the pharmacy and the doctor's office; as with cannabis, the anti-cocaine lobby emphasized the drug's popularity among minorities like African-Americans and other "undesirables." Throughout the first half of the twentieth century, cocaine remained the vice of either the lowest of the low or the modern aristocracies of Soho, the Left Bank, Broadway, and Hollywood, enjoyed by such hedonists as the actors Wallace Reid, Barbara La Marr, and Tallulah Bankhead, silent film director William Desmond Taylor, Aleister Crowley, and Art Nouveau painter Tamara de Lempicka.

Because cocaine was a processed substance from the faraway lands of Colombia, Bolivia, and Peru (unlike dried cannabis leaves and buds from California or Mexico, or hallucinogens distilled in local hideouts), its cost reflected the investment, distance, and risk taken to smuggle it: in 1973 it was estimated that ten pounds of cocaine would sell for $160,000 in the US, and a single gram usually went for $100. For many years this made it all but unavailable, and so any properties besides its basic desirability were unknown. Cocaine had always been the most expensive and most luxurious recreational drug, restricting its attractiveness to the rich and sophisticated, and as rock music gained its status as the most lucrative branch of the entertainment industry in the late 1960s, a young, large, and very wealthy market opened up. For rock musicians and those encompassed in their corona of fame and money, the social stimulant of a few bumps of coke, toot, blow, or Bolivian marching powder proffered from a decorative spoon became an almost obligatory symbol of insider chic.

Unlike marijuana or LSD, cocaine did not alter visual or audio perceptions and did not change the manner in which music was heard; there was no cocaine psychedelia. Its users instead found it made them feel not spaced-out but zoned-in—sharper, more energetic, more confident, and more in control, at least initially. It gave off no fumes that might arouse the suspicions of police, and promoted conversation and action rather than reflection and stupefaction. Cocaine inhibits the brain's receptors of the pleasure-causing chemical dopamine, thus building up an accretion of the substance, which then overloads the organ, leading to the supercharged "rush" of a cocaine high. But each successive experience of this kind produces a corresponding *drop* of dopamine as the rush wears off, leading to repeated cycles of lifts and crashes requiring a successively greater amount of the drug to attain the original sensation. Again, hallucinogens, depressants, and stimulants like cocaine do not act directly on the synapses but by playing with the brain's own chemical makeup, raising or lowering amounts of operative hormones well out of the ranges measurable under external stimuli. Also, the grainy, powdery texture of cocaine as it is sniffed can lead to long-term damage of the nasal passages, perforating the septum until the nose itself is at risk of collapse. Only gradually did cocaine's liabilities—the financial penalty, the physical deterioration, and the hellish psychological craving—become apparent to the rock 'n' roll elite. By the first years of the new decade, cocaine had permeated the lives and art of many of the top rock 'n' rollers, and its influence was to be heard on some of their best and bleakest output.

Related to this was the independence granted to rock stars by their record companies and by the very implements they used to make their music. Whereas in previous years even the most debauched performers were bound to straighten up and step into the more or less public confines of the recording studio, in the company of technicians, session players, and other staff, in the late 1960s and early 1970s studios had begun to serve as virtual homes away from home where they could carry on as they would at any party—studio work and drug use were on a continuum in the rock stars' daily and nightly lives. Engineers and producers were now expected to be confidants who gave the artists a wide leeway in writing, rehearsing, and cutting their tracks in any condition that resulted in presentable music. The baked sincerity of Neil Young's pieces with Crazy Horse that made it onto the *Tonight's the Night* album, like "Roll Another Number (for the Road)" and "Mellow My Mind," were only some of the tunes committed to tape while the control booth and studio floor were foggy with smoke, booze, and blow. "We'd just get to a point where you get a glow, just a glow," said Crazy

Horse drummer Ralph Molina. "When you do blow and drink, that's when you get that glow." Also, as professional-level recording equipment itself became more portable, many rockers elected to bring the studio to their home or other retreat and avoid the sterile atmosphere of the formal music room altogether. Country estates like Headley Grange in England or Bob Dylan and the Band's Big Pink in upstate New York were converted to makeshift recording halls where groups could get high and lay down takes over endless hours of woodshedding, jamming, and hanging out. Inevitably, the vibe of such gatherings filtered in to the finished sounds.

Sly and the Family Stone's *There's a Riot Goin' On* (1971) was one record whose lavish location and dissolute methodology are audible in just such a fashion. Stone had moved his group from their San Francisco base to the winding boulevards of Beverly Hills, renting a studio-fitted mansion from John Phillips, setting up a trailer on the grounds, and installing instruments, microphones, mixers, and tape decks throughout the premises. Instead of capturing the septet playing together in real time as he had on previous Family hits, the bandleader was now recording, rerecording, and overdubbing the members' contributions separately, and had even begun to use a primitive analog drum machine for some material, to the frustration of flesh-and-blood drummer Greg Errico. Always a high flyer, Stone lived a perpetual orgy at 783 Belair Road, inviting Phillips, Terry Melcher, R&B guitarist Bobby Womack, keyboardist Billy Preston, and jazz heavies Herbie Hancock and Miles Davis to his pad for unlimited quantities of cocaine; Stone and his guitarist brother Freddie were also taking regular doses of PCP. Vicious dogs roamed the property at will, and Stone would seduce women from nearby nightclubs by bringing them home to provide "backing vocals," which he erased after dismissing them the next morning. "[T]here was nothing but girls everywhere and coke, bodyguards with guns, looking all evil," Miles Davis recollected.

There's a Riot Goin' On is not so much a collection of individual songs as a long soundscape of shag-carpet torpor and shades-down degeneracy. The psychedelic soul of the Family Stone's 1969 singles "I Want to Take You Higher" and "Everyday People" had been superseded by the languid, menacing funk of "Family Affair" and "Luv n' Haight," and the upbeat live ambience of the group was replaced by a breathy, lo-fidelity intimacy unintentionally created by Stone's use and reuse of the same tapes over almost a year of recording. The disc was redolent of 783 Belair's druggy haze and no one, even the musicians' corporate bosses, could miss it: record executive Steve Paley reported that Sly Stone's Columbia label head Clive Davis objected, "That sounds like he's stoned. We can't put that out." "Clive, it's okay, it won't matter," Paley assured him. "It's a great record." "It was just what I observed, where I was at," Stone said many years afterward. A forerunner of the synthesized, do-it-yourself audio signatures of rap and hip-hop, *Riot* is still heard as one of the greatest albums ever made.

But nobody made drug records better than the Rolling Stones. With guitarist Mick Taylor taking over from the fired (and soon dead) Brian Jones in 1969, the Stones had survived the disaster of Altamont and other financial and emotional crises to rise to their peak period, artistically and chemically. They had come out from the shadow of the Beatles, who were on the verge of an acrimonious split, and their designation as the Fearsome Five to the Fab Four had changed to the title that would be retired with them: they had become the World's Greatest Rock 'n' Roll Band. The supremacy of the jail-dodging, sex-personifying, devil-sympathizing, dope-smoking Rolling Stones signified the cultural shift that had occurred in much of the world since 1964. As much as they disowned the controversies and danger ascribed to them, in 1970 they were thought by the chattering classes to be subversive heralds of some coming social breakdown. "If you, or the mothers of America, or anyone else, are trying to hang it on me, well, it's just the same as their lousy sexual and drug fantasies, isn't it?" Mick Jagger asked rhetorically. "They give the kids a society which they themselves have buggered up out of all sanity, and then when the kids don't buy the package deal, the decent, sensible people turn around and drop the bundle on my doorstep. You know, like I invented germ warfare. Like I have this hotline to Mao Tse-tung." If Jagger and his partner Keith Richards were leading the most popular rock act on the planet, the ideals and tastes of the rock audience had clearly been transformed.

The Stones' first album with Taylor in the lineup was 1969's *Let It Bleed*, its sanguinary title already in cutting contrast to the Beatles' re-signed *Let It Be*, and dotted with drug lyrics: "All my friends are junkies," said "Monkey Man"; "I went down to the Chelsea drugstore to get my prescription filled," said "You Can't Always Get What You Want"; "She blew my nose and then she blew my mind," said "Honky Tonk Women." These had mostly been recorded in conventional studios in London and America, but some songs from their 1971 LP, *Sticky Fingers*, were laid down at Stargroves, Jagger's home in the Sussex countryside, where the indulgence was even more liberal. *Sticky Fingers* was the first product on the band's private label, under the corporate umbrella of Atlantic Records, and as Atlantic's most valuable holding they were now granted *carte blanche* to play and say exactly as they felt. "Yeah, you got cocaine eyes," bristled "Can't You Hear Me Knocking"; "I'll be in my basement room, with a needle and a spoon," shrugged "Dead Flowers"; and a dead-of-night acoustic collaboration with Marianne Faithfull, Jack Nitzsche on piano, and slide guitarist Ry Cooder, "Sister Morphine," was surely the most depressing and most explicit portrayal of addiction and over-dose ever made. "The result of this effortless creation was not to inspire the writing of more songs but the use of more drugs!" lyricist Faithfull wrote of "Sister Morphine," as she split with Jagger and embarked on a long period of addiction and homelessness. "I became a victim of my own song." "Moonlight Mile" was a metaphor for a celestial white line, and the single "Brown Sugar," in addition to its obvious racial and sexual overtones, was named after a brand of Mexican heroin. "I don't think *Sticky Fingers* was a heavy drug album more than the world is a heavy world," defended Keith Richards.

For Richards the world had become very heavy. Though not yet the universal icon of superhuman toxicity he later became, by the releases of *Let It Bleed* and *Sticky Fingers* he had already earned a reputation in the rock community as an unusually hardy drug aficionado, blessed (or cursed) with a physical constitution that allowed him to withstand measures of cannabis, amphetamines, alcohol, cocaine, and LSD that would have felled most of his associates—and sometimes did. "I'm very lucky in that everything's always functioned perfectly, even under the most incredible strains and amounts of chemicals," he claimed. "But I think a lot of it has to do with a solid consciousness of it in a regulatory system which serves me. . . . All of the people that I've known that have died from so-called drug overdoses have all been people that have had some fairly serious physical weakness somewhere." By 1970, Richards was caught up in a heroin habit that would last several years but which showed no signs of slowing him down or diminishing his music.

In 1971 the Rolling Stones embarked on a tax exile in France, a social and economic move other British groups would emulate in response to the United Kingdom's punitive income laws and their own sizable but chaotic revenue streams; rock stars were irregularly granted windfall sums of cash but received no advice on investments and savings, nor were they given accurate pictures of their net worth and projected future earnings. In Keith Richards's spacious villa of Nellcôte on the

French Riviera, the band and friends, including producer Jimmy Miller; engineers Andy and Glyn Johns; horn players Jim Price and Bobby Keys; pianists Billy Preston, Mac "Dr. John" Rebennack, and Nicky Hopkins; and Gram Parsons, began to eat, breathe, sleep, fornicate, and get high in the creation of the Stones' next collection, a two-disc set that was tentatively named *Eat It* or *Tropical Disease* but ultimately went by the name *Exile on Main Street.*

Today hailed as the Stones' masterpiece, *Exile* is the murky audio presentation of life inside Nellcôte during Richards' residency. "The humidity was incredible," said Jagger. "It was 120 degrees. . . . That's when I got into Jack Daniel's," said Richards. "I can remember fifty people sitting down to lunch," said Mick Taylor. Alcohol, cannabis, cocaine, and heroin were on hand throughout the sessions. "Keith was getting out of it a lot and in retaliation Mick wouldn't turn up some nights," remembered the dour Stones bassist Bill Wyman. "It was obvious drugs were at the center of the problem—whatever people tell you about the creative relationship between hard drugs and the making of rock 'n' roll records, forget it." "Working on *Exile* was really long, sitting around in the south of France waiting for the band to show up," engineer Andy Johns looked back. "There was always smack around. The boredom is why I started doing it." "If you're really on some heavily addictive drug," Jagger said resentfully, "you think about the drug, and everything else is secondary. . . .[Nellcôte] was this communal thing where you don't know whether you're recording or living or having dinner; you don't know when you're gonna play, when you're gonna sing."

When the best takes were finally extracted from hundreds of idle jams and halfhearted vamps, the tracks were a red-eyed mire of gospel, country blues, honky-tonk, and rock 'n' roll, among them longtime favorites like "Tumbling Dice" and Richards's raggedly joyous "Happy," along with deep, dirty gems "Sweet Virginia," "Loving Cup," "Shake Your

Hips," "Torn and Frayed," and the spent hush of "Sweet Black Angel." While some numbers were completed or polished at proper studios in London and Los Angeles, the imperfect acoustics of Nellcôte could be detected on all four sides. The impression on first listen was of being confined in the same sweaty basement with Richards, Jagger, and guests in a permanent swelter of heat and dope as the canons of Nashville, Memphis, and the Mississippi Delta are essayed over and over and the bottles, the bags, and the vials never run out. "I did a fucking double album . . . when I was heaviest into heroin," Richards swore with hindsight. "Pills, hash, and the occasional mind-expanding drug were one thing," Wyman worried, but Richards and his codependents "were on the slippery slope."

The druggy candor of *Sticky Fingers* and *Exile on Main Street* was well received by the vast fan base that well understood their subject matter and their loose, jaded sonic mood. Keith Richards seemed to live, embody, and epitomize the spirit of the counterculture: an adult husband and father who took the personal risks of a teenage daredevil, a millionaire who roamed from continent to continent like a gypsy (he even owned a yacht named *Mandrax*), a tabloid celebrity forever running afoul of authority like an outlaw, and a sensitive and, on occasion, surprisingly eloquent musician who appeared to respectable citizens as a disheveled and lethargic creep. To his admirers he was Keef Riffhard, or the Human Riff, or the Human Drugstore, or the World's Most Elegantly Wasted Human Being, or the living incarnation of the music itself—"Keith Richards *is* rock 'n' roll," they declared. When the Rolling Stones toured North America in 1972—a triumphant return after the savagery of Altamont—photographer Annie Leibovitz snapped an iconic portrait of Richards, wearing aviator shades and a "Coke" badge that did not refer to soft drinks, slumped next to the wall of the customs area of some dreary airport in the US. On the wall beside the Human

Riff was a poster: "Patience Please . . . A Drug Free America Comes First!" In fact, during the next few years rock music moved a drug-free America, and a drug-free world society, to the back of the line.

DARK SIDE
OF THE MOON
1973-1975

Them say that herb is a dangerous drug, and poison, an' every day
I poison myself and never die....But if you smoke some nice herb an'
put your mind somewhere where inspiration flows, herb so nice.

PETER TOSH

Seventy-six million children were born in the United States from 1946
to 1964, twenty-six million more than in the previous eighteen years
and ten million more than in the two decades following. The years
1954–56 were the most fertile of a notably expansive time in American demography, and by 1973 the babies born in those months had
reached their late teens, with all the cultural and intellectual accessories of adolescence in an affluent democracy. They had been raised
in good health and provided with more than ample nutrition, had
been granted full access to entertainment in a variety of electronic
media, and had been educated in the most advanced and extensive
system of primary, secondary, and post-secondary schooling on the
globe. These young people formed the largest sector of the American
population (their numeric ranks in Canada, the United Kingdom,
western Europe, and other Allied victors of World War II differed but
just slightly), and the politics, economies, and morals of the nation

seemed to have been developed around their needs and wants. In 1970 the voting age in the US had been lowered from twenty-one to eighteen, extending the franchise to eleven million new electors, and in everything from sexual standards and censorship to hairstyles and fashion trends the impact of "the student generation," "the now generation," or "the protest generation" was felt and considered. Sometimes they were referred to as "the rock generation," and their choice of intoxicants had likewise started to affect the wider workings of the nation.

Recreational drugs, marijuana chief among them, had begun to permeate the older, more mainstream spheres outside of rock. The Rolling Stones had brought authors Truman Capote and Terry Southern on their 1972 tour to bask in the Stones' aura of youthful delinquency and report back to Middle America just how debauched these long-haired, androgynous English revolutionaries really were. "They had this doctor on the plane, about twenty-eight years old, rather good looking," the acclaimed writer of *In Cold Blood* chronicled. "He would pass through the plane with a big plate of pills, everything from Vitamin C to vitamin coke." Southern, cowriter of the films *Dr. Strangelove* and *Easy Rider* and a *Sgt. Pepper* cover subject, praised for the *Saturday Review* the Stones' generosity with Tequila Sunrises: "[T]he scarlet dash of grenadine into the orange, unstirred and allowed to seek its own cloudlike definition, lends the whole (in certain half-lights) an effect of advanced psychedelia. . . . On most planes, you can't get a drink until you're in the air—aboard *The Lapping Tongue* you usually had a drink in your hand before reaching your seat." Novelist Norman Mailer, lionized as US publishing's most outspoken and outrageous personality, had been proudly smoking pot since the 1950s and never tried to hide it: "Mary Jane . . . was the back door to sex, which had become again all I had and all I wanted. . . ."

Astronomer Carl Sagan and filmmaker Robert Altman (and many in his hip Hollywood circle) were also known to enjoy cannabis; as "Mr. X" the Cornell University professor Sagan claimed that "I have made a conscious effort to think of a few particularly difficult current problems in my field when high. It works, at least to a degree." (On the other hand, Sagan elsewhere put down "the mindless outpourings of rock-and-roll stations.") Pro athletes came forward to confess to or boast of how pot had numbed their pain or how speed had improved their game. "Uppers just make you play up to your potential when you're hungover," said baseball player Jim Bouton. Pittsburgh thrower Dock Ellis was said to have won a game where the only hit scored against him was that of the LSD he was tripping on throughout play. Thomas "Hollywood" Henderson took cocaine, stimulants, and painkillers while on the Dallas Cowboys NFL team. "The drugs that I abused playing the game, and that were abused by almost everybody around me, were codeine, Percodan, and amphetamines," he said.

Drugs' radical chic reputation, like that of donating to the Black Panthers or lining up for an exhibition of the X-rated blockbuster *Deep Throat*, went as far as the straitlaced TV host Dick Cavett, whose network talk show had featured guests like John Lennon and Yoko Ono, Jimi Hendrix, Janis Joplin, and a conspicuously fried Sly Stone. In an autobiographical account, Cavett told of his nervous initiations into hip consciousness: "I got totally high, laughed hysterically at the idea of a clock, convulsed myself over the fact that carpets were rectangular, saw the deep and cosmic humor in fingernails. . . . The last time I made moocah, or dug sweet Lucy, was with Janis Joplin, who gave me one that must have been rolled by Montezuma himself."

A backlash was already brewing—more and more forceful as the decade wore on, but at first futile. Rock 'n' roll was the bull's-eye. The Los Angeles–based Do It Now Foundation went after amphetamine use in the early 1970s and brought Frank Zappa, Alice Cooper, and even Grace Slick on board its "Speed Kills" campaign. This was one of the more credible such efforts, begun out of safety concerns as opposed to social compulsion, although singling out a drug then identified with harried housewives and long-distance truckers may have been an easy sell to hopheads and coke freaks. Jim Morrison was almost willing to tape a promo for Speed Kills but couldn't quite keep a straight face: "I sing with a group called the Doors. . . . I never, never did a song on speed. Drunk, hell yeah . . ." Another take: "Don't shoot speed. . . . Christ, you guys, smoke pot." Another take: "Speed kills. Please don't shoot speed—try downers, yeah, downers, barbs, tranks, reds. . . ." Jim Morrison never Did It Now.

The US Federal Communications Commission in 1970 began to collect data on pop songs that allegedly promoted drugs, citing the pretty obvious "With a Little Help from My Friends" by the Beatles, the Jefferson Airplane's "White Rabbit," Dylan's "Rainy Day Women #12 & 35," and the Temptations' "Cloud Nine," among others, and radio stations and record companies were pressured into ill-conceived and desultory bids to purge their rosters or playlists of supposedly drug-advocating musicians or music. The sing-along "One Toke Over the Line" by the duo Brewer and Shipley was dropped by some Top 40 broadcasters, and other titles were pulled from the airwaves, but most DJs and record executives had neither the time nor the inclination to look into the lyrics or lifestyles of every artist they promoted. Sometimes "objectionable" acts were merely unsuccessful ones, a pretext used by MGM Records head Mike Curb when jettisoning a number of soon-forgotten bands like Ultimate Spinach and Lavender Popcorn even as the company held on to commercially popular dopers like Eric Burdon and issued some 1966 live music of the Grateful Dead. "[Curb]'s spent all this money on these albums and he's putting them out even if we all have needles sticking out of our arms," snickered Dead manager Rock Scully. "Business as usual, folks." In any case, the pervasiveness of the youth culture and its range of underground outlets were such that no pressure from parents or legislators was likely to stem the tide of rock 'n' roll and its associated turn-ons.

But the pressure was coming all the way from the top. In a harbinger of executive clampdowns to come, US president Richard Nixon had spoken out against the drug culture in typically overheated terms: "To erase the grim legacy of Woodstock, we need a total war against drugs," he stated, condemning the "permissiveness" of the young against the God-fearing values of "the Silent Majority." The first shots of the War on Drugs were fired by Nixon in 1971, launching an "all-out global war on the drug menace" and recasting the shifting standards of tolerance and personal choice as a national crisis. When the congressionally mandated National Commission on Marijuana and Drug Abuse concluded in 1973 that "marihuana use is not such a grave problem that individuals who smoke marihuana, or possess it for that purpose, should be subject to criminal procedures," an angry Nixon discounted the commission's findings and continued with his calls for tougher enforcement and harsher penalties.

Despite (or perhaps because of) Nixon's prejudices, by his first term drugs had acquired their own legal defenders—not just placard-waving potheads but qualified lobbyists who launched coherent campaigns on behalf of ending the restrictions against cannabis. The serious movement to overturn the drug policies of various nations had been instigated in the 1960s and gained credence with various studies and petitions put forward in academia and the press. These were distinct from the proselytizing missions of Timothy Leary or Allen Ginsberg in that they used the restrained language of medicine and law enforcement, as opposed to claims of some impending millennial consciousness. As early as 1967 all four Beatles had put their names to an advertisement placed in the London *Times* headlined "The Law Against Marijuana is Immoral in Principle and Unworkable in Practice," which argued that "[t]he government should permit and encourage research into all aspects of cannabis use, including its medical application," and "[a]llowing the smoking of cannabis on private premises should no longer constitute an offence." Other signatories to the petition were several doctors—theatrical director and trained physician Jonathan Miller, DNA pioneer Francis Crick, and psychiatrist R. D. Laing were three of the most prominent—as well as novelist Graham Greene, playwright Kenneth Tynan, and political commentator Tariq Ali. The cost of the advertisement was paid by the Beatles' manager Brian Epstein, whose name was also attached.

In the United States, rockers were enlisted to spread the message of several pro-marijuana spokesmen. John Sinclair, a Michigan pot protester who had been busted for holding two joints, was able to attract the expatriate John Lennon to his cause, and Lennon even wrote and performed a minor song, "John Sinclair," calling for the overturn of Sinclair's conviction (which was achieved). Sinclair himself had served as manager-cum-commandant of one of the most insurrectionary groups of the late '60s, Detroit's Motor City Five (MC5), who became the musical accompaniment to Sinclair's White Panther Party with the straightforward agenda of "rock 'n' roll, dope, and fucking in the streets." It was activist Abbie Hoffman's impromptu defense of Sinclair from the stage at Woodstock that got him ejected by the Who's Pete Townshend. Sinclair recalled the ex-Beatle's recruitment: "The first time I met [Lennon], to express my appreciation for his help, we sat around and smoked quite a bit of herb, and made the fact that the stuff was illegal the object of much laughter and ridicule. . . . He was one beautiful cat." The earnest and naively radical Lennon of the early '70s also lent his credibility to the otherwise bush-league street performer and pot advocate David Peel, producing and touting his album *The Pope Smokes Dope*. (Peel wrote songs titled "I Like Marijuana" and "Show Me the Way to Get Stoned.") "I dabbled in so-called politics in the late sixties and seventies more out of guilt than anything," Lennon eventually confessed. "Guilt for being rich, and guilt thinking that perhaps love and peace isn't enough and you have to go and get shot or something, or get punched in the face, to prove I'm one of the people."

Less confrontationally, Washington lawyer Keith Stroup founded the National Organization for the Reform of Marijuana Laws, or NORML, in 1971, with a start-up grant from *Playboy* magazine publisher Hugh Hefner. NORML came to represent cannabis users from Stroup's background as a product safety advocate—"I saw the marijuana issue as a consumer question. . . . The consumers in this issue are the smokers, but we can't deal with their problems as long as we are in danger of being locked up." Stroup perceived that the millions of criminalized dope smokers were nonetheless a potentially powerful bloc of spenders and voters if they could be organized like any other interest group, and he and NORML were granted access to the corridors of power not to encourage cannabis smoking but to argue to officialdom the senselessness and waste of the laws against it. "NORML does not advocate the use of marijuana," maintained the organization's statement of purpose. "We do believe, however, that the burdensome costs of continued criminal prohibition far exceed any deterrent value of the present laws." To this end, the body distanced itself from the image of what Stroup called "the crazy freak in the street," acknowledging that the demonstrations and Be-Ins of the 1960s had become history but that "the marijuana issue is one of the few issues that does have the potential to offer the frustrated college students of the seventies some way to participate in policy making."

During this optimistic period the paraphernalia of drug use became more acceptable as consumer items, even as drugs themselves remained outside the law. Most North American urban centers had their own "head shops," retail outlets offering a selection of pipes, rolling papers, roach clips and other artifacts to discerning tokers; usually rock posters, T-shirts, and badges would be on sale nearby. In with the glossy pinups of progressive musicians would also be cartoon portraits of the "Head of the Class" (a joint-laden dude doing business from his school desk) and the often reproduced "Stoned Again" by famed illustrator R. Crumb (a glazed toker gradually melting from the brain down), which adorned many a bedroom or dormitory wall. For the bookish, author Carlos Castaneda's contemporary Don Juan trilogy (1968–72) presented an allegedly authentic (in fact fictionalized) account of the author's being introduced to the wonders of natural hallucinogens by a Mexican Indian shaman, while gonzo journalist Hunter S. Thompson's *Fear and Loathing in Las Vegas* (1971) did the same for the wonders of unnatural ones in Sin City. Rock magazines like *Rolling Stone*, *Creem*, and *Circus* featured advertisements for coyly described "smokers' needs" such as stash boxes, incense sticks, flavored papers or tobacco (to roll with marijuana or hash), and like implements, all of them legal on technical grounds, yet whose real, illicit, purposes were understood by both seller and buyer. No longer the homemade improvisations of years past, such items were ingenious and decorative necessities in any crash pad worthy of the name, and the industry of mass-produced widgets embossed with the distinctive silhouette of the marijuana leaf grew into a billion-dollar gesture of pro-drug defiance.

The drug culture—or more accurately, the drug market—even came up with its own monthly magazine, *High Times*, which first hit newsstands in 1974. Alone among hundreds of amateurish "alternative" or campus broadsheets handed out in head shops and on street corners,

High Times was a glossy periodical with international distribution, keeping readers informed on shifts in regional drug laws, prices, and quality, profiling activists like Keith Stroup, providing tips for novice cannabis cultivators, shippers, and vendors, interspersed with the comic-strip adventures of Dope Rider and Zippy the Pinhead, and lavishly illustrated with enticing "centerfolds" of primo sinsemilla, Nepalese black, or Maui Wowie spread out and ready to be rolled.

If *High Times* and head shops at home were not enough for the aspiring head, there was always travel abroad. By the 1970s the American baby boomers were eagerly discovering the convenience and adventure of jet travel—barely twenty years old at the time, building on ever more expansive routes and fleets of ever larger and faster aircraft—to take them to exotic destinations where drug prohibitions were considerably relaxed. Some journeyed to Morocco, long a preferred exile for European bohemians and US Beats and where kif (marijuana mixed with tobacco) was in ready and cheap supply; Mick Jagger, Keith Richards, and Brian Jones had fled there in the tumultuous year of 1967 and had looked into their own personal and professional abysses. "First off you go round and visit the fleshpots," explained Richards of the Moroccan itineraries, "and when you get slightly debauched and jaded, you remember, 'Ah, yes, the music . . .'" Turkey, Lebanon, India, Nepal, and the Iran and Afghanistan that predated the Islamic Revolution were further stops on the "Hippie Trail," although smokers and smugglers did run the risk of arrest, expulsion, or imprisonment, and the influx of rock-listening, dope-loving Western youths into traditionally conservative societies was not always appreciated by local authority.

Nearer to the North American sensibility was the enlightened stance of the Netherlands, which took a softer line on cannabis use (the country was also closer by air than its Middle Eastern counterparts). The coffee shops of Amsterdam began to sell over-the-counter varieties of marijuana and hashish in 1972. Though soft drugs were not fully decriminalized in that country, the government's tolerance of such substances saw the proliferation of neighborhood "hash bars" that showed the Dutch and backpacking Europeans, Americans, Canadians, and antipodeans just how civilized the marijuana community could be. One of the first such premises was the Mellow Yellow, named after the Donovan tune. The stoners' dream of walking into a safe, friendly public place and ordering a choice and quality-controlled brand of dope from a varied menu was first realized among the picturesque canals and *straats* of Amsterdam.

But the one place where a liberalized social attitude toward drugs became most closely identified with a strain of popular music was the Caribbean nation of Jamaica. A few Jamaican performers had scored international hits during the 1960s, notably Desmond Dekker and the Aces' "Israelites" and Millie Small's "My Boy Lollipop," but it was not until the advent of reggae music and its leading light Nesta Robert "Bob" Marley that the island's sounds gained a worldwide audience. With his group the Wailers, Marley had been playing and recording in the country for several years and had earned the respect of Jamaica's disproportionately poor and disadvantaged population, from which he, his band, and other reggae artists had all sprung. The rich, distinctive beats and linguistic inflections of the music had been creeping into the rock mainstream prior to the Wailers' success (e.g., transplanted Texan Johnny Nash's "I Can See Clearly Now"), but when the Jimmy Cliff–dominated soundtrack for the Jamaican outlaw film *The Harder They Come* and the Wailers' album *Catch a Fire* were released by the London-based Island Records label in 1972 and 1973, respectively, the disparate elements of reggae were crystallized into a potent and pungent showcase.

Reggae had the same African origins as American blues, gospel, and soul music (and, by extension, rock 'n' roll), but it had made a turn toward its sunny syncopation far different from the urban grit of Muddy Waters' or James Brown's music, and had taken on a brooding mysticism in the form of the uniquely Jamaican sect of Rastafarianism. An ancient blend of Judaism and Ethiopian Christianity, Rastafarianism espoused the divinity of Ethiopian emperor Haile Selassie (born Ras Tafari Makonnen) and promised a global return of the African diaspora, spread through colonialism and slavery into the Babylon of the white Eurocentric West. Significantly, via the transplanted Indians brought to work the island's agriculture in the mid–nineteenth century, Jamaica had become home to a wild and powerful strain of cannabis, which became an integral component of Rastafarian meditation and worship. Alcohol and gambling were forbidden by the creed, but what the Indians had called *ganja* was encouraged throughout black Jamaica as a folk remedy, a social lubricant, and an instrument of devotion. Officially, it was illegal under Jamaican law; unofficially, its growth and distribution was part of the national economy.

As Bob Marley and the Wailers rose to international superstardom (Marley became the "name" leader after the defection of original Wailers Peter Tosh and Bunny Livingston), what impressed many white listeners in Britain or North America as much as the songs themselves was Marley's open and constant consumption of ganja, twisted up into massive spliffs whose fumes burned around him like an aura. Even in the wake of Jim Morrison or Jimi Hendrix or Neil Young, this matter-of-fact endorsement of every hippie's most provocative pastime was unheard of among pop celebrities—but Marley was not smoking to show off. As a devout Rastafarian he was only taking a sacrament that aided him in contemplation and spiritual awareness, and besides, it came from a plant that grew freely in Jamaica's warm climate and rugged terrain. "Herb just grow, like yam and cabbage," he said. "When you smoke herb, herb reveal yourself to you." Not that he didn't get stoned out of his mind, as indicated in one interview: "I can remember the first time I hear a record when the thing was going to get popular, when Jamaican singers in Jamaica was going to get popular. . . . What were we talking about?"

More credibly than any other subcategory of classic rock, reggae made the case that something straights considered at best frivolous and at worst dangerous was actually a serious cultural phenomenon whose appeal and impact transcended border, class, race, and rhythmic style. "The whole thing seemed intelligent to me," said Marley's wife, Rita, recalling her introduction to the tenets of Rastafarianism. "It wasn't just about smoking herb, it was more a philosophy that carried some history with it." As the initial stirrings of economic and political globalization rumbled, Bob Marley was announced as the first "third-world superstar," a famous pop musician from a for once underdeveloped nation who won fans in Africa and Asia as well as in the West. The accoutrements of reggae—dreadlocked hair, knit caps, the red, yellow, and green colors of the Ethiopian flag—all became intertwined with the cannabis crusade, to a degree that the blaring of Marley's albums *Burnin'* or *Rastaman Vibration*, or his early hits like "Get Up, Stand Up" and "Lively Up Yourself," from car or apartment windows in Manchester or Minneapolis or Melbourne were virtual advertisements of the aromatic activity taking place within. Marley certainly had a broader religious and political message than mere marijuana decriminalization (although he was arrested in London and fined for possession), but he always made known his support for the cause. Asked if marijuana would ever be made legal, he replied, "I don't know if this government will, but I know Christ's government will." Other reggae performers were more vocal, especially

OPPOSITE: **Reggae superstar Bob Marley promoted cannabis as no mere recreation but the sacrament of an entire musical, social, and spiritual movement.** *(Gary Merrin / Hulton Archive / Getty Images)*

the militant ex-Wailer Peter Tosh on his incantational 1976 album and eponymous single *Legalize It,* the cover of which pictured him nestled in a lush ganja plantation: "Legalize it, don't criticize it, legalize it, and I will advertise it. . . ." Alert to a long-standing injustice, Tosh charged that the discriminatory enforcement of anti-cannabis laws were "fuckin' up the small man, 'cause only the small man at all time go to blood-clot jail for herb, and the big man just pass in him limousine." The reggae music of Tosh, Marley, and their brethren was the quasi-official soundtrack for an individual and collective resistance against many forms of oppression that would continue right up to the present day.

The drug culture's growth into an international way of life coincided with the other great social transformation of the 1960s and'70s: the sexual revolution. Not only were the rituals of male-female courtship being abandoned in favor of casual and serial relationships well outside an age-old understanding of sanctioned marriage, but so too were traditional definitions of masculinity and femininity being tested. Female and gay liberation protests were likewise upsetting religious dictates, moral truisms, family customs and state laws. Long-haired men were one thing; during the early '70s some people were challenging the very notion of distinct genders and seemed to imply a logical conclusion to the wave of sexual experimentation that would arrive when everyone turned bisexual. A number of the challengers played rock 'n' roll, and drug use was just another one of their outrages.

Glam, glitter, and gutter rock were not the LSD psychedelia of *Sgt. Pepper* or the Grateful Dead, nor were they the regal, coke-fired decadence of Crosby, Stills, Nash, and Young or *There's a Riot Goin' On.* Instead they embodied the eroticism of the nightclub bathroom stall, the uppers and downers of the Manhattan loft party, the loveless neon-lit encounter smoothed over by Valium or methedrine. They sounded the sleazy and kinky underside of rock. Lou Reed had sung with Andy Warhol's quartet the Velvet Underground—the pop artist's deadpan approximation of a pop act that took on a life of its own— and then built a respected solo career characterizing the transvestites, junkies, vampires, and weirdos of New York City. He took speed and heroin, and Velvet Underground bandmate John Cale claimed Reed once injected him: "You get a much stronger effect if you injected heroin, particularly if you shot it into a vein, but I was squeamish about needles." Reed himself mimicked shooting up on stage. In and out of the Velvets, his songs "Take a Walk on the Wild Side," "Venus in Furs," "White Light / White Heat," "Waiting for the Man," "Sister Ray" ("I'm searching for my mainline / I couldn't hit it sideways"), and "Heroin" ("When the smack begins to flow, then I really don't care anymore") were taken as harrowing vistas of the sex and drug underworlds, the sunlit pastures of Woodstock inverted into a strung-out night in the back alleys of New York's Lower East Side. "I think everybody in the Velvet Underground was aware that there was this whole area of ex- istence that was completely ignored by the rest of the music available at that time," Reed noted.

Detroit's Iggy Pop and the Stooges had come from the same bellig- erent scene as the MC5 and espoused the same unskilled minimalism as the Velvet Underground—the Stooges' "Raw Power" and "I Wanna Be Your Dog" reduced rock to three distorted chords, a grind of 4/4 time, and Iggy's (sometimes literally) naked aggression. "I took two grams of biker speed, five trips of LSD, and as much grass as could be inhaled," he said of his backstage routine. "But I remember a happy time—some fairly healthy guys smoking weed on a daily basis, growing our hair, having sex with as many young fans as we could get to come over. . . ." Of recording "I Wanna Be Your Dog" under the tutelage of the VU's John Cale, guitarist Ron Asheton recalled: "I wasn't getting really stoned when we were in the studio, but I remember we'd have some before we played, just to get into our own heads." "The inspiration for the song? I was taking a lot of acid, drinking Beaujolais, and going for long walks in the Michigan countryside," detailed Iggy. Away from the Stooges, he went through a heroin addiction and was committed to mental institutions before cleaning up down the road. "[Heroin] became a comfort, a refuge," he said. "I was trying to forge ahead, and I burned out. People around me, who weren't as intensely motivated as I, didn't get jonesed as bad."

Lou Reed and Iggy Pop were usually too abrasive or dangerous to attract much more than small hard-core followings or the occasional curious scandal seeker, but Elton John was a flamboyant and transparently gay performer who was one of the biggest names in 1970s rock. His albums *Madman Across the Water* (1971), *Honky Chateau* (1972), *Goodbye Yellow Brick Road* (1973), and *Captain Fantastic and the Brown Dirt Cowboy* (1975) were immense pop-rock hits (music by John, lyrics by Bernie Taupin), and his oversize glasses and camp costumes made him an inescapable media presence for several years. With this level of success, he was soon swept up into a predilection for cocaine, as corroborated by Taupin. "It was Jack Daniel's and lines on the console," during the making of his record *Rock of the Westies* (1975), the songwriter said, while John luxuriated in the thrill and pleasure of blow: "I felt I'd really arrived when I started taking drugs. . . . [Cocaine] invades your psyche like you wouldn't believe." In his case drugs were connected with his painful groping toward a sexual contentment. "I used cocaine basically for sex," he said. "My sexual fantasies were all played out while I was on cocaine. Sometimes when I'm flying over the Alps, I think that's like all

OPPOSITE: With "Waiting for the Man" and "Take a Walk on the Wild Side," Lou Reed delved into the sleazy, kinky underside of the drug culture—the sunshine of Woodstock inverted into a night on the Lower East Side. (*Jorgen Angel / Getty Images*)

the cocaine I've sniffed." Elton John was to grapple with substance and other health problems for another decade.

Freddie Mercury of Queen also used cocaine to augment his own same-sex binges, although underneath his and his group's florid, baroque exterior was a quartet of educated and conscientious musicians. For Mercury—born Farrokh Bulsara of Indian Zoroastrian parents in the exotic African city of Zanzibar—cocaine was but another party favor for the hedonistic superstar persona he devised to lead Queen to worldwide attention. The music was a meticulous hybrid of high camp and hard rock, put together under Mercury's soaring voice (he'd refused marijuana owing to its effects on his pipes) and his quirky private notational system, alongside the strutting guitar, bass, and drumming chops of Brian May, John Deacon, and Roger Taylor. According to his sometime partner Jim Hutton, Mercury took coke "recreationally and not that much," along with gallons of champagne and vodka, at the center of Felliniesque industry affairs with strippers, dwarves, transvestites, and live sex shows. Freddie Mercury was the rarity in rock who could take or leave drugs, and his many female and male friends and lovers have described him as a gracious and deeply private man whose outward persona, that of a rock 'n' roll Noel Coward sashaying through *Sheer Heart Attack* (1974), *A Night at the Opera* (1975), and songs like "Fat-Bottomed Girls," "Killer Queen," "We Will Rock You / We Are the Champions," and the stupendous "Bohemian Rhapsody," was all a funny, fancy burlesque. Of anyone who couldn't see Queen's talent underneath the glam Mercury would only say, "Fuck them, darling, if they just don't get it." Yet such was rock's association with drugs that even Queen's thumping 1980 hit "Another One Bites the Dust" was alleged to carry the message "It's fun to smoke marijuana" when played backward—a true enough statement, but unintentional on the part of Mercury and Queen.

More than any of the new epicenes, it was David Bowie who became the archetype of indeterminate sexuality and druggy abandon. Struggling to make it as an R&B or folk singer in his early years, he released his pivotal record *The Rise and Fall of Ziggy Stardust and the Spiders from Mars*, in 1972, whereupon he at last became a real rock star on the strength of his portraying an imaginary one. Bowie's work was part music and part theater, whereby the singer invented and reinvented a succession of personas—Ziggy, Aladdin Sane, the Thin White Duke—to act out an amalgam of futurism, fascism, cabaret, and rock 'n' roll, with the subjects of androgyny, alienation, space travel, and most of all his constantly changing self. After the landmark *Ziggy Stardust*, his discs *Aladdin Sane* (1973), *Diamond Dogs* (1974), and *Young Americans* (1975) all were big sellers, and in addition to collaborating with John Lennon ("Fame") and cultivating the careers of fellow deconstructivists Lou Reed and Iggy Pop, Bowie took to high living like the dissipated celebrity he pretended to be and therefore became.

He had contemplated "Quaaludes and red wine" in "Time," celebrated "when they pulled you out of the oxygen tent, you asked for the latest party" in "Diamond Dogs," praised an Iggy-like "Jean Genie" who was "strung out on lasers and slash back plazas . . . Talking 'bout Monroe and walking on Snow White," and pleaded with listeners to "turn on with me and you're not alone" in "Rock 'n' Roll Suicide," but by the mid-'70s Bowie had plummeted into a severe cocaine habit that left him visibly pale, dark-eyed, and emaciated. Sometimes the singer managed to harness his coke gluttony productively during all-night studio sessions, as remembered by his guitarist Carlos Alomar: "Now at 3 A.M., [Bowie] says, 'Well, it's time for you to start your guitar part.' Now if there's a line of coke which is going to keep you awake until 8 A.M. so that you can do your guitar part, you do the line of coke, because basically it just keeps you up and keeps the mind bright."

But along with suppressing the need for sleep and the appetite for food, heavy cocaine intake arouses a sense of paranoia, where all thought becomes fearful and obsessive. In 1975, Bowie had retreated to a Los Angeles abode and was convinced he was trapped there by witches and that Satan lived in the swimming pool. His wife Angela wrote that while there "his most compelling activity was receiving roadies of famous bands who would arrived with fat packages of the best Peruvian flake in their hand-tooled leather shoulder bags and leave with fatter little rolls of money, after which he'd chop and line and snort until dawn or later with his closest sycophants and whatever semi-famous showbiz coke whores happened by." Bowie agreed. "That was the wipeout period. I was totally washed up emotionally and psychically, completely screwed up.... I'd stay up for seven or eight days on the trot....Of course, every day that you stayed up longer—and there's things that you have to do to stay up that long—the impending tiredness and fatigue produces that hallucinogenic state quite naturally. Well, *half*-naturally. By the end of the week my whole life would be transformed into this bizarre nihilistic fantasy world of oncoming doom, mythological characters, and imminent totalitarianism. Quite the worst." Eventually he escaped Los Angeles ("I moved out of the coke capital of the world," he swore) and found his mental footing in Berlin, where he changed his sound yet again and recorded the albums *Low* (1977) and *Lodger* (1979) putting the drug-inspired dementia of his previous incarnations behind him once and for all. "Up until the early eighties, I had absolutely no doubt that I wouldn't be able to do anything good musically if I stopped doing cocaine," Bowie said in hindsight. "I now think that's absolute bullshit. It's the great lie."

Even the more conventional rock of the 1970s was bent toward a presumption of the artists' and the audiences' assorted indulgences. Lyrical references to drugs were not even a novelty anymore; they were gestures of solidarity and sympathy from the performers to their fans, heard in concert and on vinyl as publicly stated approval for what had become a semi-public outlaw society. Thus the decade opened with Van Morrison's yearning "And It Stoned Me," the Grateful Dead's "Casey Jones" ("Drivin' that train, high on cocaine"), Rick Derringer's "Rock and Roll Hoochie Koo" ("High all the time hope you all are too"), and the Guess Who's "No Sugar Tonight / New Mother Nature" ("A bag of goodies and a bottle of wine, we're gonna get it on right tonight"). Nineteen seventy-two heard Paul McCartney and Wings' "Hi Hi Hi" and T-Rex's "Telegram Sam" ("Sells me the good stuff!"). Keith Richards's charred vocal on the Rolling Stones' "Coming Down Again," John Denver's easy-listening "Rocky Mountain High," the New Riders of the Purple Sage's song and album *The Adventures of Panama Red*, and the Steve Miller Band's "The Joker" ("I'm a joker, I'm a smoker, I'm a midnight toker") buzzed in 1973. Eric Clapton's cover of Bob Marley's "I Shot the Sheriff" ("Every day I plant the seed. . . . He says kill it before it grows") was a chart and bong hit in '74. Seventy-six resin-ated with Boston's "Smokin'," the Steve Miller Band's "Take the Money and Run" ("Sit around the house, get high and watch the tube"), and "Kid Charlemagne," Steely Dan's tribute to Stanley Owsley ("While the music played you worked by candlelight / Those San Francisco nights, you were the best in town"); and 1977 rocked to Clapton's roiling version of J. J. Cale's "Cocaine" and Ram Jam's lone blues-metal hit "Black Betty" ("She really gets me high / Y'know that's no lie"). Over this time, meanwhile, group names like Commander Cody and His Lost Planet Airmen, Tangerine Dream, the Doobie Brothers, Rush, and the Soft Machine (after a William Burroughs novel) all suggested an industrywide empathy with the illegal pleasures of a generation. No one could miss the inferences now.

And if anyone still didn't get the joke, there were always Cheech and Chong. Comedians like Lenny Bruce and George Carlin had already used drug humor in their routines, but Richard "Cheech" Marin and Thomas Chong were the first and most popular comics whose reputation and material were almost completely tied to being high. The most common experience of a cannabis buzz, of course, is a propensity toward easy and uncontrollable amusement—just about everything seems *funny*—and whereas rock 'n' roll music blew minds, the spoken-word records and shows of Cheech and Chong busted guts. Real-life heads, Cheech and Chong dealt both friendly satires of stoner stupidity ("Dave's not here") and straight obliviousness ("Sister Mary Elephant" and "Sgt. Stadanko") that capitalized on the eagerness of the marijuana cohort to laugh at themselves, at authority, or at anything at all. "[W]e've taken dope humor off the streets and put it into the studio or on stage," Chong explained. "That's all. Obviously, not too many people were willing or inclined to do that." Both the Angeleno Cheech and the Canadian Chong were fairly accomplished improvisational actors, but they were at their best playing, or being, the hapless freaks Pedro and Man, forever looking to score some killer weed in the face of cops, squares, and their own burnt-out incompetence. Cheech and Chong's run of hit LPs, like *Big Bambu* (1972), *Los Cochinos* (1973), and *Wedding Album* (1974), made them honorary court jesters in the classic rock canon (with record sleeves resembling baggies, rolling papers, and other head-shop essentials), and their classic "Basketball Jones" number boasted the accompaniment of musicians George Harrison, pianists Nicky Hopkins and Billy Preston, and Mama Michelle Phillips. "We've sold records," said Chong. "There are a lot of top-name groups that haven't sold as many as us." "We've sold more records than the Beatles," confirmed Cheech. Right on.

A live performance by Cheech and Chong, or certainly any rock 'n' roll act of the time, was usually given for a crowd at least as wrecked as the headliners. Clouds of marijuana billowed up over the seats before the shows and again at the start of any heavy tune, and the predominantly teenage concertgoers would usually bring any other intoxicants they could smuggle into the club or arena. These might include cheap wine or spirits, over-the-counter cold or headache remedies for their tranquilizing possibilities (usually arrived at by emetic trial and error), and caches of pills like Valium or "reds," the hip, scarlet-hued barbiturate Seconal, or secobarbital. Neil Young chronicler Joel Bernstein took note of the attendees of Young's mid-'70s sets with Crazy Horse: "It was just a bunch of kids drunk and on reds for the first time. Not just beer and pot—it was reds and vodka. . . . I think Neil was too fucked up to notice." "I remember doing one entire show lying down on the stage with the microphone stand lying beside me," said Eric Clapton, "and nobody batted an eyelid. Not too many complaints came back, either, probably because the audience was as drunk as I was." "Those kids are all on downs, aren't they?" Mick Jagger gauged the Rolling Stones' concertgoers. "They take some Quaaludes and then some more downs and smoke pot and then they take heroin and then some cocaine and then some Ripple wine, right?"

After the gigs, the most attentive fans were hardly any straighter. The trend toward very casual sex between rock stars and their boldest female listeners—they were generally and not always fondly termed "groupies"—was reinforced by the spaced-out condition of many of the girls. Most found that "partying with the band" was not just a euphemism but a mandatory prelude to the more intimate bedroom action that followed, and many performers took the availability of willing women so much for granted that they expected the groupies to accompany them in getting high, and if they refused, another one would be brought in to acquiesce. Band business manager C. K. Lendt reported that one Kiss concubine was "zonked out on every imaginable type of barbiturate and at times was barely coherent, often stumbling when she tried to walk." It was all part of the lifestyle. In Los Angeles, the Girls Together Outrageously were devised by the (faithful husband and drug abstainer) Frank Zappa as a muso-sexual groupie clique, and with the occasional aid of substances GTO Pamela Miller, or "Miss P," had fallen for Jim Morrison, Hendrix bassist Noel Redding, Mick Jagger, and Jimmy Page. "He was getting real high by then," she documented of a get-together with Page in the mid-'70s, "and I happily joined him in never-never land." Another GTO, Miss Christine, OD'd on heroin in 1972, and Jimi Hendrix and Jagger's courtesan Devon Wilson (the "Dolly Dagger" of a Hendrix number) was a junkie who died in a fall in February 1971.

The narcotized condition of male and female rock listeners made them particularly responsive to the one quality of the music most palpable to a drugged nervous system: volume. Psychedelic songs were illusory trips of electronic noise, and the verses of folk rock bands or singer-songwriters spun people into meditative efforts at decryption, but it was the innovations of sheer auditory power that created the biggest and most durable subcategory of the medium. After Jimi Hendrix and Cream had taken to the hundred-watt stacks of Marshall guitar amplification—designed by the London music retailer and inventor Jim Marshall in response to the needs of gigging performers who were contending with screaming fans and inadequate public address systems—a wall of massive speaker cabinets and double-bass, multi-tom drum fortresses went from being the show's instrumental backline to inherent parts of the spectacle. The sensory assault of these implements on punters only too able to tolerate it helped create the style players liked to think of as hard rock but which longhairs in 1973 called heavy metal.

OPPOSITE: **Jimmy Page of Led Zeppelin, whose devastating extremes of volume and power were especially palpable to drugged concertgoers.** *(Robert Knight Archive / Getty Images)*

One of the pioneers in this vein was the San Franciscan trio Blue Cheer, named for a brand of Stanley Owsley LSD, who laid waste to old blues and rockabilly nuggets with medical levels of distortion and decibels. But Blue Cheer were too unhinged, musically and chemically, to last far into the 1970s; it was the expert English blues-rock of Led Zeppelin that proved to have the greatest influence through the decade and well into the next ones. Guitarist and producer Jimmy Page, vocalist Robert Plant, bassist and keyboardist John Paul Jones, and drummer John Bonham were talented professionals who first hit North America in 1969–70 with the force and loudness of a bomb, and they had the management and label support to showcase themselves in the most complimentary (and profitable) light. They too performed at awesome volumes. "Turning down?" Page asked after one early appearance. "No, we're getting louder. Our drummer is amazingly loud. I come offstage with my ears ringing." Witnesses felt the same.

Aside from their visceral clarion crunch, Zeppelin and their burgeoning crop of imitators all were tacit proponents of drugs. Page took center stage to stroke the strings of his Telecaster or Les Paul with a violin bow for spacey, moaning solos, and he also ran the curious electronic device of a theremin through his amps to elicit a squall of gothic and science-fiction effects—"Dazed and Confused" (showstopper of the debut *Led Zeppelin*) and "Whole Lotta Love" (fanfare for *Led Zeppelin II*) were punctuated with these trippy sonic conjurations. Chief lyricist Plant was a dedicated pot smoker who had led local legalization protests in England before his stardom, and stuck in numerous testimonials throughout his songs: the exquisite "Going to California" mourned a woman who "smoked my stuff and drank all my wine," while "Misty Mountain Hop" told the story of hippies being hassled by cops in the park for an all too familiar reason, and Plant's live recitations of "Over the Hills and Far Away" appended the line "I look for my dreams in a pocketful of gold . . ." with "Acapulco Gold!" to the lit-up ecstasy of the front rows. Zeppelin's British rivals Deep Purple, meanwhile, blasted off on some cosmic "Space Truckin'," and American hard rockers Aerosmith relished "livin' out your fantasy—sleepin' late and smokin' tea" in "Mama Kin" and computed "twenty million years on my brain / Synthesize overrides / Tryin' to keep from goin' insane" in "Spaced." "Drugs can be a shortcut to creativity," argued Aerosmith guitarist Joe Perry. "All throughout history, medicine men and priests in all these primitive cultures used drugs to get to that spirit place." Just as the overdriven wallop of heavy metal stood for an aural endurance test, so did its content virtually insist on a stoned audience. If you weren't on drugs, you couldn't really dig it.

Of all the great '70s hard rock bands, Black Sabbath made the most graphic evocations of getting high—and the most frightening. Out of Birmingham, England, in the train of Zeppelin, Sabbath emphasized the dissonance of heavy distortion by tuning their instruments down several steps (also to accommodate guitarist Tony Iommi's fretting fingers, partially severed in an industrial accident) and basing songs on the grating interval of the flattened fifth. "[W]e just became so fed up with people talking while we were playing that we said, 'Screw it, let's turn it up so they won't be able to chatter,'" said Iommi. "The band just kept getting louder and louder." The combination of extreme fuzz and jarring chord shifts, often played at funeral tempos, came to signify a doom-laden stoner mentality, the sludgy, slurred physiology of cannabis, barbiturates, and alcohol together in the individual consciousness. Tighter than the Stooges and less cosmopolitan than the Velvet Underground, Sabbath offered their own disenchanted reactions to the kaleidoscopic promise of drugs: they replaced the Haight-Ashbury outlook with the dead-end worldview of the slum, the unemployment line, and the rusted factory town. "We got sick and tired of all the bullshit," explained Sabbath's Ozzy Osbourne. "Love your brother and flower power forever, meeting a little chick on the corner and you're hung up on her . . . We brought things down to reality."

Way down. The members of Black Sabbath all took copious quantities of hashish and LSD, but they differed from most of their peers in their unrelentingly negative delineation of drugs, and of most everything else. Though their "occult" themes were largely a gimmick reflecting no deep commitment to Satanism or other horrors, bassist and lyricist Terry "Geezer" Butler was genuinely ambivalent about the long-term price of generational intoxication. Raised as "a severe Catholic" who aspired to the priesthood as a boy, Butler penned songs that reflected a profound guilt over chemical recreation; there is little unadulterated fun about dope in Sabbath. So 1970's *Paranoid* confronted addiction in "Hand of Doom" ("Push the needle in / Face death's sickly grin") and hallucination in "Fairies Wear Boots" ("Son, son, you've gone too far / 'Cause smokin' and trippin' is all that you do . . ."), and *Black Sabbath Vol. 4* (1972) presented one of the most chilling descriptions of cocaine abuse in rock 'n' roll, with the subzero "Snowblind": "Crystal world with winter flowers, turn my days to frozen hours / Lying snowblind in the sun, will my ice age ever come?" By then Sabbath were international stars, living and recording in Los Angeles in a wasteland of Peruvian flake. "Half the budget went on the coke and the other half went to seeing how long we could stay in the studio," Butler admitted. "So by now I'd been using cocaine for a while, and it's a twenty-four-hour drug," substantiated drummer Bill Ward. "I was loaded all the time. I mean, hash was always there for me, but I moved into hard narcotics at a relatively early age." The

OPPOSITE: **Black Sabbath's Ozzy Osbourne lived the indulgences he sang—and warned—of, in songs like "Sweet Leaf," "Snowblind," and "Hand of Doom."** *(Chris Walter / Getty Images)*

liner notes for *Vol. 4* gave thanks to "the great COKE-Cola company of Los Angeles."

Fittingly, Black Sabbath's most upbeat take on drugs is the opening cut from *Master of Reality* (1971), a dirgeful diagnosis of cannabis intake called "Sweet Leaf." The track actually begins with the sound of a planetary cough (Iommi hacking on a joint Osbourne had just produced) and launches into a reflection of stoner bliss that makes it a close rival to Dylan's "Rainy Day Women #12 & 35" in the marijuana hymnbook: "You introduced me to my mind, and left me wanting you and your kind . . ." "Sweet Leaf" even closes with Osbourne's ad lib encouragements to "try it out baby! Won't you follow the Sweet Leaf! Oh, try weed out . . ." Drug promotion didn't come much more emphatic than that, until Sabbath's later "Killing Yourself to Live" (*Sabbath, Bloody Sabbath*, 1974), which contained the vocalist's yelp of "Smoke it! Get high!" The electric threnodies of heavy metal throbbing off a vinyl disc or an eight-track cassette would become almost as much a giveaway of listeners' vices as the righteous sway of reggae.

Heavy metal's maximums of volume had been anticipated by the Who, who were among the first patrons of Jim Marshall's technical advances in amplification. One of the loudest and most popular rock 'n' roll groups of the mid-'70s, the Who were also among those most connected with the drug culture, not so much through their music as through the exploits of their drummer Keith Moon. A hyperactive kid from the suburbs of northwest London, Moon boasted a kinetic technique on his instrument that was an expression of the uncontrolled restlessness he showed in the rest of life; he did not take much to marijuana or acid after a few tries, but he devoured amphetamines, barbiturates, and alcohol in staggering portions. "A day in the life of Keith Moon was however long he was awake," explained Who singer Roger Daltrey. "He didn't have a twenty-four-hour clock like the rest of us. If he was awake for five days, that would be his day." At concerts, at home, out on the town, and especially on tour, Moon was a paragon of rock 'n' roll excess and a willing subject for journalists filing stories of rich young pop stars on the rampage—they called him Moon the Loon, and he did his best to live up to his reputation.

Keith Moon fitted his cars with portable speakers to scare motorists and bystanders with faked police messages. He dropped cherry bombs into the toilets of hotels to destroy entire floors of plumbing. He showed up at pubs and nightclubs in drag, pirate gear, and Nazi uniforms. He ran up bills at his neighborhood pub for £500 a month. He bought, sold, traded, gave away, wrecked, or discarded Rolls-Royces, Chryslers, motor scooters, a Ferrari, a Lincoln Continental, a milk truck, and a small hovercraft. After one Who tour the other three members had earned shares of concert revenues totaling four or five figures; Moon's, once the drink and hotel repair costs had been deducted, was £47. He was physically abusive toward his wife. During an inebriated fracas outside a nightclub, Moon drove over and killed his chauffeur. "At night he would wake up ten times, bathed in medicine-smelling sweat, jabbering about running over his roadie and burning for eternity," Pamela Miller reminisced. "We took handfuls of pills, and he drank vodka like he was dying of thirst." Moon gleefully took to cocaine, getting as much energy from the marching powder as from the tablets of speed he gobbled—he would stay up for days and nights on thousands of dollars' worth, then go to sleep with some downers and brandy. He set fire to a rented home tape recorder because, he said, "It ran slow." He flooded a Copenhagen hotel room with the contents of a water bed and complained to the management that it had leaked, demanding (and getting) compensation for his ruined clothes. Following a Who gig in Miami he suffered an emotional breakdown and was committed to a Florida psychiatric hospital for eight days. Impatient at an airport, he commandeered a wheelchair and sat in it as he rolled the contraption down a long flight of stairs; somehow, he remained uninjured. He cherished the surf music of California, and one of his favorite songs was the Beach Boys' limpid "Don't Worry Baby." He threw a television out a hotel window, and when an aggrieved innkeeper came to his door he said, "Next time, answer the phone when I call." He visited the actor Oliver Reed, hired to star in the film of the Who's *Tommy*, by landing a helicopter in Reed's yard. "As far as drugs went, whatever you had he'd take," remembered his acquaintance Lenny Baker of the '50s revival act Sha Na Na. "As far as booze went, whatever you had he'd drink. . . . [I]f you had something that might get him high, he'd take it." He was Moon the Loon.

For all his headline-grabbing antics, Keith Moon's instincts for destroying his relationships, his lodgings, his vehicles, and himself were in many ways more representative of rock recklessness than the more purposeful pursuits of a Jim Morrison or an Eric Clapton. He didn't consider himself a rebel. "The hippies are about as sincere as they can be," he allowed when the Who played the Monterey Pop Festival in 1967. "They never really say much, and when they do I found their comments a bit watery." Like his brother drummers Ringo Starr and John Bonham, Moon was a working-class lad of limited education who had found the sheer fame and fortune of being in a successful band more revolutionary than any Be-In and more exhilarating than any drink, pill, or powder; booze and drugs only enhanced the natural high he had been on since joining the Who at age seventeen. Moon, Starr, and Bonham were in the position of a majority of rock 'n' roll celebrities whose careers seemed an invitation to a fantastic party they could otherwise never have attended. Self-taught musicians who each in their way brought a unique

OPPOSITE: Keith Moon of the Who, living up to his reputation as Moon the Loon. Alcohol and drugs let him play the part all too well. *(Michael Ochs Archives / Getty Images)*

and hugely influential percussive style to their acts, the drummers for the Who, the Beatles, and Led Zeppelin must also have been aware how precarious their roles were—subordinate to and dependent upon their producing, singing, and songwriting mates—and how easily they might have missed out on the fun. The hotel carnages of John Bonham, nearly as infamous as Moon's, have been attributed to his simple homesickness for his farm and family in the English Midlands. The torrent of alcohol and chemicals Moon consumed was his way of affirming his position to himself and the minders, hangers-on, and friends (including Starr and Bonham) he took along for the ride. Some, but not many, of his guests and accomplices recognized the sadness of such a life and knew that Moon, daily and nightly pumped full of artificial energy, was acting a role that more and more confined him. "He had no inner self, he had no self-worth," recalled the Who's manager of the 1960s Chris Stamp for Moon's biographer Tony Fletcher. "He couldn't believe that people would love him just as he was, as an ordinary guy." His companion in drunken LA nightlife Alice Cooper noted, "If you were to ask me who had the most fun in rock 'n' roll I would say Keith Moon. Who really actually understood what rock 'n' roll was about, it would be Keith Moon. . . . I don't think he had another gear to go down to."

Before the drug culture transformed the listening habits of Western youth, pop music was commonly relayed in mono or through the tinny speakers of transistor radios, every teenager's conduit to the Top 40 of 1966—Motown mogul Berry Gordy had specifically designed the sonic signatures of the Supremes or the Four Tops to chirp and jangle over the AM signals broadcast to cars, beach parties, and high school parking lots, via what he called "the Sound of Young America." But as the technology of the studio improved and acts like the Beatles, the Beach Boys and Jimi Hendrix sought the full artistic potential of their electronic tools, the consumer market for how they were received expanded in a corresponding fashion.

By 1973 no rock fan was content with his parents' outmoded appliances, or with her kid siblings' battery-powered toys. Rock was meant for stereo, and stereos had to be constructed from a range of state-of-the-art "components," including turntables, tape decks, amplifiers, receivers (to take in the two-channel waves of the progressive new FM stations), and floor cabinets built around no less than a hierarchy of tweeter, midrange, and woofer speakers. Indeed, the mania for (and merchandising of) complex assemblies of sound apparatus during the era prefigures the computer geekdom of today, with the difference being that stereo freaks still cared about the artistic content of what their setups ultimately played. Serious stereo buffs became audiophiles: at the other end of the microphone and the mixing console were the headphone set and the reel-to-reel unit, and the equipment and investment with which rock 'n' roll was recorded demanded it be heard with a parallel commitment to punch, clarity, and acoustic imaging (the spacing of sounds across the left-right stereo spectrum). Being high made the commitment even more urgent.

"We're convinced that the Hi-Fi and stereo boom is to a great extent due to the fact that so many people are now getting stoned," wrote Jack Margolis and Richard Clorfene in their '70s head shop bible *A Child's Garden of Grass*, "because music, when stoned, becomes another world: intricate, three-dimensional, visual, and completely understandable both intellectually and emotionally." Even straights like media theorist Marshall McLuhan heard something special in stereo: "The hi-fi changeover was really for music what cubism had been for painting, and what symbolism had been for literature; namely, the acceptance of multiple facets and planes in a single experience." Though they were obviously mass-produced products whose chief buyers were the baby boomers, with their hitherto unmatched economic privileges, big-ticket sound layouts were also retailed for their mind-blowing properties as well as their ear-opening ones. The complete capabilities of a sophisticated stereo system and a fresh lid of Acapulco Gold were best discovered together with the work of Pink Floyd.

When the disintegrating Syd Barrett was replaced by David Gilmour in 1968, the Floyd's sound changed from childlike, sometimes whimsically surrealistic, to heavily abstract, sonically symphonic. Gilmour was a superior guitarist, and bassist Roger Waters was now left to compose most of the band's lyrics, as Pink Floyd moved to the vanguard of what was then hailed as "art" or "progressive" rock. Mostly British and European, progressive ensembles combined instrumental expertise and a fluency in the classical lexicon with a post–*Sgt. Pepper* knack for studio effects and cosmic imagery; some of the acts from this category included Jethro Tull; Yes; Emerson, Lake and Palmer; Genesis; the Strawbs; the Moody Blues; King Crimson; Electric Light Orchestra; Supertramp; and Roxy Music. All of them caught on with the campus drug scene. Their music was decidedly more nuanced than Black Sabbath's or the Stooges', and their low-profile public images stood in classy contrast to the publicity stunts of Elton John or David Bowie, making them the thinking stoner's choice for rock 'n' roll. The attention to detail on their album covers (Roger Dean's for Yes were masterworks of fantasy art) and in their recordings tied in with the audiophiles' quest for the perfect soundscape—the albums were made and purchased as unified entities far above the ranks of catchy AM 45s, with titles like ELP's *Brain Salad Surgery*, Jethro Tull's *Aqualung*, King Crimson's *In the Wake of the Poseidon*, Yes's *Tales from Topographic Oceans*, and the Moody Blues' *Days of Future Passed.* These were serious suites of keyboard, flute, synthesizer, and guitars, to which serious volumes of cannabis were inhaled.

What separated Pink Floyd from the prog pack was their stage shows. Even before Barrett's departure, Floyd had placed as much importance on lighting as sound, earning them 1967's accolade as "London's farthest-out group." As their venues in Europe and North America grew in size, their payload of amplification, illumination, and special props expanded as well, giving their live performances a conceptual edge over the decibel bombast of heavy metal or the sensitive "authenticity" of singer-songwriters. All the members of the group (Waters, Gilmour, keyboardist Rick Wright, and drummer Nick Mason) had studied architecture before opting for rock 'n' roll, and retained both Barrett's art school outlook and their own lessons in visual design and technical innovation. Something called an azimuth coordinator was deployed to radiate their sound through a vast arc of speakers positioned around the sites. For those tripping on LSD or magic mushrooms, or high on pot— and even for those rare punters not on anything—a Pink Floyd concert of the 1970s was an all-round sensory overload, carefully planned and executed by the artists.

Floyd themselves were only part-time dopers. "We weren't making those records under the influence of [marijuana]," Gilmour has reminded. "Rick and I would have a puff on the occasional joint—Roger and Nick wouldn't. . . . You don't have to be stoned to enjoy our stuff, but it probably helps." Mason had already been put off of acid by watching the decline of Syd Barrett, sequestered in a London flat among a hard-core LSD circle: "It was not a world the rest of us frequented." The real ambition of the band was to take the philosophical, introspective musings of Waters and set them to whatever stage or studio devices would best illustrate them, the fundamental underlay of rock 'n' roll built into a cerebral platform of ideas, ambiguity, and wattage. Their initial albums with Gilmour *A Saucerful of Secrets* (1968), *Ummagumma* (1969), *Atom Heart Mother* (1970), and *Meddle* (1971) all drove toward the fusion of intellectually challenging music and pure fantasias of sound, with vague tracks designated "Syncopated Pandemonium," "A Pillow of Winds," and "Any Color You Like." *Live at Pompeii*, the mesmeric Pink Floyd documentary of 1971 directed by Adrian Maben, captured the quartet's introverted, preoccupied performance style as they played the mind-bending cubist rock of "Echoes," "One of These Days," and "Set the Controls for the Heart of the Sun" in the Roman ruin, the cameras tracking around them with arid deliberation. "It's an image we'd like to dispel. . . . I still think most people think of us as a very drug-orientated group," Gilmour said in a *Pompeii* interview sequence. "But of course we're not. You can trust us." The film also shows them rehearsing and recording their next album, a collection of numbers around Waters's chosen subjects of alienation and withdrawal, tentatively named *Eclipse (a Piece for Assorted Lunatics)* that ultimately was released as *Dark Side of the Moon.*

In their day Pink Floyd were sometimes accused of spinning form-less electronic noises and of being dependent on advanced equipment, but the musicians were adamant that they were a band, not a labora-tory. "We were always credited with using more technology than we really did," said Mason, while Wright assured listeners, "One of the myths about Pink Floyd is that they have all this amazing electronic gadgetry, when in fact we use the same as any other group. It's our technique of using them in a different way." *Dark Side of the Moon* was a product of painstaking labor at Abbey Road Studios, employing a novel sixteen-track recorder (most albums then were made with four or eight tracks) and dropping in an unprecedented array of spoken monologues, sound snippets, vocal extemporizations, tape loops, and synthesizer drones. Mixed by engineers Chris Thomas and Alan Parsons (both alumni of the Beatles' later work), Waters' lines and the Floyd's multiply overdubbed takes cohered into a seamless audio orchestration of age, decay, and melancholy. "We'd have leads [wires] running all around the building and tape machines in the corridors outside the control rooms," Parsons detailed. "It was quite a complex arrangement." The effects—wound in and around the pristine, epic cadences of "Breathe" and "Time," and the treacherous 7/8 meter of "Money"—made the album the most spectacular headphone session ever afforded the average cannabis smoker.

Unlike *Exile on Main Street, Tonight's the Night* or *There's a Riot Goin' On, Dark Side of the Moon* did not depict the drug lifestyle of the creators—it enhanced it for the audience. The anonymous, almost sterile packaging of the record and the precision of its aural texture were not the effort of a bunch of burnouts partying through a home studio, but a polished artifact meant to set new benchmarks of recording exactitude. "I was working on using echo and making things sound *big*," Chris Thomas said; certainly Gilmour's empyrean guitar in "Time" is one of the most galactic instrumental solos ever committed to tape. "I thought to myself, 'Wow, this is a pretty complete piece of work,'" Waters recollected of finishing the LP, "and I had every confidence that people would respond to it." The album's cover and interior sleeve were designed by Storm Thorgerson and Aubrey Powell at Hipgnosis, the most prestigious graphic firm of rock 'n' roll's twelve-inch heyday, and its refracting prism was rendered by George Hardie, who had also made the equally iconic *Hindenburg* jacket for Led Zeppelin's first album. According to Waters, Thorgerson and Powell "came in with like six or seven ideas for album covers and threw them on the floor in the control room, and we all, as one man, went 'That one!' There wasn't any conversation." Together with the luminous pyramids of the interior, the package of *Dark Side of the Moon* was so devoid of the traditional motifs of promotion, and the music within so conducive to the gossamer suggestibility of the THC-boosted brain, that the disc became an almost generic drug accessory—as practical and as necessary as incense cones, roach clips, or water pipes.

"I have a suspicion that successive generations of adolescents go out and buy *Dark Side of the Moon* at about the same time the hormones start coursing around their veins," Waters opined long after, although hormones would be only one of several chemicals in the bloodstream of teenage Pink Floyd fans. Since its release in March of 1973, *Dark Side of the Moon* has gone on to sell more than thirty-five million copies in all formats and famously endured as the steadiest-selling album of the commercial pop era, registering on the trade charts of best-selling works for an unsurpassable 1,500 weeks; for many years something like 20,000 vinyl, tape, and CD releases of *Dark Side* were sold per month. These staggering numbers also served as an index to the high tide of the drug culture, the popularity of the album intersecting with that of cannabis and other illegal trips, as both rock record sales and drug use among the young peaked in the mid- to late 1970s. Yet even if there was now nowhere to go but down, many rock 'n' rollers set off on the decline by racing blindly, precipitously straight up.

THAT SMELL
1975-1980

The greatest rock stars, living in the moment of performance
and on the edge of psychic derangement, rewarded in their youth
beyond their wildest dreams, became their generation's
Byronic exemplars of action and experience.

STEPHEN DAVIS, *OLD GODS ALMOST DEAD*

The eldest members of the baby boom entered their third decade of life
in 1976: the generation that had once been warned not to trust anyone
over thirty was itself hitting that dreaded milestone. Though barely
eight years gone, the hippie gatherings of Woodstock or San Francisco
had become hopelessly passé in the time of disco, jogging, oil shocks,
and Gerald Ford, and the long-haired, peace-signing eccentric was now
almost as obsolete a figure as the Zoot-suited hepcat of the 1940s or the
goateed Beatnik of 1957. On April 30, 1975, the last American embassy
staff and military personnel were airlifted out of Saigon, Vietnam, as the
war whose youthful opponents had been so galvanized by rock music
and drugs came to an ignominious end.

Neither drug use nor rock 'n' roll was on the wane, of course, at least
not in terms of economics. The stadiums were packed with hordes of
stoners flocking to see Deep Purple, Elton John, and Yes, and rock

was now a cornerstone of the entertainment industry, with revenues totaling in the billions; relative to the investment of signing artists, producing material, and distributing product the medium was undoubtedly far more profitable than film or television. Likewise, illicit drugs were a booming business, not only because of demand among a huge international age class but because the very restrictions against the various substances allowed sellers at all stages of distribution to impose giant markups on prices as compensation for the perils of growing, processing, and smuggling. But inevitably both the ubiquity of cannabis and cannabis-inspired music would lead to an adverse reaction among users and listeners for whom both had become stale. Moreover, the growth of the baby boomers out of their phase of rebellion and experimentation—and the substantial drop of births in America and other democracies after the early 1960s—promised a parallel tapering-off of young people's cultural dominance. Without anyone realizing it, after 1975 the prime years of pop records, rock stardom, and getting high had passed.

Getting high had turned rock stardom itself into a dangerous job. More names were added to the list of overdosed musicians in the later 1970s, among them Deep Purple's new guitar hero Tommy Bolin in 1976 (heroin overdose), Little Feat's slide maestro Lowell George in 1979 (heart attack brought on by weight and drug problems), and Wings guitarist Jimmy McCulloch the same year (he was found dead with a joint in his fingers and morphine and alcohol in his system, though an inquest concluded with an "open verdict"). The most spectacular drug death was that of the King himself, Elvis Presley, found lifeless in his bathroom in August 1977 after an apparent heart attack but clearly

OPPOSITE: The King of Rock 'n' Roll deplored the use of illegal drugs but declined and died owing to the pharmacy of legal substances he ingested. *(Michael Ochs Archives / Getty Images)*

suffering from overmedication or, as one obituarist termed it, "polypharmacy." The difference here, aside from his fame and influence, was that Elvis's drugs were all legal.

Presley had been introduced to Benzedrine while serving in the US military in 1958–60 and thereafter came to rely on a steady supply of speed, barbiturates, and painkillers, acquired from his personal physician Dr. George Nichopoulos. "Dr. Nick" supplied the singer and his gang of lackeys with Demerol, Dexedrine, Dilaudid, Lomotil, Percodan, Quaaludes, Tuinal, and Valium, among many other prescriptions, and the emotionally adrift King of Rock 'n' Roll spent his last few years sinking into obesity and a drug-induced haze—an autopsy revealed his blood contained Valium, Placidyl, pentobarbital, butabarbital, and phenobarbital (all downers) when he was dethroned. But because these were clinical drugs obtained through a licensed doctor, neither Presley nor many of his fans made the connection between his obvious dependencies and the proscribed ones he deplored in the younger rock market. In December 1970, Elvis, concerned over the antiauthoritarian attitudes of the Woodstock nation, was granted an audience with President Richard Nixon after assuring him via letter that "[t]he drug culture, the hippie elements, the SDS [Students for a Democratic Society], Black Panthers, etc., do not consider me as their enemy or as they call it The Establishment." Presley requested and got from Nixon a badge certifying him as an honorary federal narcotics officer.

For the "hippie elements" and other proponents of easing the laws against marijuana, hopes were raised by the election of Jimmy Carter in the United States in 1976. After the discredited Nixon, Carter looked to introduce (or at any rate back) legislation that recognized the mildness of weed: on August 2, 1977, the White House issued a formal message asserting in part that "[p]enalties against possession of a drug should not be more damaging to an individual than the use of the drug itself; and where they are, they should be changed. Nowhere is this more clear than in the laws against possession of marijuana in private for personal use... The National Commission on Marijuana and Drug Abuse concluded five years ago that marijuana use should be decriminalized, and I believe it is time to implement those basic recommendations." The American federal penalties for marijuana in 1977 stood at up to a year in jail or a $5,000 fine if found guilty of possession, and up to five years' imprisonment or a $15,000 fine if convicted of selling or distributing pot. In 1978, Willie Nelson, performing for the president at a state function in Washington, defied these regulations to sneak up to the White House roof and smoke a joint. "That was an incredible moment, sitting there watching all the lights," said the braided outlaw. "I wasn't aware until then that all roads led to the Capitol, that it was the center of the world."

Carter's presidency, however, went through a series of domestic and foreign crises (e.g., the taking of American hostages in revolutionary Iran), and most of his political plans were derailed. His announcement of an amnesty for Vietnam-era evaders of the US draft, far from healing the war's social divides, only prolonged them. As well, his special assistant for health issues, Dr. Peter G. Bourne (who advised him on the drug issues), was caught writing an illegal prescription for Quaaludes; the doctor was also said to have taken cocaine with Keith Stroup of NORML and the legendary drug-fried author Hunter S. Thompson. During the Carter administration frightened moms and dads formed pressure groups like the National Federation of Parents for Drug-Free Youth and the Parents' Resource Institute for Drug Education. There would be no significant reform of US drug laws under Jimmy Carter, and indeed a reversal of them would be enacted under his successor in the Oval Office.

Rock music was now guilty by association. If previous bids to censor or suppress drug-related songs or singers had proven impotent, pop hits were detected as first indicators of illegality by the growing bodies of parents and educators on the zealous lookout for teens in trouble. Public service documentaries used generic electric guitar backings as soundtracks to dramatizations of Bobby's or Jenny's descents into the madness of marijuana and LSD, and police and teachers rang alarm bells with legends of clean-cut, straight-A kids who went to rock concerts and were never the same again. This propaganda was on the same plane with the tales that Led Zeppelin had sold their souls to the devil or that the group name *Kiss* stood for "Knights In Satan's Service." Precursors of the Moral Majority evangelical lobby (which would become far more vocal in the next decade) took lonely stands against Mick Jagger and other degenerates: "Where have we gone wrong that our twelve- and thirteen-year-old daughters are making him a millionaire—YET AGAIN?" thundered upstanding columnist Steve Dunleavy. "Here is this person, a convicted drug offender, preaching the gospel according to Jagger to our teenagers. . . ."

A handful of pop artists signed up to do TV commercials or other testaments of drugs' dangers—"If you become a pothead, you risk blowing the most important time of your life," gravely intoned a leisure-suited Sonny Bono. The 1971 adolescent "diary" *Go Ask Alice* took its title from the Jefferson Airplane's "White Rabbit," and its hyperventilating protagonist confided her introduction to drugs in the proximity of her friends' record collection: "I was a part of every single instrument, literally a part. Each note had a character, shape, and color all its very own. . . . The lights and music and sound of San Francisco were part of me and I was part of them." With its high school confidential depiction of the US drug menace, *Go Ask Alice* was a best seller throughout the 1970s (just like Deep Purple and Yes LPs), although it was later discovered that the work was a composite of many teen journals, edited and embellished by a staff of adult counselors.

In the United Kingdom, meanwhile, the first stirrings of a revolt against the established rock aristocracy and their drugs were heard in 1976, as the punk movement played its first shows and made its first headlines. Johnny Rotten, née Lydon, the figurehead of the most visible punk act, the Sex Pistols, was notoriously first tapped for the role when seen wearing a Pink Floyd T-shirt over which he had inked "I HATE" above the creators of *Atom Heart Mother* and *Dark Side of the Moon.* Punk acts and their followers quickly moved to distance themselves from the romanticism of flower power, the dreaminess of psychedelia, and the lethargy of prog rock. For them, the frenzied clench of amphetamines made the music. "I was so into speed. . . . I don't even recall making the first album," said Mick Jones of the Clash. In fact, cannabis was not at all forsaken by the British and North American punk and New Wave bands, and recreational drug use was hardly diminished in the scene: the Clash's Joe Strummer was a heavy toker infatuated with reggae, Johnny Rotten was fined for amphetamine possession, the quasi-glam and proto-punk New York Dolls were addicts of one kind or another (drummer Billy Murcia overdosed in 1972), and Sex Pistol Sid Vicious (John Ritchie) OD'd on heroin in 1979 after being implicated in the death of his girlfriend Nancy Spungen.

What punk did change, though, was the stereotype of dope smoking as the undisputed indicator of nonconformity or decadence. Punks resented the opulent lifestyles of the rock 'n' roll jet set and the middle-class comforts of their fans, and at impoverished punk squats even the cheap high of inhaling solvents and adhesives was known to have been resurrected: "My first drug experience was sniffing glue," said Johnny (Cummings) Ramone, whose pseudo-fraternal band titled a song "Now I Wanna Sniff Some Glue" on its premier 1976 record. "It was a good high, but it gave you a bad headache." Bongs, strobe lights, and South American crystals lined up on a mirror formed no part of the punk identity. After the Sex Pistols, the Clash, the Damned, the Buzzcocks, Siouxsie and the Banshees, the Ramones, and their safety-pinned compatriots, marijuana, acid, cocaine, and magic mushrooms looked as threatening as the mellow suburbanites and millionaire rockers who still preferred them.

Like Paul McCartney. The ex-Beatle was still one of the richest and most famous performers in the world, even if many believed his work leading Wings was a pale imitation of his achievements with *A Hard Day's Night*, *Revolver*, or *Abbey Road*. He was also still a regular cannabis consumer, and his affable public image was not hurt by several run-ins with the police over his choice of relaxants. "He and Linda [McCartney's wife] did smoke a fantastic amount of the stuff by anybody's standards," recalled Wings guitarist Denny Laine. "They smoked joints the way ordinary people smoke cigarettes." In 1972 the McCartneys were arrested in Sweden and fined the equivalent of £800; the same year Paul was also busted for growing a small plot of marijuana at his farm in Campbeltown, Scotland, and had to pay up £100. "I don't think [cannabis] is dangerous," McCartney told reporters after his court appearance. "It should be like homosexuality—legal among consenting adults." In 1975 the couple were stopped again in Los Angeles and Linda was found with seventeen grams of weed, warranting another trip to the station house. As a sign of how acceptable soft drugs had become, McCartney maintained his stature as the cute Beatle.

The Grateful Dead were not so lucky. They too had survived the passage from the freaky, Acid-Testing fringes of the counterculture to somewhere nearer the mainstream but were still singled out by police. In January 1970 the Dead and their patron Stanley Owsley were nabbed

OPPOSITE: Despite his steady appetite for marijuana and several arrests for it during the 1970s, solo artist Paul McCartney remained the Cute Beatle. *(Jan Persson / Getty Images)*

for marijuana possession in a New Orleans hotel, immortalized in their song "Truckin'": "I'd like to get some sleep before I travel / But if you got a warrant, I guess you're gonna come in. . . ." Over the decade, the band grew into a self-contained conceptual nation of musicians and "Deadheads," the roving tribes of fans who accompanied them to every concert and set up their own villages of fun, friendship, and open-air drug transactions. During the 1970s these first-generation Deadheads were both followers of the music, who made and exchanged their own annotated recordings of each performance, and also an independent and unabashed community of 1960s survivalists who clung together for safety in tie-dyed numbers. Without the regular jobs, homes, or hesitations of casual listeners, some of the Deadheads became as addled as the players they cheered.

Backstage, the Dead's caravans were awash in pot, cocaine, and opiates, the drug expenses now a substantial part of the group's overhead, as much as transportation, accommodation, and stage management. Owsley's mad-genius sound systems alone came with a $350,000 price tag. "China White [heroin] is eating up more and more of our money," worried their manager Rock Scully, who did a short jail stint in 1977 for his involvement in a marijuana-smuggling scheme. "We had also used certain drugs like cocaine and speed as road tools," Scully remembered. "The band, the crew, everybody was using coke to get going. Working until four in the morning, crash, wake up with a line, hit the road." By the mid-'70s Scully, Dead head Jerry Garcia, and other members of the group and its attendants were all on hard drugs, and their constant touring schedules gave them little respite from temptation. "As these things have a habit of doing," Dead bass player Phil Lesh looked back on Garcia's slide, "the drug gradually took over his life, first his domestic affairs, and then his music and his relationships with the other band members, to the exclusion of all else."

In 1976, John "Scooter" Herring, roadie for Dixie rockers the Allman Brothers, was tried and convicted for selling pharmaceutical cocaine and the narcotic painkiller Demerol to keyboardist and vocalist Gregg Allman, mostly through the testimony of Allman himself after the singer was granted immunity from prosecution. The ill will generated by the trial broke up the band: "There is no way we can work with Gregg again, ever," said guitarist Dickey Betts. Sad as the outcome seemed (Herring's lengthy sentence was eventually reduced and the outfit reformed in various permutations), the case was illustrative of how prominent rock performers, like the Allmans, Paul McCartney, and the Grateful Dead, seemed to be ripe targets for criminal persecution but ended up with lighter penalties than average citizens. Better-paid lawyers, deeper reserves of bail or fine money, and their own examples as hedonists or bohemians who nevertheless appeared to live productive and independent lives—the Allmans had given beneficial fund-raising concerts for Jimmy Carter's presidential campaign—gave them a legal protection most of their listeners never had. Johnny Rotten's complaints about "the entire superband system," where the most lucrative acts existed on a far higher plane of prosperity, indulgence, and deference than any of the punters whose money put them there, were not without justification.

The rock stars themselves had little idea just how sheltered they were. Most lived and traveled with an entourage of paid and unpaid gofers, handlers, agents, sidekicks, and bodyguards, picking up after them and enabling drug intakes that would have soon debilitated anyone with the mundane concerns of work, school, bills, shopping, parenting, cleaning residences, or driving cars. "To be on the rock & roll road was to glide through the universe on cruise control," concluded *Rolling Stone* journalist Daisann McLane after a jaunt with Aerosmith. "For weeks, often months, decisions were made and problems resolved by managers, lawyers, publicists, and accountants. Wake-up calls came at noon, road managers collected luggage from outside one's hotel room door. . . . The myth of the rock & roll road was freedom; the reality was that one emerged from this pampered bubble as dependent and querulous as a spoiled adolescent." Consequently, many of the most famous rock performers drifted through the later '70s oblivious to all but their few obligations—showing up for gigs and studio sessions—and their many needs, a steady supply of drugs chief among them.

Aerosmith definitely needed drugs. A funky American combination of Led Zeppelin's whiplash riffery and the Rolling Stones' or the Peter Green–led Fleetwood Mac's raunch, the Boston-based act had become a prime stadium attraction with its 1975 album *Toys in the Attic* and the following year's *Rocks.* They had liked to party when they were struggling musicians sharing a pad, and headlining fame didn't change them. Vocalist Steve Tyler's stage attire of gaudy scarves draped over his neck and shoulders was where he kept his stash: "I would stuff it full of Tuinals [addictive barbiturates similar to secobarbital]," he confessed. "That was my drug of choice—cocaine and a couple of Tuinals." The quintet became rich quickly and spent the money sooner, "but there was no guidance financially," said drummer Joey Kramer. "It was like everybody was just doing what they wanted, and who knows how much money I was spending on drugs at the time." This was the dissolute luxury of the rock 'n' roll life lived by young men who were true fans and true believers. "I got a chance to ride in the front seat of a roller coaster with Hendrix once," Tyler recalled wistfully. "We were both doing poppers [amyl nitrate]. . . . Because coming up with it, you're getting high to be able to drive from here to Tempe, Arizona, for a few shows, and so you smoke a little pot, and then you hear your

OPPOSITE: One half of the Toxic Twins, Aerosmith's Steve Tyler: livin' out his fantasy, sleepin' late and smokin' tea. *(Ian Dickson / Getty Images)*

record on the radio and you get caught up in the *wowness* of it all, you do a little blow. . . . And some beautiful girl and her girlfriend decide to enjoy each other as they whip out a needle, and so you try shooting coke as you're getting blown. . . ."

Black Sabbath were on their own spree. Though their record and ticket sales had slowed after 1975, they still had enough momentum to pull significant numbers and afford premium coke. "I was stoned all the time," Ozzy Osbourne told it. "I was into sex, drugs, and rock 'n' roll, and the rock 'n' roll was paying for my sex and drugs." Geezer Butler dated the band's personal decline from 1974: "*Sabbath Bloody Sabbath* was our last coke-inspired album. We were still doing coke after that, but it was horrible—it had turned round on us by then, and was starting to kill us." Sabbath slogged through the uneven LPs *Sabotage* (1975) and *Technical Ecstasy* (1976) before the lineup collapsed during the making of the contrary *Never Say Die* (1978). "[W]e'd go down to the sessions and have to pack up because we were too stoned," recalled Bill Ward. "Nobody could get anything right. We were all over the place." "We were all doing a lot of coke, a lot of everything," said Tony Iommi. "We were supposed to be rehearsing and nothing was happening and it got worse." Osbourne was fired in 1979, and both he and the original players were briefly able to revive their careers even as their chemical descents accelerated. "I ended up in the Park Hotel in Los Angeles, and I didn't open the drapes for three months," the singer recounted. "My dealer dropped off the coke every day, and I sent out for booze and pizza."

David Crosby was by these years an epic cocaine user, sporadically collaborating with Stephen Stills or Graham Nash for concerts and albums (CSN's *CSN* in 1977, and Crosby-Nash's *Wind on the Water* in '75 and *Whistling Down the Wire* in '76) but increasingly preoccupied with getting his next nonmusical hit. His septum was perforated from frequent snorting: "That was me, Ol' Crusting and Bleeding." Stephen

Stills was similarly far gone into cocaine paranoia, imagining he had actually seen combat as a soldier in Vietnam. Neil Young mourned coke's effects on CSN's once glistening harmonies: "Screwed up the pitch. Made everything sharp. Made 'em play too fast." On his and Crazy Horse's *Rust Never Sleeps* (1979) Young sang regretfully that he had "searched out my companions, who were lost in crystal canyons. . . ."

With his nostrils ravaged, Crosby turned to drinking cocaine mixed in glasses of wine, then took to smoking it via the novel technique of freebasing, where the drug is distilled down to its purest form through a process of filtration using ammonia and ether. "The nature of base smoking is that once you get started, you do it a lot," Crosby admitted. "You become obsessive with it immediately." He was sustained by his record company (now Capitol, after CSNY's glory days on Atlantic), but his unreliability as an artist and his out-of-control freebase habit were open secrets. "The word had already been everywhere that he was unfit to make records," remembered Capitol representative Bobby Colomby. "Nevertheless, Capitol somehow made a deal with Crosby that was ridiculous." Money was fronted to Crosby from the record label with one of the singer's homes as collateral, and when he was proven incapable of making releasable music, Colomby "pleaded his case and pointed out the publicity would look bad for the company if we actually repossessed his home and evicted him to get our advance back." Crosby's health continued to deteriorate under the effects of freebase. "Working in that studio was like [working in] a tomb," said producer Stanley Johnson. "It smelled of ether and all those chemicals and although I don't know what morgues smell like, I bet it's close."

Sly Stone, too, was coming down from a peak. After *There's a Riot Goin' On*, his subsequent records with the Family Stone, *Fresh* (1973) and *Small Talk* (1974), were decent but inevitably anticlimactic; he went solo in 1975 with *High on You*, then cobbled a "new" Family together for *Heard Ya Missed Me, Well I'm Back* and *Back on the Right Track* in 1976 and 1979, respectively. The upbeat titles fooled no one. Since the early '70s he had been less and less dependable as a performer, often skipping whole itineraries of concerts and corralling a patchy run of players and sitters-in for his fitful studio bookings. "There were discussions with him, and eventually he tried rehab programs," equivocated record executive Al DeMarino. "I would talk to him, others would talk to him—as opposed to the hangers-on, who were always looking to get some free blow—and I would say, 'Sylvester, what are we doing here?' And he'd respond, 'I know you love me, and I'm in control.' Famous last words." Stone's manager David Kapralik had himself become a suicidal cocaine addict, and Stone was also beginning to freebase. "You expected people like the David Kapraliks, the people who were adults, had been in the music business, and who, in theory, had some knowledge, to be telling Sly the truth," observed Kitsaun King, sister of Stone's occasional partner Debbie. "But they weren't telling the truth. They were just going along with Sly's program. And Sly's program was totally substandard, because he was high all the time."

So was Marvin Gaye. The aftermath of 1971's *What's Going On* saw him lurch from more hits (soundtracks for the film *Trouble Man* in 1972 and *Let's Get It On* in 1973) to an ill-judged move to Hollywood and schmaltzy duets with ex-Supreme Diana Ross. He was busted and bailed for marijuana possession in Los Angeles in 1973. Never a careful businessman, he was spending far more than even his considerable royalties paid him, most of the money going to women, tax debts, alimony, and cocaine—he was officially declared bankrupt in 1978. "How much have I spent on toot over the years? I don't even want to think about it. . . . My attitude has always been, [W]henever good blow is around, buy it, regardless of price," he confessed. The paranoia of cocaine and his fading career made him suicidal. "I just wanted to be left alone to blow my brains away with high-octane toot. It would be a slow but relatively pleasant death, certainly less messy than a gun." It got worse when he took to freebasing. "The pipe is very, very deep. . . . I lost myself by smoking cocaine." He drifted around Europe for a few years, giving shows intermittently, before making the fateful decision to return to America and reside with his parents, still addicted.

Another star who was coasting on past successes was John Phillips. The Mamas and the Papas had lasted only from 1965 to 1968, but Phillips's reputation as a talented songwriter and arranger gave him a free pass to the '70s rock stratosphere (aside from Scott McKenzie's "San Francisco" he had also authored a Grateful Dead favorite, "Me and My Uncle," and put out a single solo album, *John the Wolfking of LA* in 1970). He had always been a voracious drug user, and by 1975 he had added heroin to his list of habits. "I have no idea what my music would've been like without the drugs," Phillips summed up. "What would the *Titanic* have been like if it hadn't sunk?" The addiction soon spread throughout his dysfunctional household. "My dad was a pleasure seeker, a hedonist," said his actress daughter Mackenzie, only in her teens when she too became hooked; his third wife, Genevieve, and their son Tamerlane were taking junk as well. "Getting drugs becomes the most important thing in your life," Phillips verified later. "Family, ethics—all of that goes to the bottom of the list." Like others with expensive vices to support he took to dealing as well as buying drugs, and with his many connections in and out of the music industry and his humongous personal cache of cocaine and opiates, he was arrested and charged with conspiracy to distribute narcotics after a near-fatal car crash near his home on Long Island in 1980. Phillips served little time but did community service alongside his daughter to warn others of the dangers of drug abuse. When he went into a rehabilitation clinic his hands were turning black as his blood circulation deteriorated under the regular puncture of syringes.

The sinking commercial and mental conditions of so many rock 'n' roll celebrities were aspects of a vicious circle that could only have existed in these most profligate years of the recording business. Artists were attached to labels with generous contracts that nourished them over several releases, unlike the binding agreements of later eras, which would grant performers only one chance to make a blockbuster debut. Thus the likes of Aerosmith, Black Sabbath, David Crosby, Sly Stone, and John Phillips were still flush with cash even as their chart heights sank or ticket sales dwindled. The catch was that they were typically paid with an advance against future royalties, meaning their day-to-day expenses, and the fees for more lavish purchases like custom cars and fabulous homes, would be subtracted from any income to be generated by prospective album grosses or publishing rights; as the much-maligned "corporate rock," most of these corporations were in the red more than they ever scraped into the black. The labels themselves enjoyed guaranteed revenue flows, while the musicians could only be assured of money doled out for single events, i.e., concert appearances. "When you're much younger and on top, they tell you, 'Don't worry 'bout nothin'. Hey, you're an artist, just worry about your music,'" remarked an embittered Sly Stone. "I'd be getting into a Lear jet, on my way somewhere, and they'd say, 'Before you get to the next place, can we see you, sweetheart? Sign this right quick.'" "Much of the time, when we weren't onstage or in the studio, we were in lawyers' offices trying to get out of all our contracts," Black Sabbath's Geezer Butler repeated. "We were literally in the studio, trying to record, and we'd be signing all these affidavits and everything." Players who first took costly drugs to give them energy for a punishing circuit of shows now found they had forced themselves to do punishing circuits of shows to pay for costly drugs.

Only the biggest acts could get and stay rich while still choosing where and how often they were to perform in public, and in 1975, Led Zeppelin was the biggest rock act in the world. In fact, their most popular (and to many, best) records had been made and issued in a dizzying thirty-six months between the fall of 1968, when *Led Zeppelin* was produced, and the autumn of 1971, when their untitled fourth album had hit the record stores—timeless though many of their songs have become, Zeppelin had reached their artistic zenith early. But they continued to move product by the truckload, and their relative lack of press coverage gave them a mysterious allure that made their North American tours of '73, '75, and '77 huge spectacles of volume, light, and endurance, with sold-out attendance at every gig and fan riots at ticket outlets. Their two-disc *Physical Graffiti* (1975) and 1976's downbeat *Presence* were sprawling documents featuring visionary marathons like "Kashmir," "In My Time of Dying," and "Achilles Last Stand." The band's manager Peter Grant had succeeded in winning for his clients immense shares of concert profits, telling local presenters: "You don't have to 'promote' Led Zeppelin—just announce on the radio that they're playing Madison Square and an hour later there won't be a ticket to be had. . . . The days of the promoter giving a few quid to the group against the money taken on the door are gone." Though Grant was far different in personality than the Los Angeles hustler David Geffen, both operated on the principle that their respective clients didn't need to be hyped in an economy where buying rock 'n' roll albums, rock 'n' roll posters and T-shirts, and passes to rock 'n' roll shows were already how millions of young people around the world spent their discretionary incomes. You know and I know what these people are worth, ordered the moguls—just pay up. The Zeppelin organization was so surfeited with wealth, they had their own boutique record label, Swan Song, under the umbrella of Atlantic Records, shrugged off the theft of $200,000 in cash from their New

York hotel, and in the midst of a global energy crisis rented a private Boeing 720 four-engine jet to shuttle them from city to city at a cost of $2,500 per hour. That still left plenty of money to buy drugs.

"The record industry was fuelled by cocaine, sex, and music," explained Led Zeppelin publicist B. P. Fallon. "Except in the world of Led Zeppelin, the norm was magnified a million times." Zep's founder, producer, and guitarist Jimmy Page was by 1975 a clinical cocaine and heroin addict, with drummer John Bonham, road manager Richard Cole, and Peter Grant himself not much healthier. Page later joked that the inadequate footage of dates at Madison Square Garden in 1973 was attributable to a stoned camera crew—"Everybody was stoned at the time, but at least we did *our* job." Singer and Zeppelin pal Michael Des Barres admired Page for unbeatably "being the stonedest person in the room." The relentless funk of *Physical Graffiti*'s "Trampled Underfoot" went out with Robert Plant's telltale repeats of "I can't stop talkin'. . . . I can't stop talkin' about love. . . . I can't stop talkin'," while *Presence*'s "For Your Life" numbly charted the vertiginous ups and downs of a coke bender. On board the Zeppelin tour plane, they were doing lines of blow followed by sniffs of cherry snuff and quick dabs of Dom Pérignon champagne for flavor. "I'd stay up for five nights on the trot," said Page. "Everything was so exciting—why would you want to go to sleep? You might miss something." Before two performances at Oakland Coliseum in July 1977, impresario Bill Graham was asked to deliver a $25,000 advance of cash in expectation of greater sums taken at the gate, which he took to the group's hotel. "They announced me and I walked into this anteroom," Graham recounted. "There sat the dealer. Then it hit me for the first time: this is *drug* money."

Led Zeppelin's 1977 American tour was their last, marred by drug-related arrogance and violence that left even veteran onlookers like Graham shaken. The entourage included an on-call doctor, who, like the Beatles' Dr. Robert, did minimal consulting with his patients before dispensing various forms of medication, and the road crew was known to pile into city pharmacies on their stops and help themselves to the stock, exiting with a toss of $1,000 in hundred-dollar bills across the counter. Jimmy Page, the charismatic guitar hero of "Whole Lotta Love" and the towering "Stairway to Heaven," was withdrawn into his dependence: rock writer Ben Fong-Torres attempted to conduct an interview with him and found his questions relayed through a personal assistant, while Page's solos were meandering fumbles of notes and he was said to have been barely able to find his way to the stages or remain standing for complete sets. His posture at shows was part swagger, part stagger, part spasms of opiate and stimulant reaction. He retired to his hotel during Bonham's half-hour drum solo. Bottles of Jack Daniel's bourbon were chugged in the dressing room. "We were doing three-and-a-half-hour concerts," a sober Jimmy Page defended years later. "By the end of that, you come offstage and you're not going back to the hotel to have a cup of cocoa. Of course it was crazy; of course it was a mad life." Few rock musicians of the time were as conspicuously, unapologetically strung out as the dazed and confused leader of Led Zeppelin in the quartet's long twilight.

Only Keith Richards stood out more. He too was hooked on heroin and had been since the late '60s, dragging in his wake of headlong self-destruction the Rolling Stones and introducing his most dangerous of proclivities to co-guitarist Mick Taylor, rock journalist Nick Kent (who had coined the "Elegantly Wasted" description), producer Jimmy Miller, engineer Andy Johns, saxman Bobby Keys, and others reckless enough to try to keep up—it was in the company of Richards that John Phillips had acquired his own fixation, and Richards's closest companion in heroin addiction was his own wife, Anita Pallenberg. "The Rolling Stones destroy people at an alarming rate," the guitarist marveled. Richards's gaunt, corroded features and his long history of drug offenses over the Stones' presence in the media for the pop eternity of ten years won him the apocryphal title of the Rock Star Most Likely to Die. It was meant as a compliment.

Since the 1967 Redlands affair, Richards had faced police and judges from many nations several times. His French villa of Nellcôte was raided in 1972, and heroin, cocaine, and hash were found; he left the country in a fog of accusations and legal negotiating. Anita Pallenberg was caught with marijuana in Jamaica and her husband came up with a $12,000 bribe to bring her back to England. In 1973, Richards's London home was searched by detectives who discovered Mandrax, heroin, drug paraphernalia, and weapons; he was fined. On tour in the US in 1975 he was arrested for carrying an illegal knife (as a "concealed weapon") and cocaine while driving around the Deep South; the charges were dropped. In England in 1976, a police search in the aftermath of a car accident turned up a cocaine spoon and traces of LSD; another fine. Through all this, Richards and Pallenberg were parents of two young children, and a third died in infancy in 1976.

The Rolling Stones' recorded work of Richards's lowest heroin period—*Goat's Head Soup* (1973), *It's Only Rock 'n' Roll* (1974), and *Black and Blue* (1976)—are worthy albums that embellished their jaded reprobate personas, and their portrait on the cover of *Black and Blue* by photographer Hiro is alone a classic visualization of stoned, seen-it-all grandeur. But writing and rehearsing the songs now happened only as the senior guitarist's mood and physiological competence suited him, leading to long jams, overdubs in separate studios around the world, and all-night retakes of the same material. The finished LPs

OPPOSITE: **Rolling Stone Keith Richards, here with partner Anita Pallenberg, had regular run-ins with the law over drug offenses. Critics lauded him as the World's Most Elegantly Wasted Human Being.** (*Wesley / Getty Images*)

were assembled from miles of tape that spooled out while the parties dragged on, with guests like keyboardists Billy Preston and Nicky Hopkins, or horn players Bobby Keys and Jim Price, sharing in the treats. Neophyte acts would never have been given the same leeway. Bored of the routine, tired of waiting for Richards to perfect his parts hours or days after he had learned his, and a despairing heroin user, Mick Taylor quit the Stones in 1974.

Audiences rejoiced in Keith Richards as the ultimate symbol of rock 'n' roll heedlessness, but the fans who tried to mimic his style learned the hard way how Keef Riff-Hard made it look easy. What appeared attractive from afar turned out to be seedy and embarrassing to familiars. Photographs showed a romantic, piratical icon; in-person encounters exposed a stumbling, slurring junkie. His teeth had rotted out and were replaced with a false set. Close inspection showed that the instrumentalist had lost much of his musical chops, falling onstage drugged within an inch of his life and making desultory swings at his instruments while the rest of the Rolling Stones held the sound together. "All his guitars had capos on them so he didn't have to play barre chords [fingers across all strings]," revealed Nick Kent. "There was a different guitar for every song because he was too fucked up to make the effort." One deathless rock urban legend held that he had his scrawny frame's entire blood supply drained and exchanged for clean contents, allowing him to pass through customs (in fact it was medically cleansed but not replaced). On a '75 US circuit, his heroin was allegedly supplied by the FBI in a deal with the tour sponsor, guaranteeing their investment in the act and the ongoing presence of its second-most-famous attraction. Posted concert times were only approximate—the Rolling Stones would be shepherded to their venues in an armada of police-escorted limousines only after Richards had secured his fix. Critic Lester Bangs, no stranger to heavy substance intake, chided that Richards was in part responsible for "a drug culture that he perpetuates by making it seem glamorous to appear half-dead. People consider him to be Mr. Rock 'n' Roll, but if your last shred of charisma is a guy who doesn't play much anymore, who seems half-dead by his own choice, then who the hell cares about the Rolling Stones or rock 'n' roll?" "I don't think there is such a thing as a 'recreational drug,'" opined the far more conservative Mick Jagger, "but anyway, heroin certainly isn't it." Bill Wyman, unlike most outsiders, knew that "Keith didn't have to live by the rules of normal society. Money afforded him that luxury, if indeed it is a luxury."

Photographer Annie Leibovitz: "A rock 'n' roll tour is unnatural. You're moving through time and space too fast. The experience is extreme. There is the bigness of the performances and then the isolation and loneliness that follows." Like Jimmy Page and the handful of other rock 'n' rollers who could play to teeming football stadiums where tens of thousands of people cheered their every strum or lick, Keith Richards needed drugs to reinforce the awesome rush of a live gig. "I can't live without being on the road," he claimed. "Every minute spent off the road I either turn into an alcoholic or a junkie 'cause I've got nothing else to do. . . . I mean, most people that do things at least have the opportunity of doing it pretty regularly. We're in this unique, so they say, position of not having to expose ourselves too much. So you've got these horrible extravagances of people saying, 'I don't want to work *this* year.'" The excruciating drops from mass adulation to virtual anonymity were an emotional roller coaster only rock stars understood and only rock stars tried to remedy.

In Toronto in 1977, Keith Richards and Anita Pallenberg were found first with hashish at the airport and later with heroin and cocaine at their hotel. The quantities were such that he was charged with trafficking, although all of it was of course reserved for the couple. Both were arrested, tried, and eventually released, although the Rolling Stones played a court-ordered benefit concert for the blind—Richards's lawyer had invoked Vincent van Gogh, F. Scott Fitzgerald, Billie Holiday, and Dylan Thomas in his defense. While the drugs were confiscated, Richards went through the feverish, vomiting agony of involuntary withdrawal. "I was so stoned throughout that whole period that I just accepted it as part of doing what I was doing," he looked back. Margaret Trudeau, estranged wife of Canadian prime minister Pierre Trudeau, after partying with the other Stones was brought to Richards's suite by his tearful son Marlon: "Dad's lying on the floor crying—what shall I do?" the boy asked. His father was dragged to bed and covered with a blanket. "I couldn't just abandon the child," Trudeau wrote later, "so, clearing a space among the dirty plates, empty bottles, and garbage that littered the room, I settled down on the floor to help him glue together a model airplane. He had a lot of very expensive toys he couldn't understand, intended for far older children."

After the Toronto case—where the quintet's fate lay in the balance as Richards was looking at serious jail time—the Human Riff weaned himself from heroin, although cocaine, cannabis, and alcohol were there to ease the process and remained on hand for many years. Drummer Charlie Watts and Taylor's replacement Ron Wood acquired heroin and freebase cocaine problems of their own; following Wood's 1980 arrest for coke a police officer reported, "He looked really beat, like a typical drug user." "When we were in Woodstock, New York, rehearsing for the 1978 tour," Wood later documented, "[the dealer] had so much coke for Keith and me that, suddenly, it was three days later. We sniffed five grams up each nostril and set off through our blissful high."

Keith Richards's improbable survival gave him a lifelong air of indestructibility that admirers relish to this day: the later trend for "heroin chic" that plagued the runways and photo shoots of the fashion industry was doubtless inspired by his pallid, nodding, kohl-eyed visage of the late

1970s. "Being Keith Richards is a job and he's got it down to a fine art," summed up Anita Pallenberg, who split with the Stone as she continued a descent into heroin that culminated with the death by self-administered gunshot of a teenage friend. "He's very sheltered and shuttered and that helps him keep it going. . . . Everybody knows what he wants, what he likes, what he needs." Richards's biographer Victor Bockris had once asked him, "Do you ever get worried that [drugs] will finally get you?" "Well, I mean if they haven't done it by now, no," he answered. "I mean, 'cause it must be fairly obvious to everybody now that they've had a go with trying." They had tried very, very hard, and Keith Richards had come very close to being another famous rock 'n' roll casualty. Being a famous rock 'n' roller may have been what saved him.

Or not. In a last-ditch attempt to cure his rampant alcoholism, in the late summer of 1978 the hitherto indestructible rock 'n' roller Keith Moon of the Who had obtained a quantity of Heminevrin, a powerful sedative made of the drug chlormethiazole, which should have been administered only under doctor's supervision. On September 7, he overdosed on thirty-two of the pills and was found dead in the same apartment where Mama Cass Elliot had died four years previously. He had ingested one tablet for every year of his short, fast life.

The entertainment business in the final years of the 1970s was a blizzard of cocaine that buried not only the artists and performers but the behind-the-scenes managers, producers, functionaries, and technicians as well. Everyone knew about it; no one bothered hiding the spoons and the mirrors anymore. The 1976 farewell concert for the Band, filmed as Martin Scorcese's documentary *The Last Waltz*, was performed in front of a backstage whiteout where some of the biggest names in rock music were getting zonked. It was a spectacle of "all these heroes of the world pulling up in their limousines, coked out of their heads, smacked out of their brains, bumpin' into walls," said the Band's onetime employer Ronnie Hawkins. Eric Clapton arrived with his new partner, the former Mrs. George Harrison: "Pattie and I flew over a couple of days before and started some hard-core partying." Among Bob Dylan, Joni Mitchell, Van Morrison, Ron Wood, and Ringo Starr, Neil Young was coming off his own exhausting tour schedule. Said Young, "They were there, and a lotta people did drugs and I did drugs and there's nights where I did way too many drugs and I was stupid. . . . I was fried for *The Last Waltz*. I was on my way out, falling onstage, and someone said, 'Here, have some of this.'" Young's duet with the Band and an offstage Joni Mitchell on "Helpless" had to be cinematically doctored in the editing room to obscure the lump of cocaine hanging from one of his nostrils.

"I think cocaine is one of the biggest industry-dismantling vehicles," said Family Stone saxophonist Jerry Martini, who had watched his leader Sly Stone disintegrate under a freebase avalanche. "The downfall of the most famous bands was largely due to the affiliates, the hangers-on, the dealers, the doctors. . . . Everybody we were on tour with, it happened to most of the other bands back then." "Everybody in the music business was involved, even upper-level executives," said the Eagles' new guitarist Don Felder, hired in 1975. "One of the presidents of a very large label probably had the biggest cocaine habit I knew of. . . . We were generally well coked up before we ever appeared on stage, but our roadies had instructions to leave lines of blow on our amps so that between songs we could go back an bend over as if we were adjusting the knobs, when actually we were snorting in front of an entire live audience." Concerts of that age often opened with a fast, compelling number like the Stones' "Brown Sugar," Aerosmith's "Back

OPPOSITE: Guest performers at the Band's farewell concert were partying heavily backstage. "I was fried for *The Last Waltz*," admitted Neil Young, here with Joni Mitchell. *(Larry Hulst / Getty Images)*

in the Saddle," Blue Öyster Cult's "R U Ready 2 Rock," Black Sabbath's "Tomorrow's Dream," or Led Zeppelin's eruptive "Rock and Roll," the musicians bouncing on to the boards in the supercharged moments after sniffing up a fat white rail just offstage.

Cocaine had altered not only how the music was played but how deals were brokered and contracts fulfilled. Its use and value were factored into getting studio time, tour bookings, and especially radio airplay: sometimes it was a "gift" from promotional staff to disc jockeys, sometimes a perk for a record label's sales force, sometimes an accepted expense of celebratory meet-and-greets between artists and reporters. "In the advertising world, it's the martini—in the music world, it's cocaine," an unnamed producer was quoted as saying. The payola of the 1950s had become drugola in the 1970s. The Grateful Dead's "Truckin'," which indeed laments a "Sweet Jane" who is now "livin' on reds, vitamin C, and cocaine," became a hit song with help from some friendly persuasion portioned out on a mirror. "Fuck me, it actually works!" exclaimed Rock Scully. "And to think all you have to do is lace the deejays with an eight ball [an eighth of an ounce] of blow, a few luncheons, and the occasional new Cadillac. . . . 'Listen to this record, man, just listen to thirty seconds of it! Okay, now do another line and listen to it again.'" "Drugs did decimate this business," concluded artist manager and industry player Ron Stone. "It sent lifestyle shock waves through the whole system."

The American center of cocaine importing was Florida, and just as Mexican pot had earlier been a fringe benefit for LA session work, so the local snowdrifts of Peruvian or Colombian blow made Miami a choice locale for recording. New York, Los Angeles, San Francisco, Nashville, London, and Paris still had their appeal, but Miami was where the purest arrivals could be bought fresh off the boat. The city's Criteria Studios was chosen by everyone from the Bee Gees and Crosby, Stills and Nash to Black Sabbath, Aerosmith, and Eric Clapton for *Layla* and

461 Ocean Boulevard, the latter named for his Miami address. "We had scored masses of coke and smack before we left Florida and took it on tour with us," Clapton said of undertaking engagements as Derek and the Dominos.

The proximity of so many drugs available for purchase, in the Sunshine State or elsewhere, meant that the management or travel organizations around the acts could drift into selling drugs themselves to finance their own hoards (a venture that brought down the out-of-control John Phillips), or cooperating with dealers in laundering cash, making deliveries, or otherwise edging into organized crime. "In Alabama, a team of beefy drivers who looked like linebackers stuffed into sweatpants and zipper jackets made it clear they could get 'anything you want,' including cocaine and prostitutes," recalled Kiss business manager C. K. Lendt of a limousine service he'd hired. "They ran a ring of local working girls and did drug deals when they weren't driving." Some musicians reacted in disgust to the swamp of payoffs and addictions around them, as did FM-friendly songster Steve Miller: "My career has been blocked and stopped by certain formats and opened up by others," he said. "And all along I just refused to pay payola. . . . I went from one-and-a-half million [records sold] to 26,000, and said, 'Fuck this. I don't even want to be in this business. I'm so sick of this graft and corruption and this Mafia bullshit and their cocaine.' It just became a cesspool." "I saw the cocaine thing become this insidiously destructive juggernaut in the lives of friends," contended American heartland rocker Bob Seger. "When I thought the whole coke thing couldn't get any worse in the late seventies, that's when it exploded as a hemispheric plague, wrecking governments in South America and threatening to ruin a generation [in the US]."

One band that laid down takes at Criteria Studios was Lynyrd Skynyrd, coming down from their home in Jacksonville, Florida. Skynyrd

were the biggest and baddest of the southern rock 'n' rollers and set
the fatalistic denim pace for other blue-collar boogie acts like Molly
Hatchet, AC/DC, and Motörhead. Discovered by Dylan accomplice
Al Kooper in 1972, they had a sound that was hard rock honky-tonk, a
rural white man's protest against commitment ("Call Me the Breeze,"
"I Ain't the One"), authority ("Gimme Back My Bullets," "Workin' for
MCA"), and patronizing outsiders ("Sweet Home Alabama," "Whiskey
Rock-a-Roller"). Their triple-guitar attack sometimes evoked banjos run
through a fuzz box and a Marshall, and singer Ronnie Van Zant adopted
the yee-haw vocal inflections of country casualty Hank Williams and the
everyman balladry of Woody Guthrie. "Wild, crazy, drinking, fighting
rednecks with a capital R, and proud of it," their original manager, Alan
Walden, said of the group.

But Skynyrd also defied the stereotype of unrepentant good ole
boy racism—though they hung Confederate flags at their shows and
doffed rebel gear, Van Zant also checked into hotels under the blues-
man's pseudonym of Robert Johnson and wrote "The Ballad of Curtis
Lowe," a sympathetic tale of white-black companionship, and "Saturday
Night Special," his full-bore anti-gun invective aimed straight at the
south's National Rifle Association demographic. Named after Ronald
Reagan, Ronnie Van Zant found his favorite lyricist in the contrarian
outlaw Merle Haggard. Lynyrd Skynyrd's take on drugs likewise rebelled
against the audience's expectations, as they served up both the long-
hair's jailbreak of "Double Trouble" ("Those men that's dressed in blue
never done so right by me / Some of the times I was innocent but the
judge said guil-ty") and the tortured heroin admonition of "The Needle
and the Spoon": "I've been feelin' so sick inside, Gotta get better, Lord,
before I die. . . ."

The darkest of Van Zant's messages was "That Smell," today an FM
radio standard and one of the most explicit drug sermons in the genre

of classic rock. "I had a creepy feeling things were going against us, so I thought I'd write a morbid song," he said in July 1977. "Unfortunately, that song is kind of about me and a lot of other people," conceded Skynyrd guitarist Gary Rossington, with Van Zant a central personage in the band's rowdy offstage behavior. "I was doin' Quaaludes and drinkin' and went out on Labor Day weekend. . . . We got crazy, and on the way back home I ran into an oak tree, knocked some teeth out, and got in trouble. That song's just about getting caught up in the times." Written by Van Zant and Allen Collins, "That Smell" describes a party pack of intoxicants and where they ultimately lead: "Whiskey bottles, and brand-new cars, oak tree in my way / There's too much coke, and too much smoke, look what's goin' on inside you. . . ." The ominous titular scent of the song is of death itself—ironic, then, that only three days after the album on which the track appeared, *Street Survivors*, was released in October 1977, Ronnie Van Zant, guitarist Steve Gaines, and Gaines's sister, backup singer Cassie Gaines, were killed in a plane crash near McComb, Mississippi, along with the two pilots and Skynyrd road manager Dean Kilpatrick. Other musicians and road crew aboard were severely injured. It was not cocaine, heroin, or Quaaludes that destroyed Lynyrd Skynyrd but a skidding impact with the southern swampland they had been proud to call home. "Y'all do what you want to," Ronnie Van Zant told his nervous bandmates before setting out in the aircraft. "If it's my time, it's my time."

As Skynyrd went down, Fleetwood Mac rose from the ashes. Anchored and named by the rhythm section of drummer Mick Fleetwood and bassist John McVie, the group had gone through a number of personnel changes since the late '60s when they settled on a lineup that by 1975 included American guitarist Lindsey Buckingham and singer Stevie Nicks, both songwriters, taking center stage with McVie's wife Christine McVie on keyboards and vocals. The combination of two not-always-happy couples in one group was fraught from the beginning, and the additional factor of being based in coke-crazed Los Angeles spelled trouble too. "There was a lot of cocaine around that studio," Fleetwood remembered, "and we recorded our album in a somewhat Peruvian atmosphere." The music, however, had been transformed from the gutbucket blues of Peter Green's tenure into an agreeably feminized, sensitized Californian glow, highlighted by Buckingham's idiosyncratic guitar, Christine McVie's lithe "Say You Love Me," and the enchantress Nicks's pensive "Landslide" and "Rhiannon." The success of *Fleetwood Mac* and the remade band's live concerts spurred them to embark on a follow-up, named for the tangle of estrangements, jealousy, and in-nuendo that had risen around and between the musicians: *Rumours.*

Stevie Nicks: "*Rumours* took twelve months because we were all trying to hold the foundation of Fleetwood Mac together, and trying to speak to each other in a civil tone, while sitting in a tiny room lis-tening to each other's songs about our shattered relationships." Mick Fleetwood: "It was like a cocktail party all the time. The studio was full of weirdos we'd never seen before, partying with each other while we tried to work. . . . There was one coke dealer who kept us supplied with high-grade Peruvian flake, and we were so grateful to him that I considered (in my state of dementia) giving him some kind of credit on the album jacket." John McVie: "Amazing. Terrifying. Huge amounts of illicit materials, yards and yards of this wretched stuff. Days and nights would just go on and on." Christine McVie: "In those days, it was quite natural to walk around with a great old sack of cocaine in your pocket and do these huge rails, popping acid, and making hash cookies."

Rumours was not really about drugs in the way that, say, *Sticky Fingers* or *Paranoid* had been, but it reverberated with the post-Water-gate, post-Vietnam triumphalism of the baby boomers' dope culture, where at last the straights had been overthrown and the heads had been vindicated. This Fleetwood Mac was at the top of the "soft rock" pyramid, the roster of mellow, smoothened acts like Bread, Seals & Crofts, and America, who nevertheless lived and espoused a velvety hedonism hardly different from that of the Stones or Black Sabbath. Suffused with bubbly SoCal philosophies of relationships ("You Make Loving Fun," Buckingham's gorgeous "Never Going Back Again") and personal growth ("Don't Stop," the irresistible "Go Your Own Way"), *Rumours* was the right album at the right time, selling some twenty-six million copies since 1977; its momentum drove Fleetwood Mac on into the next decade with the ambitious, expensive double album *Tusk* (1979) and regal expectations of servitude. "The refreshment rider written into our contracts with the local promoters provided an immense backstage buffet for an army of California gourmands," Mick Fleetwood said, "although many of us were too coked up and glazed over to actually eat anything. A king's ransom was spent on keeping the tour's cocaine supply adequate." The one song on *Rumours* that addressed drug use was Stevie Nicks' eerie "Gold Dust Woman," which she had in fact composed in her lean years as a duet with Buckingham that predated her own cocaine habit, acquired during her time as the Mac's resident mystery woman. "Rock on, gold dust woman / Take your silver spoon, dig your grave," she sang in her feathery vibrato. "Everybody said it was okay, recreational, not addictive," she remembered before the flake nearly caused her facial cartilage to cave in. "Nobody told you that you may end up with a hole through your nose the size of Chicago."

The only artists who exceeded Fleetwood Mac as avatars of Los Angeles rock royalty were the Eagles, winging skyward after *One of These Nights* (1975) and the addition of guitarist Don Felder, bringing a crunchier tone to their older sepia-toned efforts—which had been made under the supervision of producer Glyn Johns, who forbade drug use in the studio. But by 1976 the Eagles too were rent with personal rivalries and creative conflicts, all of them aggravated by cocaine. "[T]he drugs did erode our objectivity," divulged singer, drummer, and lyricist Don Henley. "They brought out the worst of our personalities. While I don't believe things would have been a great deal different if we hadn't been doing drugs, drugs had the effect of speeding up and exacerbating the separation process." "There was a time during 1976, 1977, where the record business went crazy," attested singer and songwriter Glenn Frey. "Led Zeppelin might argue with us, but I think we might have thrown the greatest traveling party of the seventies."

With the hard-rocking, hard-living Joe Walsh brought in to replace Bernie Leadon for the band's next album, the vibe became more intense. "Coke really allowed me to focus, and alcohol took the edge of the cocaine," Walsh explained. "I could go in the studio and stay fresh for hours. I was crazy on alcohol and drugs." Felder was right there with him. "Cocaine and alcohol with Quaaludes thrown in was bad medicine, even if it did smooth off the edges," he put in. One reason Eagles and Fleetwood Mac records were taped over months and months of pricey recording time was the perfectionism cocaine instigated, musicians, engineers, and producers all colluding to splice in the best moments from dozens of separate takes to make the sweetest final cut—both the Eagles' LPs and *Rumours* were vilified by punk rockers for the cold gloss of their production. "You don't do all those Eagles albums without joining in," producer Bill Szymczyk said of the silver-spoon hospitality on hand at the mixing deck. "Those wonderful seventies—I'm sure glad I went through them, I'm even happier I survived them." The constant sharing of white powder engendered a quick aside between Eagles

OPPOSITE: "I was crazy on alcohol and drugs," said the Eagles' Joe Walsh of his recording and performing regimen in the 1970s. The Eagles defined the coked-out splendor of the pop music industry at its indulgent peak. *(Bobby Bank / Getty Images)*

pointing out traces left on the others' nostrils just before a gig or public appearance—"Hey buddy, you're showing." They went to Florida for another round of all-night studio sessions, although the music they made in Miami's Criteria Studios emerged as a love-hate homage to their adopted state of California.

Hotel California jousted with *Rumours* at the top of the US album charts after its debut in the fall of 1976, and like the Fleetwood Mac disc is one of the most commercially successful rock records of all time (more than fourteen million copies sold) and one of the most vivid evocations of place and mood in the classic rock pantheon. *Hotel* is a slick folk-rock update of Nathanael West's 1939 novel *The Day of the Locust*, depicting the dreams and delusions of the migrating flocks of Americans seeking redemption or reinvention in the paradises of Hollywood, Malibu, Venice Beach, or Big Sur—with the new complications of serial partners and recreational drugs thrown in. Here the edgy optimism of *Rumours* is offset by the disillusionment of realizing the Mamas and the Papas' 1965 California dreams and finding them empty ten years later. Aside from Felder and Henley's hypnotic, labyrinthine title track, the music showed what Henley called "the more superficial aspects of life in [Los Angeles]" through a cocaine-flecked prism, scarring the casual romance and double meaning of "Wasted Time" ("And the shadows come to stay / So you take a little something to make them go away"), the environmentalism of "The Last Resort" ("We satisfy our endless needs, and justify our bloody deeds / In the name of destiny, and in the name of God"), and the unexpected face-to-face regrets of "Pretty Maids All in a Row" ("Why do we give up our hearts to the past / And why must we grow up so fast?").

The devastating "Life in the Fast Lane" is the Bel Air equivalent of Lynyrd Skynyrd's "That Smell," telling the scary fable of a spoiled young couple driving and living at high speed: "There were lines on the mirror, lines on her face / He pretended not to notice, he was caught up in the race. . . ." "It's been mistaken as a song glorifying that kind of lifestyle, when in fact it's not," Henley warned. "I'm just trying to give others the benefit of my experience." Despite the album's popularity, the Eagles only managed one more record, 1979's *The Long Run*, after which they collapsed in a squabble of money grudges and cocaine-propelled resentment. Bassist Randy Meisner quit on the *Hotel California* tour, and recording with replacement Tim Schmit ground on until "finally," Felder looked back, "we exhausted ourselves, exhausted our patience, and took so many drugs that nobody could see any further solutions except to finish what we had and walk away from it. . . . Being high allows for a false sense of camaraderie, but as soon as the drug wears off, you realize how fake it all is." "Although we were flying high," Henley said of the Eagles' flight, "it was going to come to a screeching halt in not too many years." In November 1980 his LA home was raided by police, and pot, cocaine, Quaaludes, and a sixteen-year-old girl were found—he was charged with contributing to the delinquency of a minor. His own life in the fast lane had careened off the road.

The minor news story of Henley's arrest was overshadowed by a much bigger one at the same time: the election of Ronald Reagan to the US presidency on November 4, 1980. Himself a Midwestern boy who'd sought (and found) stardom in the tinsel factory of Hollywood, Reagan had served as a two-term governor of California from 1967 to 1974, over the very years and in the main locale of the sex, drugs, and rock 'n' roll counterculture. Ready with a trained geniality and reflexive patriotism, Reagan personified the uptight, ignorant square who would never comprehend the intentions or ideals of the young. Campaigning for governorship he said he was "sick at the sit-ins, the teach-ins, the walk-outs," and in office described the typical student demonstrator, of whom he faced many, as someone who "dresses like Tarzan, has hair like Jane, and smells like Cheetah." His wife Nancy was even more cloistered in her beliefs. "I admit I'm getting tired of jeans and long hair," she told an interviewer in 1972. "From a woman's standpoint, it frightens me when I see students shouting obscenities." When her pot-smoking daughter Patti moved in with, of all people, Bernie Leadon of the Eagles, her parents disowned her. "It wasn't because she was living with a rock musician, although the Eagles were not exactly a mother's dream," said Nancy. "It was that they were living together, which we just couldn't accept."

Ronald Reagan's occupancy of the White House, like his ally Margaret Thatcher's of 10 Downing Street from 1979, was seen as the inevitable swing of a political pendulum back from the previous sixteen years' protests, liberations, revolutions, freedoms, and free festivals. Or was there really far to swing? "The same people who had always been in control were still in control," noted Don Henley. "While we were out taking drugs and preaching flower power and having rock concerts and love-ins, people were running the country." Under Reagan's administration it was not particularly the president who devised policy, but rather his spouse, cabinet, and staff who, emboldened by Reagan's blinkered certainty that the upheavals of the 1960s and 1970s were mere aberrations and that "American values" would always prevail, set out a punitive agenda against a perceived fringe of malcontents and radicalism. Reagan the leader could in fact do little to bring down rock music or its psychotropic accessories, but Reagan the symbol would stand for a social retreat after which neither the pop nor the drug industries would ever be the same.

TOMORROW
NEVER KNOWS

I suspect that the rock addiction, particularly in the absence
of strong counterattractions, has an effect similar to that
of drugs. The students will get over this music, or at least
the exclusive passion for it.

ALLAN BLOOM, *THE CLOSING OF THE AMERICAN MIND*

In bare monetary terms, neither rock 'n' roll nor drugs was much
troubled by the trend toward social conservatism that began in the
late 1970s and accelerated through the 1980s. The business of popular
music adapted to new style cycles and media venues to immense profit,
with figures like Michael Jackson and Madonna made into worldwide
celebrities scaling or surpassing the heights reached by the Beatles, Bob
Dylan, Bob Marley, or Pink Floyd. Likewise, the international trade in
illegal intoxicants went truly global, threatening to topple some governments while fatally compromising others, and earning billions of
dollars in an underground market whose size rivaled or exceeded that
for many legitimate commodities. But changes in politics, technology,
demographics, and cultural habits did diminish the place both rock and
drugs had once occupied in contemporary life—still broadly obtainable
and widely distributed, between 1980 and the present both the songs

and the substances would lose most of the mystique and urgency they had together found in prior decades.

The twelve years of Republican administrations under US president Ronald Reagan and his successor, George H. W. Bush, did much to reverse the tide that had seemed to be culminating in a popular acceptance of most drugs and even a legalization of marijuana. Capitalizing on a general public fatigue with the liberal platforms of civil rights, feminism, youth activism, and the humiliations of Vietnam and the energy crisis, Reagan, like Richard Nixon, seized on drug use as a law-and-order issue with which to frighten the American middle classes and distract them from his own ideology of laissez-faire capitalism. In 1982, Reagan created the White House Drug Abuse Policy Office and later advanced mandatory minimum penalties for persons convicted of drug crimes; the Drug Enforcement Administration (DEA), formed under Nixon, was joined by the Organized Crime Drug Enforcement Task Force in 1983, the National Narcotics Drug Policy Board in 1984, and the Office of National Drug Control Policy in 1988.

Because so many average young people were implicated as at least occasional smokers of cannabis, it was now the dealers who became vilified, even though among marijuana users the distinction between vendors and purchasers was often a nebulous one. Reagan appointed Carlton Turner, the first in a line of officials bearing the unintentionally sinister title of "Drug Czar," to carry out his prohibitionist agenda. "We have to start focusing on the users and make them pay the price," Turner declared in 1985, "and we ought to have the death penalty for drug dealers." Here the once grievous, desperate lyrics of Steppenwolf had won the chief executive's sunny seal of approval: "If I was the president of this land, I'd declare total war on the pusher man. . . ."

It was Reagan's first lady, Nancy, however, who took up the anti-drug mania as her pet crusade. Utilizing the bland slogans of "Hugs

Not Drugs" and the immortal "Just Say No," she turned back the legal clock from the complexities of public health and personal privacy to the fire-and-brimstone (albeit garbed in designer fashions) posture of Harry J. Anslinger. "The final answer lies in taking the customers away from the product," she said, which would have had her ejected from the Republican Party had she been discussing any other sector of the national economy. "We've got to do it, and I need your help." Though, like her husband, Nancy Reagan was undeniably sincere as she made the rounds of rehab centers and clinics while solemnly hearing patients' tales of misery, or coaching school children in the Just Say No mantra in front of a posse of newsmen, the results of her campaign would prove devastating to America.

Simply put, by creating a climate of unthinking hostility toward drugs of all kinds, borrowing the tactics and terminology of the military and intelligence services in attempts at international curtailment, and encouraging tougher sentences for drug criminals of any stripe, the first lady made the sale of drugs all the more profitable for those willing to risk it. Organized crime had always played a role in the drug underworld, of course, but ventures into gambling and prostitution were usually found to offer greater and more predictable sums of cash. Before the War on Drugs was begun under Richard Nixon and intensified under Ronald Reagan, the distribution chains of smuggled or homegrown marijuana were often loose and spread among a broad range of low- or middle-level growers, dealers, and transporters. As the police intervention grew more aggressive, it paid to have a more coordinated system in place, run by heavily armed full-time criminals warring over territory (including sovereign states) and murderously enforcing contracts just as in the era of rumrunners, speakeasies, and Al Capone. The sense of fraternity and pacifism that had characterized the hazy atmospheres at Monterey or Woodstock, or the earnest proselytizing of Stanley Owsley at the Acid Tests, would be supplanted by a ruthless competitiveness among hard-core gangs like the Hells Angels or offshore magnates like Pablo Escobar of the Medellín, Colombia, cartel.

Paradoxically, too, the judicial pursuit of cannabis growers in Mexico (where plantations were sprayed with chemical herbicide that found its way into the lungs of smokers) and cannabis traffickers in the US led many drug suppliers to turn to the far more addictive cocaine. Since the punishment for carrying pot was about equal to that for carrying coke, and the payoffs for coke much larger, the choice was an easy one. "It's easier to handle, easier to fly, and easier to hide," said one apprehended cocaine trader. By the early '80s what had once been the exclusive treat of the Jimmy Pages or Elton Johns was now available at drastically reduced prices affordable to any office worker or college sophomore; even the DEA allowed that the amount of cocaine imported into the United States rose from an estimated thirty-six to sixty-six tons of blow in 1981 to sixty-one to eighty-four tons in 1984. The price per kilogram dropped from $60,000 in 1982 to $15,000 in 1989. A 1977 study showed that only 10 percent of those in their late teens and early twenties questioned said they had tried coke, a number that grew to one-third of respondents eight years later.

The glamorous, jet-setting symbolism of cocaine decayed further as crafty dealers began to dispense it in the form of crystallized lumps that could be smoked: crack. Crack was cheaper still than powdered cocaine—only $5 for a rock—but the resultant high was far more pleasurable and far shorter in duration, making crack one of the most viciously habit-forming drugs available. Derived from the freebase technique to which David Crosby, Sly Stone, Marvin Gaye, and Ron Wood had succumbed, crack quickly infiltrated into the ghettoes of America in a

OPPOSITE: The anti-drug campaigns of the 1980s marked the end of an era in pop music and society at large. *(Diana Walker / Getty Images)*

storm of press alarmism, which only served to boost curiosity among the foolish and cynicism among the greedy. "The first hit is totally euphoric," Wood said of freebasing, "but you never get back there, so you're always chasing that first time." Even ignoring the media overkill, the crack epidemic did genuinely blight the already bleak African-American urban centers, and a generation grew up in and around the squalor of crack pipes, crack houses, crack prostitution, and addicted crack babies born to teenage crack mothers. Even Gaye's "Inner City Blues" had never imagined anything like this. Crack was the drab, colorless psychological negative of Jimi Hendrix's lysergic Experience.

President George H.W. Bush extended the War on Drugs and launched the US military against Panamanian leader General Manuel Noriega, accused of shipping huge tonnages of cocaine through his country, laundering the profits, and keeping much of the proceeds for himself. While attempting to extradite Noriega, the American soldiers blasted recorded rock music at him in attempt to draw him out of his Catholic sanctuary, what the fugitive considered "scorching, diabolical noise," but which others would hear as, among other tunes, the Rolling Stones' "Time Is on My Side," Black Sabbath's "Paranoid" and their apocalyptic "War Pigs," Pink Floyd's "Run Like Hell," Led Zeppelin's "Your Time Is Gonna Come," the Animals' "We Gotta Get Out of This Place," and Jimi Hendrix's searing rendition of "The Star-Spangled Banner" live at Yasgur's farm. It went unmentioned that most of the music's authors were heavy drug users.

In the waning days of the Reagan presidency and the early days of Bush's, it transpired that the US government had previously enlisted Manuel Noriega's aid in illegally diverting arms to neighboring Nicaragua's anticommunist contra rebels, to whom they were sympathetic, and that the same aircraft used to transport weapons to the contras were then flown north transporting drugs into America. The US Senate's

Foreign Relations Narcotics Subcommittee eventually concluded, "Individuals who provided support for the Contras were involved in drug trafficking, the supply network of the Contras was used by drug trafficking organizations, and elements of the Contras themselves knowingly received financial and material assistance from drug traffickers." Years afterward, President Bush's son George W. Bush all but confessed to having tried marijuana and cocaine, some of which presumably came via Panama, as a dissolute young man in the 1970s. Ronald Reagan's departure from office in 1989 saw the overall totals of illegal drugs consumed in the US sitting at the same levels they were when he came in.

Other drugs were being introduced or reintroduced in the 1980s, many of them more toxic than the pharmacopoeia enjoyed by Neil Young or Ozzy Osbourne. Ecstasy was the new name given to MDMA, tablets of which had been tried by the hippies of the 1970s and in some more experimental therapeutic settings, but the drug, which remained legal since its development in the Merck labs in 1912, did not catch on as a recreational trip until 1984. As its nickname suggested, Ecstasy ("E" or "X" to adherents) produced a powerful feeling of happiness, empathy, and affection in the user, together with a skyrocketing rush of energy and an almost painful fixed smile as they went "rolling" while "loved-up" for several hours. When finally made illegal in 1985, Ecstasy became increasingly available at straight and gay dance clubs while its cost rose and quality fell, another unintended but entirely foreseeable consequence of prohibition. Though not addictive in the manner of crack or heroin, Ecstasy when taken frequently was discovered to bring on heart arrhythmia and brutal crashes that drove the taker to go rolling again; a small number of deaths were attributed to Ecstasy impairment, sometimes due to exhaustion, heatstroke, or dehydration while dancing.

The dance clubs where Ecstasy was favored were also prime centers for other drugs that enhanced the charged atmosphere of twisting bodies, synthetic beats, and throbbing lights. GHB (gamma hydroxy-butyrate), a liquid depressant sipped from vials that produces effects similar to drunkenness—relaxation, giddiness—became popular in the 1990s, as did the pill Rohypnol (flunitrazepam) and the sniffed powder ketamine, both strong anesthetics that can trigger hallucinations, amnesia, and extreme disorientation. "E," "G", and "Special K" all formed part of rave culture, a lifestyle among young middle-class partiers dancing long, dizzying nights and wee hours away in huge warehouses or halls with names like Parallel Youniverse, Nocturnal Audio and Sound Awakening (NASA), Ministry of Sound, or Paradise Garage, grooving to the remorseless drones and meters of techno music pumped through state-of-the-art speaker systems. Some raves drew almost 30,000 attendees. It was all reminiscent of the Grateful Dead's Acid Tests or the Unlimited Freak Outs of early Pink Floyd—with the exception that the music was artificial, not live, and the dancers were not really there to listen but to feel.

Though there were obvious parallels between the rave scene and that of the earlier psychedelic rock, a major distinction was that the sounds presented at raves—techno, trance, ambient, acid house, trip-hop, and so on—were devised by DJs using an elaborate array of turntables, samplers, and sequencers to juxtapose and intersperse snippets of pre-existing tracks rather than human performers improvising together. Many artists and songs were associated with Ecstasy, like Candy Flip, Flowered Up, and Josh Wink's "Higher State of Consciousness," and the Shamen's "Ebeneezer Goode," but the genre produced few lasting players whose work could truly transcend its setting. Because the songs themselves were modeled from a diverse range of other tunes (Motown, Arabic or Indian pop, movie soundtracks, and the futuristic prog rock of Kraftwerk or Tangerine Dream, to name a few), there was a constant flux of "remix" and "dance mix" versions to be heard at any one period,

essentially confining their appeal to the dance clubs where they originated and were best appreciated. At the same time, a fluctuating round
of guest DJs might jump from studio to studio or turntable to turntable
holding little longtime affiliation with a single "act" in the conventional
sense. Rave music was not made by anyone outsiders would recognize
as rave stars. The repetitiveness of techno's rhythms and the calculated
programming of its sonic movements made the music more of an orna-
ment to the drug experiences than a representation of them. "House
and techno producers have developed a drug-determined repertoire
of effects, textures, and riffs that are expressly designed to trigger the
tingly rushes that traverse the Ecstatic body," gushed rave writer Simon
Reynolds, describing a clinical methodology different from the subjective responses intended by the Jefferson Airplane's "Crown of Creation"
or the Doors' "Break On Through."

Ecstasy, GHB, ketamine, and Rohypnol were each the subject of media titillation and parental backlashes, but none of them was much more
dangerous than LSD, STP, amphetamines or reds; they were merely the
next generation of "designer drugs" invented by pharmaceutical companies and adulterated, embellished, coarsened, diluted, and abused as
they were made illegal and treated as contraband. Some injuries, deaths,
and long-term mental damage were blamed on the drugs, especially
when taken in quantity or with a miasma of other chemicals, and Rohypnol took on a reputation as a "date rape" substance after cases came
to light where it was slipped into drinks and victims were assaulted in
a virtually comatose condition. In terms of sheer lives destroyed, relationships ruined, careers failed, and dates raped, by far the deadliest
drug of all remained alcohol.

But some new highs warranted concern. Most of these were isolated to college or high school campuses or seedy downtowns, like
the stimulant methcathinone ("cat" or "goob") and the smoked form

of methedrine called ice, both of which attracted disproportionate attention from opportunistic political candidates seeking free rides on Nancy Reagan's Just Say No publicity. Methamphetamine and its solidified derivative crystal meth, however, became widely taken in the 1980s and 1990s and, in a sad and stupid irony so common to the War on Drugs, were introduced as a cheap, homemade substitute for the closely pursued (by police) cocaine and crack. A sort of souped-up moonshine amphetamine that could be cooked with household equipment and over-the-counter ingredients, meth or "crank" use spread throughout the United States, particularly among rural whites, leading to its designation as "the hillbilly crack." Sickeningly addictive, methamphetamine is one of the harshest and most caustic street drugs: like chocolate, orgasms, or cocaine, meth releases dopamine in the brain, but at vastly higher extents than any comparative rush, and can bring on catastrophic episodes of heart attack, stroke, convulsions, and organ failure. Methamphetamine affects blood circulation and suppresses the appetite so much that addicts—and by some measures over 90 percent of first-time meth takers get hooked—lose weight, skin elasticity, and teeth, are prone to paranoia and outbursts of uncontrollable violence ("tweaking"), and acquire sores and infected welts around their bodies. When they hallucinate that insects are on or under their skin, they scratch and pick continuously, leading to an even more horrific appearance. Long-term meth use causes loss of motor coordination and permanent memory loss. "It was shocking," said one professor of neurology after examining methamphetamine's rotting of sample brain tissue. "It was like a forest fire of brain damage." Meth addicts, both heterosexual and homosexual, are more likely to have indiscriminate unsafe sex and contract HIV/AIDS. Though medical, law enforcement, and legislative authorities disagree on the severity of the methamphetamine problem in North America, none deny the destructiveness of the drug. Needless to say, there is no known category of pop music that describes, accompanies, or celebrates it.

The old standbys of cannabis and LSD have now been part of post-industrial democracies for several generations—it is possible that grandparents who smoked up and tripped out in 1966 now have children and grandchildren who have done the same, perhaps even to recordings of the same music or, in the case of the Rolling Stones, a concert by the same musicians. This very familiarity of both pot and acid has made them the least threatening illicit drugs, although the circumstances in which they are produced and consumed have changed considerably. Lysergic acid diethylamide has made something of a comeback in the psychiatric establishment, with some recent studies suggesting it can be useful in the treatment of alcoholism and obsessive-compulsive disorder. Others note that LSD is today weaker in strength than the tabs dropped in Haight-Ashbury. According to one academic researcher, "LSD is now taken in smaller doses [than in the 1960s]. The effect is a euphoric high similar to that of marijuana, and powerful mind-altering states are neither desired nor achieved." In 2006 the US Supreme Court voted to allow the use of the hallucinogenic DMT in the rituals of certain Native American groups in New Mexico, on the basis of religious freedom.

Cannabis, for its part, is still the most widely used illegal substance and, in political debate if not broad public opinion, the most controversial. It is estimated that between one-quarter to well over one-third of all people in the United States have tried pot at least once, a count of over ninety-six million citizens. Around the world, the United Nations International Drug Control Program has cited a figure of 3.5 percent of the planet's population over the age of fifteen as regular cannabis smokers—147 million people. Statistics suggest that the portion of American twelfth-grade students who claimed to have smoked dope in the most recent thirty days peaked at about 35 percent in 1978, dropped to about 10 percent in 1992 after the Reagan-Bush years, and has risen again, to about 20 percent in 2005.

Marijuana is one of the most lucrative cash crops on the earth, and in some parts of the United States and Canada its revenues exceed those for corn, wheat, and timber; in California alone the cannabis industry is worth about $14 billion per annum. Because of the increased monitoring and interception of marine or overland marijuana smugglers out of Mexico or Jamaica in the 1970s and 1980s (hence the "Save the Bales" stoners' T-shirts), most weed sold in North America is now homegrown. Some of this is bred secretly in farmland or wooded areas, but a large crop is sourced from indoor "grow ops," where complicated and expensive systems of nurturing, watering, and lighting enable the grower to harvest more and stronger generations of cannabis in shorter periods than would be farmed naturally. The strains of marijuana thus produced, with names like Sour Diesel, Bubba Kush, Purple Urkel, Blueberry, Lavender, Jedi, and LA Confidential, carry a sumptuous range of colors, tastes, and effects, with the most desirable retailing for over $5,000 per pound. As with many other agricultural products—olive oil, wine, lettuce, or balsamic vinegar—today there is a far greater selection of specialty weed for the discriminating shopper to choose from than even Bob Dylan or Allen Ginsberg could have scored in 1964. Over the years the THC content of good-quality pot has risen from less than 1 percent to over 6 percent, although the higher number is still well below a concentration that would imply toxicity.

The laws against cannabis in many places are convoluted, confusing, subject to frequent challenges and counterchallenges from prosecutors and lobbyists, and unevenly enforced. Although more than 800,000 Americans were arrested for marijuana crimes in 2006 (the vast majority for possession only), many of these were either let off with a warning (with their stash confiscated), fined, or sentenced to short stays in the local jail. Depending on the location, someone caught with a small amount may walk away or do time, with considerably more lenience shown to tokers in big cities like Los Angeles or Vancouver than to their brethren in small-town Oklahoma or Saskatchewan. Within the United States, different jurisdictions mete out a range of different punishments for the same charge: in New York an ounce of dope will earn the owner a $100 fine, while in Louisiana he might get twenty years. For some marijuana crimes prosecuted under a draconian "zero tolerance" policy, cars, homes, and other possessions can be confiscated by the state, and some individuals implicated in trafficking schemes have been sentenced to life imprisonment in penitentiaries with murderers and rapists. In other instances, the most peripheral members of a grow op or smuggling ring receive the stiffest jail terms (since they cannot or will not barter a deal by fingering anyone else), or growers will alert police to rival pot dealers and so increase their own business. The growth and traffic of cannabis, while still a federal crime in the US, are now in the same vague legal arena as gambling and adult entertainment venues, where prosecution or tolerance is determined by community standards and police initiative. "It's ridiculous to have this constant battle between federal and state laws," noted Los Angeles city council member Bill Rosendahl. "The War on Drugs is out of control—it's become a war on people."

To add to the uncertainty, since the 1990s experts have contended that marijuana has legitimate medicinal benefits for patients suffering from glaucoma, AIDS, chemotherapy-induced nausea, and other chronic health conditions. This has led to the proliferation of quasi-sanctioned cannabis outlets in Canada, the US, and elsewhere, where adults with a doctor's approval can buy and smoke pot on the premises. There is continued dispute over exactly how helpful marijuana can be to the ill—it is smoked, after all, and contains as much or more tar than tobacco, although many smokers both fit and unfit prefer the cleaner drags of bongs or water pipes. How strictly the prescriptions are evaluated is another question. In California, physicians might attest that a patient requires marijuana for "anxiety." Many operators of cannabis dispensaries, as well as the professionals who direct people to them, admit that the medical standards are lax but say that since pot is no stronger a psychotropic drug than legal ones like Prozac, there is no reason it should not be recommended and administered for the same generalized ailments.

In consequence of the myriad contradictions, hypocrisies, and ineptitudes surrounding the War on Drugs, many articulate voices have been raised calling for the crusade to be abandoned altogether. Outlaw Willie Nelson, a beloved country star whose persona embodies the American virtues of rugged independence and heartland honesty, has become an outspoken advocate on behalf of marijuana and its non-intoxicating twin, hemp. He has promoted hemp as an agricultural alternative for cash-strapped farmers, appeared on the cover of *High Times*, and reminded fans that the original US Constitution was written on hemp paper. Arrested in Texas in 1994 with the remains of a joint in his car's ashtray, he fought the bust in court and complained, "It's becoming apparent in this country that we are losing our rights one after another. . . . I think [marijuana] should be taxed and regulated like your cigarettes." The case against him was dismissed.

Even the political Right in America has raised doubts about the anti-drug efforts. Premised on libertarian grounds, various commentators have argued that while drug use may be morally wrong, the money and time devoted to suppressing it is an inappropriate use of state power and an unwanted intrusion into the private affairs of otherwise upright citizens. In 1996 the conservative writer and intellectual William F.

Buckley bluntly reported, "The War on Drugs is lost," and pointed out in his erudite style that "we are willing to build more and more jails in which to isolate drug users even though at one-seventh the cost of building and maintaining jail space and pursuing, detaining, and prosecuting the drug user, we could subsidize commensurately effective medical care and psychological treatment." Since then, the laws in the US, Canada, Australia, Britain, and Europe have continued to fumble back and forth between de facto decriminalization and expedient "tough on crime" bills that mean a seesaw of violent criminal competition for an inherently nonviolent buying population, the brutality of the one raising public outcries against the supposed naivety of other—ignoring the fact that the very illegality of marijuana is what brings on the violence.

There is one aspect of the drug issue that has not carried over from the 1960s and '70s: the prominence of popular music in the debate. Although lone performers like Willie Nelson, Blues Traveler, roots -rockers the Black Crowes, and rap groups Cypress Hill and the Wu-Tang Clan have all loudly proclaimed their fealty to the cause, and although hits like Tone Lōc's "Cheeba Cheeba" and Dr. Dre's *The Chronic* have spread a cannabis-positive message, no broad movement of sex, drugs, and rock 'n' roll appears to be storming the citadels of straight society. Other than at marijuana decriminalization rallies themselves, protest is dissociated from pot. With drugs from marijuana and acid to crack and crystal meth staple subjects in popular culture, journalism, politics, and family life for over forty years, drug use is now viewed as either an almost time-honored adolescent ritual or a mounting urban scourge, but in either case divorced from any particular trend in mass entertainment.

News stories of pop and rock stars' drug habits continue to make good copy (the "Dirty Laundry" sung about by ex-Eagle Don Henley), yet these are now met with shrugs from an audience that assumes all that celebrities party to the extreme and that court dates and rehab sessions are just good publicity. In recent years players who have made reputations as druggies include singers Pete Doherty, Amy Winehouse, and Whitney Houston; the Stone Temple Pilots' Scott Weiland; Phil Anselmo of Pantera; Culture Club's Boy George; Perry Farrell and Dave Navarro of Jane's Addiction; Slash of Guns n' Roses; and all four members of the veteran hair-metal outfit Mötley Crüe. Drug-related deaths have piled up, including the Red Hot Chili Peppers' Hillel Slovak's in 1988, Nirvana leader and heroin addict Kurt Cobain's suicide in 1994, Shannon Hoon of Blind Melon's cocaine OD in 1995, and Super Freak (and ex–Neil Young collaborator) Rick James's death in 2000. But the predictable cycles of near-fatal burnout and cowed reform have been played out so many times by earlier generations of rock 'n' rollers that today's crashes and comebacks are not the scandals they were for Keith Richards, Eric Clapton, or David Bowie; the cleaned-up rock star is now as much a cliché as the wasted one. Even heroin looks derivative, something done in slavish emulation of the undisputed Human Riff. Why else would Guns n' Roses' Duff McKagan take it? "To be like Keith, man," said the bassist. "That's what it comes down to, and if any guitar player tells you different, they're high on heroin, and they're lying like every heroin addict does. . . . He's Keith, man." In the 1988 documentary *The Decline of Western Civilization II: The Metal Years*, Aerosmith's freshly sober Steve Tyler bragged, "Joe [Perry] and I are the Toxic Twins, baby," but was asked, "Are you proud of it?"

"Uh, no." Tyler paused, thinking it over. "You know, yes, that I went through it, but no, in that all the people think that that's the way to do it, you know, and that isn't the way. . . . That's not the way at all, because we painted ourselves into a major corner."

Rockers from the era of Richards, Clapton, Bowie, and Aerosmith, when drugs were wholeheartedly embraced and their risks blithely discounted, have paid to a disproportionate degree the ultimate price for their choice. Some have died as a direct consequence of drug overdose or addiction, while others have passed away prematurely after many years of sustained intoxication. A few artists remain technically alive yet indisputably the worse for wear from their bacchanals of yesteryear, like the fragile Sly Stone and his faltering reunions with the Family Stone, or the reality TV clown Ozzy Osbourne, whose dazed demeanor as head of a Hollywood household served to render the once-dreaded Sabbath singer a lovable cartoon. "I've done so many drugs that I've fucked up my brain somewhere," he has been quoted as saying. "Everybody says, 'Ozzy, you're a legend.' But behind the façade is a sad, lonely, wet fart of a person." Living or dead, these are the members of the first and perhaps final class of pop musicians to have been let loose in a period of unexampled hedonism and its unexamined hazards.

Several of Bob Dylan's backing musicians were victims of drugs. Blues guitarist Mike Bloomfield, who played on *Highway 61 Revisited* and Dylan's earliest electric gigs, was found expired in his car in February 1981. He was thirty-six and had been a longtime heroin addict. Harmonica player Paul Butterfield, Bloomfield's employer and also there at the landmark Newport Festival in 1965 and the Last Waltz in 1976, died at age forty-four in 1987, worn down by years of drugs and alcohol. In 1986 keyboardist Richard Manuel of the Band, battling depression, alcoholism, and the legendary group's relegation to the oldies circuit, hung himself in a Florida hotel room after finishing off some liquor and cocaine. His song "Whispering Pines" (1969) is one of the most haunting ballads in rock 'n' roll. He was forty. Band bassist Rick Danko died at age fifty-six in 1999, a few years after he had been arrested for heroin possession in Japan. The Canadians Danko and Manuel were with Bob Dylan on his first plugged-in tours in the US and Britain after Dylan recruited them, plus guitarist Robbie Robertson and keyboardist Garth Hudson, from

Ronnie Hawkins' Hawks. Dylan had once told Keith Richards that his sidemen of ex-Hawks were "the greatest band in the world."

Three accompanists of Eric Clapton became drug casualties. Bassist Carl Radle, who had worked with Clapton for most of the 1970s, was hooked on heroin and died in 1980 of kidney failure. "[D]eep down I felt partly responsible for it," said Clapton, who had managed to break his own junk habit if not his lesser ones at that point. Journeyman bass man Rick Grech of the guitarist's supergroup Blind Faith and a member of Family, Traffic, and Ginger Baker's Air Force, had also lived hard and died in obscurity in 1990 at age forty-three. Most poignant of all was the fate of drummer Jim Gordon, cowriter of "Layla" and a highly respected session hand for the likes of Clapton, George Harrison, Carole King, Joe Cocker, and many others, who got into hard drugs while serving as one of Derek's Dominos and later developed acute schizophrenia, the condition very probably worsened by his substance abuse. In 1983 the delusional Gordon murdered his own mother and was incarcerated the following year. He has been institutionalized to this day.

Marvin Gaye became another cocaine paranoiac and took to brandishing guns and threatening associates and family members. In 1983 the strung-out, broke, and suicidal singer moved back with his mother and father in Los Angeles, where he stayed in his room doing coke, not changing clothes or washing, watching porn videos, and fighting with his father, toward whom he had borne resentment since childhood. On April Fool's Day, 1984, a violent altercation between Marvin Gaye and Marvin Gaye Senior ended with the elder man's shooting his son twice. Gaye died instantly the day before his forty-fifth birthday. His father was given probation after accepting a sentence of voluntary manslaughter in self-defense in the face of his child's drug-induced rage.

Dennis Wilson, the one member of the Beach Boys who was genuinely the athletic surfer dude the others only harmonized about being, got into alcohol, cocaine, and depressants in a bad way as the band's golden years drifted further into the past. Never thought to be a strong musician, he only played drums at live gigs, while most of the Beach Boys' tracks featured studio experts keeping the beat. He married and divorced a number of times and had a short, sodden relationship with Fleetwood Mac's Christine McVie and a shorter one with Ronald Reagan's daughter Patti, before, shortly after Christmas 1983, he dove from his boat in a California marina and drowned. He was drunk, as he often was, and had been taking cocaine and Valium. "The problem with Dennis was that he was totally out of control," his brother Brian said. Dennis Wilson was buried at sea.

Phil Lynott, vocalist and bassist of the great Irish hard rockers Thin Lizzy ("Jailbreak," "The Boys Are Back in Town"), passed away in early 1986 with blood poisoning and an infected kidney—he had been a heroin addict. Arranger and producer Jack Nitzsche died at sixty-three from a cardiac arrest in 2000, after scratching out a living in the music industry as a composer of film scores but mostly being considered a high-risk has-been. "His attitude was you could be old and still rock," his friend Denny Bruce was quoted as saying. "Any real businessman didn't want to take a chance on him." Keyboardist Billy Preston, who had played with Little Richard, the Beatles, the Rolling Stones, and Sly Stone, died in 2006 at the age of sixty. He had been a working musician since his teens, and his cocaine use began shortly thereafter, eventually leading to arrests, jail time, and a kidney transplant in 2002. "All he knew was that they passed lines of coke when he was onstage," explained his manager. "He got caught up in it." The deaths of Jimi Hendrix Experience bass player Noel Redding in 2003 and drummer Mitch Mitchell in 2008 were both attributed to natural causes. They were fifty-seven and sixty-one, respectively. John Entwistle of the Who, regarded as one of the most innovative bassists in all of rock 'n' roll (and the most grounded of the foursome), succumbed to a heart attack in Las Vegas in June 2002 before he was to embark on a tour with the group; traces of cocaine were found in his body, and his ingestion of the drug was believed to have arrested his already weakened organ. He was fifty-seven as well. "I just hope God has got His earplugs ready," said the Who's Roger Daltrey. "He'll have to reinvent thunder."

Rick Wright of Pink Floyd died of cancer in September 2008 at age sixty-five. Euphemistic "personal problems" had forced him from the band's lineup during the making of *The Wall* (1979), although he rejoined the latter-day Floyd as a salaried member. After years in seclusion, Pink Floyd's founder Syd Barrett suffered diabetes (necessitating the amputation of some of his fingers) and loss of vision, and fell to pancreatic cancer in 2006. He was sixty. Still submerged in the mental night that had enclosed him in the early 1970s, he had had no further contact with his old bandmates, and they had at first failed to recognize him when he appeared at a studio as early as 1975. His psychological condition was generally regarded, though never confirmed, as having been brought on by his heavy diet of LSD during Pink Floyd's formative years. Floyd drummer Nick Mason, who survived to grow rich and indulge in the sport of competitive auto driving, concluded, "Rock 'n' roll, in comparison to motor racing, is so much more dangerous. I've known so many more people who have been really awful casualties of the music business and drugs. It's higher-risk than most people realize."

The rock 'n' roller whose death put the drug culture in the least favorable light was the Grateful Dead's Jerry Garcia. Through the 1980s the Dead had enjoyed a resurgence in popularity on the strength of hit singles like "Touch of Grey" and a tour with Bob Dylan, and their geographically and musically wandering performances had attracted a second flowering of young Deadheads. More affluent and more stable than the original acolytes, the Dead's newest fans took from the concerts a fresh appreciation for cannabis and psychedelics, and a new wave of tripped-out "jam bands" like Phish rose out of the revived cult. The Grateful Dead themselves looked to have adapted to the times well enough, a harmless collection of old hippies who might have indulged too much in the Summer of Love but who had managed to remain a prosperous, functioning act with a loyal following and a catalog of famous tunes—there was even a brand of ice cream, Ben & Jerry's "Cherry Garcia," named for their leader. But Jerry Garcia was still on hard drugs. By the summer of '84, the Dead's manager Rock Scully saw, "Garcia's condition is worsening daily. He never sleeps or lies down. . . . He lives on a diet of ice cream, M&Ms, Persian [heroin], and cigarettes." The Dead head was arrested for cocaine and heroin possession in 1985, struggled with his weight, and in 1986 slipped into a diabetic coma. "I didn't know whether it was drugs, his health, or his marriage," remarked Phil Lesh of Garcia in 1994, "but he seemed to be aging before my eyes." He finally checked into a clinic to confront his heroin problem in 1995. On August 9, at the Serenity Knolls institution in California's Marin County, he was found dead of an apparent heart attack. Captain Trips was fifty-three years old.

Jerry Garcia's death from the stress of drug withdrawal prompted a rethinking of the entire way of life that he had epitomized. In the midst of a hyperbolic "culture war" in the United States, with a president who had campaigned with Fleetwood Mac's "Don't Stop" as a theme song and who had infamously admitted to trying but not inhaling cannabis while exempt from military service in the 1960s, the terminus of the Grateful Dead's road show seemed to symbolize a closure of the baby boomers' collective reckless youth. By then, many other American political leaders than Bill Clinton had been forced to disclose callow "experimentation" with soft drugs—Vice-President Al Gore and Congressional majority leader Newt Gingrich, to name two—and as Garcia was laid to rest, Clinton made appropriate noises about "self-destructive behavior" and radio blowhard Rush Limbaugh memorialized the musician as "a dead doper."

The anti-drug, family-values lobby could now crow that drugs got everyone in the end, that drugs were undoubtedly a social problem, that drugs had eroded the principles of responsibility and deferred gratification on which civilization was built, that drugs infantilized their users and warped their ability to reason, et cetera. Even the politically neutral agreed that getting high or dosed had not brought about the worldwide utopia the Deadheads had long attempted to create in microcosm: "I find myself worrying about the lost souls who know nothing but the parallel world of the Grateful Dead," said one. It was author and Yale law professor Steven B. Duke who raised cogent objections to the sneers of Limbaugh and his kind. "Why do so many conservatives preach 'individual responsibility' yet ardently punish people for the chemicals they consume and thus deny the right that gives meaning to the responsibility? Newt Gingrich, Charles Murray, and other conservatives are rightly concerned about the absence of fathers in the homes of so many of America's youngsters. Where are those fathers? At least half a million are in prison, often for nothing worse than possessing drugs."

In fact, considering the graveyard of rock stars whose deaths were blamed on drugs, it is noteworthy how many of them—Brian Jones, Jim Morrison, Jimi Hendrix, Richard Manuel, Dennis Wilson, Keith Moon, and more—had also been drinking when they passed away. Several major figures succumbed to alcohol alone, either from a bender or from compounded mental and physical decay. Among them were the Dead's Ron "Pigpen" McKernan (who usually *refused* drugs) in 1973, folkie Phil Ochs by suicide in 1976, and Led Zeppelin drummer John Bonham and AC/DC vocalist and lyricist Bon Scott in 1980. Two men as culpable as anyone for the birth and flourishing of the drug culture, *On the Road*'s inspiration Neal Cassady and its author Jack Kerouac were each bombed when they died in 1968 and 1969 respectively. Cassady passed out near a Mexican railroad track after walking home from a wedding party dressed in only a T-shirt and jeans in the February rain. He was forty-one. Jack Kerouac especially had disowned the hippies and their pot, peace, and protesting ways: "I'm bored with the new avant-garde and the skyrocketing sensationalism. . . . I like to hang around with non-intellectuals, as you might call them, and not have my mind proselytized, ad infinitum." He was a miserable alcoholic upon his death at age forty-seven, his liver ruined. Among alcohol, tobacco, cocaine, heroin, barbiturates, amphetamines, and all the other legitimate and illegitimate drugs that have been taken by humans over centuries, there is but one to which no deaths of anyone, anywhere, anytime have been directly ascribed: marijuana.

What has perhaps been transformed more than the social dilemma of mind-altering drugs, the political dialogue surrounding their legal limbo, or even the advancing age of the first and most populous body of users to try them on a generational scale, is the cultural gravity of rock 'n' roll itself. During the 1960s and '70s, rock music addressed many subjects, including sex, mysticism, war, societal tension and conflict, race, individuality, and environmentalism, but the single matter where the performers and their audiences most understood each other was in that of drugs. The echo of a definitional popular and private experience by a mass-marketed medium was never as loud, as relevant, or as memorable as in the medium now considered "classic rock."

Classic rock increasingly signifies an irreplaceable era in modern times, its prime figures today revered or denounced for an influence that will long outlive them, or already has. There will one day be a world without Rolling Stones. There will one day be no Doors left, no Eagles, no Stooges, and no Doobies. Bob Dylan will go to rock 'n' roll heaven, and so will Joni Mitchell, David Crosby, Sly Stone, and Neil Young. Eric Clapton will one day be jamming with Mike Bloomfield, Stevie Nicks with Janis Joplin, and David Bowie with Freddie Mercury. There were once four ex-Beatles; then there were three surviving Beatles and there are currently two remaining Beatles. There will one day be no more Beatles.

Of course, there is already a vast mythology built up around "rock legends," whose biographies cram airwaves, video collections, and book shelves, and whose songs can readily be found in stores or in a quick scan of the radio dial or search of the Internet, or being used to sell shoes and cars and food and drinks. Many of them are among the biggest-selling recording acts of all time. A few are knighted; several make annual "rich lists"; numerous others have received some sort of "lifetime achievement" award from trade or fan associations. Their relics—a Jimi Hendrix guitar, a Freddie Mercury costume, a John Lennon Rolls-Royce—fetch hundreds of thousands of dollars at auction. Concerts by reunited or resuscitated acts like Led Zeppelin or the Eagles sell out at hundreds of dollars per ticket. Critics, though, counter that this mythology is just that—a self-serving, profit-driven fiction of glib imagery that really only marks an intermediate point in pop music's descent from melody, restraint, and grace into rhythm, amplification, and coarseness, chronologically and aesthetically the halfway mark between R&B and techno, between bebop and hip-hop. Demographers speak of classic rock as nothing more than the soundtrack for the baby boom, something those born before 1945 are bound to ignore and those born since 1965 obligated to resent. To everyone bored of the boomers and their self-satisfaction, the safe and familiar songs are not classic but comfort rock.

Despite the hagiographies upheld by the Rock and Roll Hall of Fame and disc jockeys on rigid-format FM radio, many of the detractors are correct. Yet neither the music's opponents nor its defenders have quite articulated its lasting importance. First hailed as the voice of the rebellious young, now derided as the shame of sold-out middle age, classic rock was actually aiming for something else entirely. In all the sneers that rock 'n' roll's peak performers and prime cohort merely grew up, grew old, got clean, and cashed in, there is the unspoken admission that they were once thought to be above such compromises. No one harbored similar hopes for Frank Sinatra or Ella Fitzgerald, and no one now holds R. Kelly or Arcade Fire to the same ideal. Love it or hate it, classic rock is the "before," and we exist in the "after."

Classic Rock's composers, vocalists, instrumentalists, and producers at their best sought to remind their publics of the widening chasm between folk art and pop culture by daring to straddle the void, daring listeners to guess where artistic expression ended and manufactured commodity began. Their music's distinction lies not in its "authenticity"—always a dubious proposition in the realm of corporate entertainment—but *spontaneity*, its anomaly as a naive, frequently imitative local or regional form brought to and then enriched on an international assembly line. To understand how this element has been drained out of contemporary culture, the unique aspects of classic rock need to be isolated and evaluated.

Most classic rock was written and played intuitively—self-taught, often improvised music of drunk, stoned, very earnest, and very young people. Heard as anthems decades later, many songs began as scrawled reportage of casual sex (Steppenwolf's "Hey Lawdy Mama," Lynyrd Skynyrd's "What's Your Name"), the road (Bob Seger's "Turn the Page," Creedence Clearwater Revival's "Travelin' Band"), or assorted misadventures, many drug-related (the Beatles' "She Said She Said," the Dead's "Truckin'," the Stones' "Sister Morphine"). Many classic rockers considered themselves neither poets nor visionaries but primarily working entertainers, and gauged their real strengths by the quality of their interaction with their audiences. Most acts, even those that still enjoy lucrative careers, accomplished their greatest albums and shows within a space of five years or less. The erratic temperament of instruments, amplifiers, and other equipment, and the elusive quest for close harmonies and solid backbeats, meant that many classic rock pieces were the combined results of rigorous rehearsal and cosmic serendipity. Some million-selling records and sold-out concerts were performed by men and women whose inherent musical gifts were small.

That said, classic rockers adhered to standards of craftsmanship and professionalism that later became almost completely discounted. They may have lowered the artistic bar set by Louis Armstrong or Benny Goodman, but they never took on the willful primitivism of punk rock and punk-descended acts like Nirvana or Green Day. Virtually every folk, blues, funk, or rock 'n' roll name of the '60s and '70s had climbed a ladder of small-time engagements where musical discipline was tested night after night to little reward, whereas the wannabes featured on *American Idol*, YouTube, and similar amateur showcases do not endure the often torturous screening for stamina, instinct, and raw ability through which classic rock performers passed. Today's electronica and hip-hop can claim some striking sonic surfaces and sampled juxtapositions, but they have none of the humanity, orchestration, or attention to detail of a David Gilmour solo, a Family Stone arrangement, or a Beach Boys production. "The great jazz drummer Elvin Jones gave me my hands; I emulated his technique," reflected John Densmore of the Doors. "Are today's drummers emulating Japanese electronics?" By and large, classic rockers *chose* to play what they did, embellishing the basic formulas of their predecessors (R&B, country, gospel, folk, and so on) with their own whims, audacities, and mind-expanding experiments. The subsequent generations of rockers and their relatives, in contrast, have more and more resorted to playing only what they can.

Secondly, classic rock stars achieved in their day a balance of celebrity, autonomy, and humility that no luminaries before or since have ever found. They were of the generation that had begun to see through media and marketing and the Dream Factories of Hollywood, Madison Avenue, and Fleet Street—the "star-maker machinery behind the popular song" Joni Mitchell sang of in "Free Man in Paris," her mini-bio of industry shark David Geffen. The public visibility that embarrassed and annoyed the most famous of them ("We were always meeting the wrong people, Lord Mayors and police chiefs," griped George Harrison) was what made them all the more appealing, as they demonstrated an I-can't-believe-it-either honesty and modesty that was seldom convincing in movie and sports idols. Classic rockers were hyped, of course— Andrew Loog Oldham first flogged the Rolling Stones as the anti-Beatles and Jimi Hendrix was cast as "the Wild Man of Pop"—but not by such a publicity engine as exists today. Stardom was not then equated with saturation. Supporting players, such as Keith Moon, Experience bassist Noel Redding, or Pink Floyd's Rick Wright, epitomized a novel type of celebrity: the performer who, alone, could have been anybody, but with three or four companions was an indispensable component of a superstar whole. Long before pop cognoscenti ever thought of scanning "under the radar," much of classic rock was already there.

That equilibrium between distance and intimacy has been lost. The lively and sincere communities of Deadheads, Zepheads, Beatlemaniacs, the Kiss Army, Dylanologists, and other classic rock fan bases are obsolete in the new millennium, as every budding pop tendency soon collapses into its own opponents, and any mystery or secrecy or word of mouth around any act soon dissipates over the Internet and the five-hundred-channel universe. Urban legends that Jim Morrison had faked his own death, that Stevie Nicks was an ordained witch, that Keith Richards had had his blood changed, that "Lucy in the Sky with Diamonds" stood for LSD or that Jimmy Page had sold his and his bandmates' souls to Satan would not last a week in 2010. Even Richards is a family-friendly presence in the *Pirates of the Caribbean* summer blockbuster franchise, his costar Johnny Depp basing his characterization of the wobbly Jack Sparrow on the World's Most Elegantly Wasted Human Being and cooing that pirates were "the rock 'n' roll stars of the eighteenth century." Meanwhile, torrents of digital chatter wash over Next Big Things whose meager recorded output and infrequent live gigs are just not enough to sustain a durable listeners' consensus, so cults of Richards, Morrison, Bob Marley, and Syd Barrett go on, while spasms of excitement around Marilyn Manson or Eminem or Oasis fade away.

Technology has changed the music, too. The sonic gadgetry embraced by classic rockers and their psychedelicized fans was primitive next to the computer programs and digital devices employed from the 1990s onward. In 1968 or 1977, chops still mattered, and amateurish guitar riffs or drum rolls could not be tweaked with electronics. Today even relatively inexpensive equipment and software enables solitary technophiles to construct their own *Tommy* or *Layla*, piling any amount of synths or samples on each other, track over track, without needing to play either to or with anyone else, or to "play" in a traditional sense at all. Aspiring rockers who once looked with envy on Jimi Hendrix's Stratocasters, Paul McCartney's Hofner, or John Bonham's Ludwigs— and then went to their neighborhood music store to invest in their own axes or tubs—content themselves with computer simulations in 2010. "So far as the records I made [in the 1960s], I made records back then just like a lot of other people who were my age and we all made good records," Bob Dylan has said. "The high priority is technology now. It's not the artist or the art. It's the technology which is coming through."

With musical proficiency or ensemble compatibility no longer part of the performance equation, the Information Age has cheapened the audience's experience as well. Pocket accessories like iPods and their earpieces shrink the soundscapes of *Dark Side of the Moon* or *Are You Experienced* to tiny, tinny reproductions that cannot do justice to the full stereo spectrums intended by their creators. Hundreds of thousands of old and new songs are for sale or downloaded for free online, and almost unlimited collections of material are now being copied at little or no cost by anyone with a modem and a mouse. Music retailers and old-style record labels are in terminal decline. Inevitably, the sheer convenience of pop music has rendered it almost a piped-in public utility, stored not on physical discs or tapes but as data—"disposable" culture at its literal extreme. But classic rock albums, especially, were thought of as single entities ("Stairway to Heaven," "A Day in the Life," and "Little Wing," to name three album cuts, were never released as 45s), and iconic album covers like Supertramp's *Breakfast in America*, Floyd's *Wish You Were Here* or the Grateful Dead's *American Beauty* were inseparable from the melodies and lyrics they showcased, as well as being handy joint-rolling platforms. The dominance of file sharing and iPods over vinyl and CD has erased much of the music's original character, just as the dominance of video over live recital has flattened it.

Finally, as confused, simplistic and contradictory as classic rock's "statements" could be, they did command public interest and popular respect in a way that is simply no longer granted to mass artists of any medium. Computer games like *Guitar Hero* and *Rock Band* now place the anthems and stadium gestures of dope-smoking, coke-snorting, acid-tripping rock 'n' rollers alongside competing representations of World War II or medieval sorcery, all of them equally distant and un-real to the adolescents who play them. A special edition of *Guitar Hero* licenses material from Aerosmith to play along with—do the sprawled suburbanites clicking away at their plastic guitars know that Steve Tyler was once believed dead of an overdose onstage? (A Beatles version of the amusement was issued for 2009.) Whether advocating self-knowledge, emancipation, or commonwealth; or peace, love, and understanding; or sex, drugs, and rock 'n' roll, the original music was linked to genuine social upheavals that were perhaps less defined—or, in the end, less successful—but no less insistent than the bohemian movements that preceded them, and far more insistent than the self-consciously blasé trends that followed. Classic rock was quite likely the last form of industrial entertainment that might be called irony-free. The waning consumer draw of modern pop music precludes it from taking on the political, sexual, criminal, or chemical significance associated with classic rock by friends and enemies of the genre alike. For a short and likely exceptional historical moment, the most commercial branch of commercial media was also the most contentious.

Thirty or forty years later, the legacy of this is still ambiguous. It is hard to deny that the most celebrated rock 'n' rollers often cast psychotropic drugs in a brazenly upbeat light and made egregiously unrealistic promises of their potential. Drugs may have helped them realize their full artistic gifts but could not embellish what gifts (or formal musical training) they already possessed; a stoned Ringo was no substitute for a straight Paul, and a healthy Springsteen achieved more with his talent than a deathly David Crosby with his. Cannabis may or may not be a "gateway" drug whose use inexorably leads to more harmful habits, but it is anecdotally understood to be a routine prelude to whatever more harmful habits do develop; few addicts start off with heroin or crack before trying anything else. But it may be fairer to suggest that the drugs classic rock put to the forefront of international awareness would probably have leached into the social fabrics of the world anyway and that the songs and songwriters only identified a phenomenon that might otherwise have been even less understood—and less reasonably assessed—than it was. Divisive and emotional as the drug question can be, it at least carries the weight of many moderate, informed opinions and eloquent first-person evidence. To repeat, the long-term importance of classic rock lies not so much in *what* it said than in the many millions of people who heard its wisdom as an accurate and unadulterated summary of what they were already thinking and doing.

In its day, of course, the music was hit with the same accusations thrown at its successors—that it fed a manufactured public appetite, had no true merits, and was ultimately a fraud planned by scheming businessmen and carried out by duped nobodies. In 1964 the conservative British historian Paul Johnson broadsided rock 'n' roll and its followers in an essay titled "The Menace of Beatlism": "The huge faces, bloated with cheap confectionery and smeared with chain-store makeup, the open, sagging mouths . . . the shoddy, stereotyped, 'with-it' clothes: here, apparently, is a collective portrait of a generation enslaved by a commercial machine. . . . At 16, I and my friends heard our first performance of Beethoven's Ninth Symphony; I can remember the excitement even today. We would not have wasted thirty seconds of our precious time on the Beatles and their ilk."

"This moaning about the Beatles is the same as our parents who never stopped talking about the goddamn Second World War," an exasperated John Lennon said in 1980, shortly before he was murdered. "I think that's pathetic. I mean forget about that. Listen to Beatles records, but dig . . . whatever is going on now." As quick to debunk himself and his work as any stodgy critic, he lashed out at his image as a psychedelic Pied Piper: "It took our whole life, a whole section of our youth—during a time when everybody else was just goofing off and smoking dope, we were working twenty-four hours a day. I was doing it and doing it and doing it and there was no switching off. . . . We were there to provide whatever the Beatles provided. We are not there to save the fucking world." As early as 1971 he downplayed the part drugs had played in his music, arguing, "It's like saying, 'Did Dylan Thomas write *Under Milk Wood* on beer?' What the fuck does that have to do with it? The beer is to prevent the rest of the world from crowding in on you. The drugs are to prevent the rest of the world from crowding in on you. They don't make you write any better. I never wrote any better stuff because I was on acid, or not on acid, you know."

Is classic rock, then, just druggy nostalgia for something phony to begin with? The music was once considered by its earliest fans' parents to be as frivolous or as subversive as *their* parents had considered the jitterbug and gin joints, and now even the jitterbug and gin joints warrant serious scholarship and soft-focus romanticizing seventy years later. So who can be sure that the Ecstasy, hydroponic chronic, and interactive website of today isn't the LSD, Panama Red, and *Revolver* of tomorrow? No one—but few would dispute that classic rock and its lifestyles were far less manipulated and monitored than anything spilling out of our present media maelstrom. Buyers and boosters of contemporary clothes, computer games, snack foods, and pop music not least of all are subject to constant market testing and trolling by researchers and promoters and the unpaid hip, so that an honest cultural conversation among artists, outlaws, and their public constituencies is instantly smothered. A critical mass of production and promotion means that there is less and less to distinguish where advertising begins and the advertised artifact or activity ends. Junk becomes inflated into treasure almost immediately, and then decays back into junk all the sooner. What John Lennon was self-effacing enough to think of as sentimental bias turns out to have been something like objectivity. What Paul Johnson saw as an enslaving commercial machine appears with hindsight to have been an organic, democratic freak of history.

The genres that preceded and anticipated classic rock—blues, jazz, folk, the Beats—spoke of African and European traditions furtively intersecting at the smoky margins of North American life; classic rock spoke of the intersection of individualism and Information in a Dionysian revel heard around the world for some sixteen years, and closed with the displacement of the imaginative, inspired, and more or less independent creator by a technological and mercantile colossus. The point is not that these particular singers and players were unsurpassed talents of unimpeachable motive leading faultless personal lives and dispensing unassailable good sense, but that post-industrial global culture has evolved styles very different from—and by most measures, less skilled, less discriminating, and less soulful than—those of the 1960s and '70s, which were established in the face of ignorant prejudice by an extraordinary group of misfits, eccentrics, innocents, and believers, who foolishly and brilliantly practiced what they preached. Rock is dead. Long live rock.

AUGUST 28, 1964
THE AFTERMATH

In the wake of their pot party at New York's Delmonico Hotel, the work of **Bob Dylan** and **the Beatles** grew in lyrical depth, musical sophistication, and public acclaim.

Bob Dylan has become an icon of American and international popular culture. He has sung for Pope John Paul II, been awarded a Pulitzer Prize, Grammy Awards, an Academy Award for Best Song, and was honored by the John F. Kennedy Center for the Performing Arts in 1997, where President Bill Clinton lauded, "He probably had more impact on people of my generation than any other artist." His music has earned significant attention from scholars of literature, philosophy, and musicology, and is of ongoing fascination to countless listeners. He has probably played more shows per year for more years than any other rock 'n' roll performer in history, and continues to feature "Rainy Day Women #12 and 35" in concert.

George Harrison made several popular solo records during the 1970s and '80s, and joined Bob Dylan in the group the Traveling Wilburys in the 1990s, although he took a skeptical view of celebrity and rock 'n' roll. "I'm really quite simple," he wrote in his 1980 autobiography. "I don't want to be in the business full-time, because I'm a gardener. I plant flowers and watch them grow. I don't go out to clubs and partying." He did, however, record songs like "Try Some Buy Some," and it was said that Harrison bested a considerable cocaine habit in the 1980s. "Out of the LSD madness," Harrison recalled, "there came a few 'zaps'. . . . Since then it has been a matter of trying to hold on to that little shining light which one's lucky to have glimpsed, and manifest the light more and more and more until you become that."

He suffered a violent attack by a mentally disturbed person at his home on the night of December 30, 1999, and battled cancer until he succumbed to the disease (and, likely, the injuries sustained during his assault) on November 29, 2001. His ashes were scattered in the Ganges River in India.

Ringo Starr had an erratic career after the Beatles disbanded, making some hit records and more that found obscurity; he also acted in films, did narration for children's television programs, and lent his image to advertisements. During the 1970s he sang the hilarious drug ditty "No No Song" ("No thank you please, it only makes me sneeze / Then it makes it hard to find the door") and recovered from a major drinking problem in the 1980s where he and his wife, actress Barbara Bach, reportedly put away sixteen bottles of wine per day together. Starr subsequently settled in to a placid semi-retirement in England, although he has performed and recorded with his All-Starr Band alongside other famous and reformed rockers such as Dr. John, Billy Preston, and Joe Walsh. He has been drug- and alcohol-free for many years, although he still performs "No No Song" in concert, and the jaunty psychedelia of "Yellow Submarine" and "With a Little Help from My Friends" remain his signature tunes.

John Lennon had several successful solo years after the Beatles' split, becoming as well known for his political activism as his pop music. Between 1973 and 1975 he fell in with heavy partiers such as Alice Cooper, Keith Moon, and Harry Nilsson, and his public drunkeness was widely reported. Though he cleaned up after his "lost weekend," Lennon acknowledged in his final interview that "A little mushroom or peyote is not beyond my scope, you know, maybe twice a year or something. . . . If somebody gives me a joint, I might smoke it, but I don't go after it."

He was murdered by a deranged fan's gunfire on December 8, 1980, outside his New York home of the Dakota Apartments, not far from the Delmonico Hotel. He was forty. Millions of people around the world mourned his death, and his songs "Imagine" and "Give Peace a Chance" have become antiwar anthems.

Sir Paul McCartney was knighted by Her Majesty Queen Elizabeth II in 1997, despite numerous run-ins with the law over cannabis infractions (the most serious being his arrest and incarceration for several days in Japan in 1980). As recently as his 2008 divorce settlement proceedings, his ex-wife Heather Mills alleged that he still regularly smoked marijuana, which was one of her more plausible claims against him. Notoriously reticent regarding his personal habits, McCartney nonetheless stated in a 1997 biography, *Many Years from Now*, "I think the 'Just Say No' mentality is so crazed. . . . 'No, no, all drugs are bad. All drugs are bad. Librium's good, Valium's good, ciggies are good, vodka's good. But cannabis, ooooh!' I hate that unreasoned attitude."

The most commercially successful and wealthiest rock star in the world, he continues to compose, perform, and record, with work ranging from his trademark bright pop to electronic music and well-received classical opuses like *Liverpool Oratorio*. He is widely considered to be one of the greatest popular musicians of all time, and has never refuted the existence of the Seven Levels.

Brian Epstein, the Beatles' devoted mentor and manager, was increasingly sidelined by the band's retreat from touring in 1966 and their pursuit of studio-based creativity and the wisdom offered by figures like the Maharishi Mahesh Yogi. While he remained close to all four Beatles, his personal life was troubled and he died of an accidental overdose of sleeping pills on August 27, 1967. He was thirty-two.

Derek Taylor worked as the Beatles' press officer between 1963 and 1966, and again between 1968 and 1970. He promoted the careers of the Byrds, the Beach Boys, and the Grateful Dead, and helped organize the 1967 Monterey Pop Festival. Active in the record industry for many years, author of several books and the liner notes for the Beatles' *Anthology* collections of the 1990s, he died of cancer in 1997 at age sixty-five. He was remembered for his intelligence, wit, and taste for psychedelics—the Beatles' friend Harry Nilsson described him as "Ronald Colman on acid." His 1987 memoir, *It Was Twenty Years Ago Today*, acknowledged his sobriety and stated, "While the book has to deal fairly and squarely with the enthusiastic ingestion of illegal drugs of an explorative nature during the period covered in the mid-sixties, there is no intention to encourage anyone at all to follow suit."

Mal Evans, the Beatles' original minder and roadie, was left adrift following the group's breakup in 1970. Separated from his wife and heavily involved with drugs and alcohol, he was shot and killed by police in a Los Angeles hotel on January 5, 1976, when he allegedly produced a gun during an incident with a female companion.

Victor Maymudes served as Bob Dylan's assistant and road manager through the 1960s and again from 1986 to 1996. Following a brain aneurysm he died in Los Angeles, surrounded by his family, on January 26, 2001. His obituary noted his belief that "song is the ultimate repository of human civilization—it's a resting place for one heart and translates the soul of culture for all." Elsewhere he was eulogized as appreciating "a well-turned phrase and a good joint." He was sixty-five.

Neil Aspinall was hired as the Beatles' aide in 1961 and was with them through their active career and after, running their Apple business and overseeing the band's archival releases on compact disc and video. Perhaps the one man among the group's friends and confidantes with the best claim to the title of "Fifth Beatle," he never parlayed his connection into a book deal or other insider's account and rarely gave interviews. He died of cancer on March 23, 2008, at age sixty-six.

Al Aronowitz was a widely published music journalist whose subjects included the Rolling Stones, Frank Sinatra, Johnny Cash, Ray Charles, and Miles Davis. Sometimes called "the Godfather of Rock Journalism," he was among the first reporters to credibly cover Beat writers, jazz legends, and rock 'n' roll musicians for a mainstream audience. However, many of his relationships with famous performers (including Bob Dylan) ended badly, and following his wife's death in 1972 he descended into hardcore drug addiction. "I eventually joined many others of the sixties in smoking cocaine freebase, now more commonly known as crack, which drove me crazy enough to alienate myself from just about everybody I ever knew," he recalled. He finally recovered, established the website blacklistedjournalist.com, and died of cancer on August 1, 2005. Though his final years were reclusive and he was described by his son Joel as "a very bitter man," he was also lauded by luminaries like the

Band's Levon Helm, who said, "Al's good cheer, advice, and insight kept all of us focused on the music," and songwriter Gerry Goffin, who told him, "Don't ever let anyone tell you you haven't led a successful life."

Aronowitz recounted his introduction of Dylan to the Beatles: "My aim was to make happen what did happen, which has been some of the greatest music of our time. I was pleased by the thought I was engineering, participating in and chronicling a milestone moment in history. . . . I'd hate to think that putting Bob together with the Beatles is the only thing I'll ever be remembered for, but I think it certainly was the right thing to do. Hasn't the whole world benefited?"

Author's Note

George was very curious. It smelled funny!
Suddenly his head began to turn. Then he felt
as if he were flying. Then rings and stars danced
before his eyes, then everything went dark. . . .

H. A. REY, *CURIOUS GEORGE TAKES A JOB*

I was sprung into the world on the early morning of June 18, 1967—the week of the Mick Jagger–Keith Richards drug trial in England following their Redlands bust, not quite two weeks after the release of *Sgt. Pepper's Lonely Hearts Club Band*, just a few hours before the Who, the Grateful Dead, and Jimi Hendrix played the Monterey Pop Festival, and the same day Paul McCartney celebrated his twenty-fifth birthday. Also, like millions of others in my age range, I have consumed a sizable amount of drugs, much of it while listening to the songs and albums discussed here. Between my middle teens and my middle twenties I was a frequent smoker of marijuana, hashish, and hash oil; I later became an intermittent user of cocaine, and I took LSD on several occasions, psilocybin on several more, and mescaline once or twice. Once some friends and I, over a long afternoon, evening, and late night, smoked weed, hash, and hash oil, dropped acid, ate magic mushrooms, and greeted the dawn polishing off a liquor cabinet by taking shots of cream liqueur curdled with vodka—it went down like alcoholic cottage cheese. That was a party. The soundtrack that day included David Bowie's *The Man Who Sold the World*, Willie Nelson's *Red-Headed Stranger*, *Led Zeppelin II*, and I think some T-Rex.

My vinyl copies of *The Beatles* and *Rubber Soul* are smeared with remnants of hash oil where spliffs were rolled, and some of my Black Sabbath and ZZ Top cassette cases still bear traces of the hash chunks that I assembled on the surface before they were burned and inhaled off the end of a cigarette. A glossy hardcover Rolling Stones photo book in my possession made a convenient and appropriate plate on which to cut lines of blow. In high school one of my prized garments was a T-shirt depicting the well-known Annie Leibovitz portrait of Keith Richards slumped nearly comatose in a backstage chair on a '70s Stones tour, with the emblem "Shattered." Keith was a hero to my generation, but not only for his music. Where my poster of Jimmy Page raising his Gibson double-neck has gone I have no idea, although a plectrum stamped with a leafy "Reefer" logo is still packed away with one of my guitars.

At almost every concert I ever attended—by the Rolling Stones, Neil Young, Rush, Jimmy Page and Robert Plant, AC/DC, ZZ Top, and a thousand others—I was stoned. But the smokiest show I ever witnessed was by the resuscitated Lynyrd Skynyrd in the Pacific Coliseum in 1997, crowded with bikers, aging hippies, and, well, British Columbians. I think even the band were taken aback. My weirdest experience in this field was catching the original Black Sabbath at Vancouver's Thunderbird Stadium, where they headlined Ozzfest. I had failed to rendezvous with a buddy arriving from elsewhere and so I saw the entire Sabbath set alone and completely straight. How odd, I thought, that when the concert was over Ozzy Osbourne himself reminded the audience, "If you've been drinking or doing dope tonight, make sure you go home with someone who hasn't been drinking or doing dope." Huh? Two hours of anthems about paranoia, hallucinations, acid, cannabis, and cocaine and Ozzy makes a plea for sobriety? Trudging out of the site to the city bus loop I at last met my friend, and when we boarded public transit together with hundreds of other fans we were surprised by a very sensible operator who told the passengers, "I know you've all been having a good time, so you can still smoke but just don't open any bottles." A great cheer went up in the vehicle, then a battery of joints were fired up and passed down the aisles from friend to stranger, me included. I can't imagine what the riders we picked up later in the route thought when they stepped on and paid their fare, and I heard a guy behind me go, "Wow, I've never hot-boxed a *bus* before!" I'll always remember that understanding bus driver; we all gave him an appreciative round of applause as we disembarked. I love you, Sweet Leaf.

On the other hand, I sat through an unfortunate number of mediocre TV programs while stoned. Coughs, hangovers, and a loss of short-term memory that took the term *absentmindedness* to extremes were for me a way of life, with a walk from the living room to the kitchen turning into a deeply searching session of regression therapy: Why'd I come in here again? The pleasure of hearing music —be it Bob Dylan, the Beatles, Chet Baker or Guns n' Roses—was certainly enhanced by drugs, but music is music under any mental condition. Gradually I found that the sensory or conceptual insights afforded by cannabis or shrooms would be there in any case, and to this day my personal doors of perception have remained open long after I threw away the keys. No less an expert than William S. Burroughs once wrote that "I have now discontinued the use of cannabis for some years and find that I am able to achieve the same results by nonchemical means. . . . [C]annabis, like all the hallucinogens, can be discontinued once the artist has familiarized himself with the areas opened up by the drug" As Neil Young, himself a veteran toker, told his biographer Jimmy McDonough, between music and drugs, "music is much better. You don't come down."

Bibliography

Nearly every biography, autobiography, history, or musicology of rock musicians and rock music acknowledges the pervasiveness of drug use in the genre, especially during the 1960s and 1970s, and the concurrence of a worldwide rise in the popularity of cannabis, LSD, and other highs with rock 'n' roll's commercial and creative explosion is widely recognized. Most people, even (or especially) those not fond of rock, are familiar with the litany of drug arrests, overdoses, deaths, and dismissals that is part of its mythology, and even celebrated abstainers, like Bruce Springsteen or Frank Zappa, have been forced to explain their own refusals to indulge. For the cultural historian, the task is to isolate the drug anecdotes or confessions of the various performers without overemphasizing them, extracting from thousands of available sources the most relevant facts and quotations pertaining to their good and bad encounters with illegal intoxication while still treating their work as their most important legacy.

Some of the references cited here make only glancing allusion to drugs, while in others—biographies of Keith Moon, Janis Joplin, or Keith Richards, say—they are necessarily front and center. Some artists have only discussed their excesses in embarrassed or dismissive terms, while others have openly boasted of them; in some cases the clearest accounts are from their associates or passing acquaintances rather than the prime figures themselves. I have tried to balance the juicy with the judicious, presenting the most relevant or intimate depictions of nasty habits alongside broader appreciations of creative development.

Aside from any firsthand personal evidence, of course, the songs and albums are often the best illustration of a given ensemble or player's feelings about or representations of drug sensations. It's notable that the life stories researched for this book correspond in chronology with the progress of rock 'n' roll generally, all of the principals making their initial and often most stimulating records somewhere between the ages of nineteen and twenty-seven. Thus, as the Beatles and Bob Dylan were born between 1940 and 1943, the birthdates of Crosby, Stills, Nash, and Young span from 1941 to 1945, the Grateful Dead's from 1942 to 1950, Bob Marley and the original Wailers' from 1944 to 1947, David Bowie and the Stooges' from 1947 to 1949, Aerosmith's from 1948 to 1952, and so on. Again, the parallels between the musicians' youthful ventures into recreational chemicals and that of the society that contained them are unmistakable.

Many studies of drugs specifically were also consulted for this book, and here again, while there is a diversity of focus and opinion on the different effects, uses, risks, and penalties of different natural and man-made substances, there is a general agreement that that they are unlikely to disappear as contemporary moral, medical, and legal issues. Statistics and clinical analyses vary according to time and place, but no one now pretends drug taking, drug marketing, or indeed drug advocacy can ever be eradicated. As well, even the sternest conservatives (such as the late William F. Buckley) have expressed serious doubts about the efficacy of the War on Drugs, and a nearly unanimous conclusion has been reached that the statutory clampdowns on the milder pleasures of cannabis should at minimum be eased and better yet abandoned altogether—a conclusion I hope the personalities, performances, persecutions, and pop culture examined in *Out of Our Heads* will strengthen.

Books: Music

Amende, Coral. *Rock Confidential: A Backstage Pass to the Outrageous World of Rock 'n' Roll.* New York: Plume, 2000.

The Beatles Anthology. San Francisco: Chronicle, 2000.

Bockris, Victor. *Keith Richards: The Biography.* New York: Poseidon Press, 1992.

Boot, Adrian, with Chris Salewicz. *Bob Marley: Songs of Freedom.* London: Bloomsbury, 1995.

Booth, Stanley. *The True Adventures of the Rolling Stones.* New York: Vintage, 1985.

Bowie, Angela, with Patrick Carr. *Backstage Passes: Life on the Wild Side with David Bowie.* New York: G. P. Putnam's Sons, 1993.

Boyd, Pattie, with Penny Junor. *Wonderful Tonight: George Harrison, Eric Clapton, and Me.* New York: Harmony Books, 2007.

Brown, Peter Harry, and Pat Broeske. *Down at the End of Lonely Street: The Life and Death of Elvis Presley.* New York: Dutton, 1997.

Buckley, David. *Strange Fascination: David Bowie: The Definitive Story.* London: Virgin, 1999.

Carr, Ian. *Miles Davis: A Biography.* New York: William Morrow, 1982.

Case, George. *Jimmy Page: Magus, Musician, Man: An Unauthorized Biography.* New York: Hal Leonard, 2007.

Clapton, Eric. *Clapton: The Autobiography.* New York: Broadway Books, 2007.

Collier, James Lincoln. *Benny Goodman and the Swing Era.* New York: Oxford, 1989.

Collier, James Lincoln. *Louis Armstrong: An American Genius.* New York: Oxford, 1983.

Cooper, Alice. *Alice Cooper, Golf Monster: A Rock 'n' Roller's 12 Steps to Becoming a Golf Addict.* New York: Crown, 2007.

Cott, Jonathan, and Christine Doudna, eds. *The Ballad of John and Yoko.* Garden City, NJ: Doubleday, 1982.

Cott, Jonathan, ed. *Bob Dylan: The Essential Interviews.* New York: Wenner Books, 2006.

Crosby, David, with Carl Gottlieb. *Long Time Gone.* New York: Doubleday, 1988.

Cross, Charles R. *Room Full of Mirrors: A Biography of Jimi Hendrix.* New York: Hyperion, 2005.

Dalton, David, ed. *The Rolling Stones: The First Twenty Years.* New York: Alfred A. Knopf, 1981.

Davies, Hunter. *The Beatles* (Second Revised Edition). New York: McGraw-Hill, 1985.

Davis, Stephen. *Hammer of the Gods: The Led Zeppelin Saga.* New York: Ballantine, 1985.

Davis, Stephen. *Old Gods Almost Dead: The 40-Year Odyssey of the Rolling Stones.* New York: Broadway Books, 2001.

DeCurtis, Anthony, and James Henke, eds. *The Rolling Stone Illustrated History of Rock & Roll.* (Revised Edition) New York: Random House, 1992.

Densmore, John. *Riders on the Storm: My Life with Jim Morrison and the Doors.* New York: Delacorte Press, 1990.

Des Barres, Pamela. *I'm with the Band: Confessions of a Groupie* (Updated Edition). Chicago: Chicago Review Press, 2005.

Dylan, Bob. *Chronicles, Volume One.* New York: Simon & Schuster, 2004.

Echols, Alice. *Scars of Sweet Paradise: The Life and Times of Janis Joplin.* New York: Henry Holt, 1999.

Einarson, John. *Neil Young: Don't Be Denied—The Canadian Years.* Kingston, Ontario: Quarry Press, 1992.

Faithfull, Marianne, with David Dalton. *Faithfull: An Autobiography.* Boston: Little, Brown, 1994.

Fleetwood, Mick, with Stephen Davis. *Fleetwood: My Life and Adventures in Fleetwood Mac.* New York: William Morrow and Company, 1990.

Fletcher, Tony. *Moon: The Life and Death of a Rock Legend.* New York: Spike, 1998.

Gaar, Gillian G. *She's a Rebel: The History of Women in Rock & Roll.* Seattle: Seal Press, 1992.

Garbarini, Vic, and Brian Cullman. *Strawberry Fields Forever: John Lennon Remembered.* New York: Bantam, 1980.

Gillespie, Dizzy. *To Be or Not to Be-Bop: Memoirs.* New York: Doubleday, 1979.

Giuliano, Geoffrey. *Behind Blue Eyes: The Life of Pete Townshend.* New York: Dutton, 1996.

Giuliano, Geoffrey. *Blackbird: The Life and Times of Paul McCartney.* Toronto: McGraw-Hill Ryerson, 1991.

Harrison, George. *I Me Mine.* New York: Simon & Schuster, 1980.

Hart, Mickey, with Jay Stevens. *Drumming at the Edge of Magic: A Journey into the Spirit of Percussion.* San Francisco: Harper San Francisco, 1990.

Herman, Gary. *Rock 'n' Roll Babylon.* London: Plexus, 1994.

Hertsgaard, Mark. *A Day in the Life: The Music and Artistry of the Beatles.* New York: Delacorte, 1995.

Holt, Sid, ed. *The Rolling Stone Interviews: The 1980s.* New York: St. Martin's Press, 1989.

Hopkins, Jerry, and Danny Sugerman. *No One Here Gets Out Alive.*
New York: Warner, 1980.

Hoskyns, Barney. *Across the Great Divide: The Band and America.*
London: Pimlico, 2003.

Hoskyns, Barney. *Hotel California: The True-Life Adventures of
Crosby, Stills, Nash, Young* [...]. Hoboken, NJ: John Wiley & Sons,
2006.

Humphries, Patrick. *A Little Bit Funny: The Elton John Story.* London:
Aurum Press, 1998.

Jones, Lesley-Ann. *Freddie Mercury: The Definitive Biography.*
London: Hodder & Stoughton, 1997.

Kaliss, Jeff. *I Want to Take You Higher: The Life and Times of Sly and
the Family Stone.* New York: Backbeat, 2008.

Kennealy, Patricia. *Strange Days: My Life With and Without Jim
Morrison.* New York: Dutton, 1992.

Kureishi, Hanif, and Jon Savage, eds. *The Faber Book of Pop.* London:
Faber and Faber, 1995.

Larkin, Colin. *The Virgin Encyclopedia of Dance Music.* London:
Virgin in association with Muze UK, 1998.

Larkin, Colin. *The Virgin Encyclopedia of Reggae.* London: Virgin in
association with Muze UK, 1998.

Lemke, Gayle. *The Art of the Fillmore 1966–1971.* New York:
Thunder's Mouth Press, 1999.

Lendt, C. K. *Kiss and Sell: The Making of a Supergroup.* New York:
Billboard Books, 1997.

Lennon, Cynthia. *John.* London: Hodder & Stoughton, 2005.

Lesh, Phil. *Searching for the Sound: My Life with the Grateful Dead.*
New York: Little, Brown, 2005.

Levinson, Peter J. *Trumpet Blues: The Life of Harry James.* New York:
Oxford, 1999.

MacDonald, Ian. *Revolution in the Head: The Beatles' Records and the Sixties*. London: Pimlico, 1995.

Maggin, Donald L. *Stan Getz: A Life in Jazz*. New York: William Morrow, 1996.

Marley, Rita, with Hettie Jones. *No Woman No Cry: My Life with Bob Marley*. New York: Hyperion, 2004.

Marsh, Dave. *Born to Run: The Bruce Springsteen Story*. London: Omnibus, 1988.

Marsh, Dave, and Kevin Stein. *The Book of Rock Lists*. New York: Dell, 1984.

McCabe, Peter, and Robert D. Schonfeld. *John Lennon: For the Record*. New York: Bantam, 1984.

McDonough, Jimmy. *Shakey: Neil Young's Biography*. Toronto: Random House Canada, 2002.

Miles, Barry. *Paul McCartney: Many Years from Now*. London: Secker & Warburg, 1997.

Miles, Barry. *Zappa: A Biography*. New York: Grove Press, 2004.

Murray, Charles Shaar. *Crosstown Traffic: Jimi Hendrix and Post-War Pop*. London: Faber and Faber, 1989.

Nelson, Willie. *The Facts of Life and Other Dirty Jokes*. New York: Random House, 2002.

Norman, Philip. *Shout! The True Story of the Beatles*. London: Penguin, 1993.

Norman, Philip. *Symphony for the Devil: The Rolling Stones Story*. New York: Dell, 1984.

Olsen, Eric, with Paul Verna and Carlo Wolff. *The Encyclopedia of Record Producers*. New York: Watson-Guptill, 1999.

Osbourne, Ozzy and Sharon. *Ordinary People: Our Story*. New York: MTV Books, 2003.

Palmer, Robert. *The Rolling Stones*. Garden City, NJ: Doubleday, 1983.

Patoski, Joe Nick. *Willie Nelson: An Epic Life*. New York: Little,
    Brown, 2008.

Randolph, Mike: *The Rolling Stones' Rock and Roll Circus*. San
    Francisco: Chronicle, 1991.

Ritz, David. *Divided Soul: The Life of Marvin Gaye*. New York: Da
    Capo, 1991.

Rosen, Steven. *Black Sabbath*. London: Sanctuary, 2002.

Rosenthal, Elizabeth J. *His Song: The Musical Journey of Elton John*.
    New York: Billboard Books, 2001.

Sacks, Oliver. *Musicophilia: Tales of Music and the Brain*. Toronto:
    Alfred A. Knopf Canada, 2007.

Sandford, Christopher. *Springsteen: Point Blank*. New York: Da Capo,
    1999.

Santelli, Robert. *The Bob Dylan Scrapbook: 1956–1966*. New York:
    Simon & Schuster, 2005.

Scaduto, Anthony. *Bob Dylan: An Intimate Biography*. New York:
    Signet, 1973.

Schaffner, Nicholas. *The British Invasion: From the First Wave to the
    New Wave*. New York: McGraw-Hill, 1982.

Scully, Rock, with David Dalton. *Living with the Dead: Twenty Years
    on the Bus with Garcia and the Grateful Dead*. New York: Little,
    Brown, 1996.

Shapiro, Harry. *Waiting for the Man: The Story of Drugs and Popular
    Music*. London: Helter Skelter, 2003.

Sheff, David. *The Playboy Interviews with John Lennon & Yoko Ono*.
    New York: Berkley, 1982.

Slick, Grace, with Andrea Cagan. *Somebody to Love: A Rock-and-Roll
    Memoir*. New York: Warner Books, 1999.

Taylor, Derek. *It Was Twenty Years Ago Today: An Anniversary
    Celebration of 1967*. New York: Simon & Schuster, 1987.

Walker, Clinton. *Highway to Hell: The Life & Times of AC/DC Legend Bon Scott.* Portland, OR: Verse Chorus Press, 2001.

Wenner, Jann. *Lennon Remembers.* New York: Fawcett, 1972.

White, Timothy. *The Nearest Faraway Place: Brian Wilson, the Beach Boys, and the Southern California Experience.* New York: Henry Holt & Company, 1994.

White, Timothy. *Rock Lives: Profiles and Interviews.* New York: Henry Holt & Company, 1990.

Wilson, Brian, with Todd Gold. *Wouldn't It Be Nice: My Own Story.* New York: Harper Collins, 1991.

Wood, Ronnie. *Ronnie.* London: MacMillan, 2007.

Wyman, Bill. *Rolling with the Stones.* London: Dorling Kindersley, 2002.

Books: Culture and Drugs

20th Century Day by Day. New York: Dorling Kindersley, 2000.

Anonymous. *Go Ask Alice.* New York: Simon Pulse, 2006.

Berne, Emma Carlson. *Methamphetamine.* San Diego, CA: Reference Point Press, 2007.

Booth, Martin. *Cannabis: A History.* New York: St. Martin's Press, 2003.

Bugliosi, Vincent, with Curt Gentry. *Helter Skelter.* New York: Bantam, 1975.

Carroll, Will. *The Juice: The Real Story of Baseball's Drug Problems.* Chicago: Ivan R. Dee, 2005.

Castaneda, Carlos. *A Separate Reality: Further Conversations with Don Juan.* London: Penguin, 1973.

Cavett, Dick, and Christopher Porterfield. *Cavett.* New York: Bantam, 1975.

Davenport-Hines, Richard. *The Pursuit of Oblivion: A Global History of Narcotics, 1500–2000.* London: Weidenfeld & Nicolson, 2001.

Davidson, Keay. *Carl Sagan: A Life.* New York: John Wiley & Sons, 1999.

Davis, Patti. *The Way I See It.* New York: G. P. Putnam's Sons, 1992.

Edison, Mike. *I Have Fun Everywhere I Go: Savage Tales of Pot, Porn* [...]. New York: Faber and Faber, 2008.

Egendorf, Laura K. *Heroin.* San Diego: Reference Point Press, 2007.

Elliott, Emory, ed. *American Literature: A Prentice Hall Anthology.* Englewood Cliffs, NJ: Prentice Hall, 1991.

Evans, Mike. *The Beats: From Kerouac to Kesey, an Illustrated Journey Through the Beat Generation.* London: Running Press, 2007.

Gitlin, Todd. *The Sixties: Years of Hope, Days of Rage.* New York: Bantam, 1987.

Hersh, Seymour M. *The Dark Side of Camelot.* New York: Little, Brown, 1997.

Hoskyns, Barney. *Beneath the Diamond Sky: Haight-Ashbury, 1965–1970.* New York: Simon & Schuster Editions, 1997.

Huxley, Aldous. *The Doors of Perception / Heaven and Hell.* London: Flamingo, 1994.

Inglis, Brian. *The Forbidden Game: A Social History of Drugs.* London: Hodder and Stoughton, 1975.

Johnson, Haynes. *Sleepwalking Through History: America in the Reagan Years.* New York: W. W. Norton, 1991.

Karson, Jill. *Club Drugs.* San Diego: Reference Point Press, 2008.

Kelley, Kitty. *Nancy Reagan: The Unauthorized Biography.* New York: Simon & Schuster, 1991.

Kerouac, Jack. *On the Road.* London: Penguin, 1976.

King, Francis X. *Witchcraft and Demonology.* London: Hamlyn, 1987.

Langton, Jerry. *Iced: Crystal Meth: The Biography of North America's Deadliest New Plague.* Toronto: Key Porter, 2007.

Leamer, Laurence. *Make-Believe: The Story of Nancy and Ronald Reagan.* New York: Harper and Row, 1983.

Love, Robert, ed. *The Best of Rolling Stone: 25 Years of Journalism on the Edge.* New York: Doubleday, 1993.

Marcovitz, Hal. *Marijuana.* Farmington Hills, MI: Lucent Books, 2007.

Margolis, Jack S., and Richard Clorfene. *A Child's Garden of Grass.* New York: Ballantine, 1984.

McCage, Crystal. *Hallucinogens.* San Diego: Reference Point Press, 2008.

McLuhan, Marshall. *Understanding Media: The Extensions of Man.* Toronto: Signet, 1969.

Miles, Barry. *Jack Kerouac: King of the Beats: A Portrait.* London: Virgin, 1998.

Mills, Hilary. *Mailer: A Biography.* New York: Empire Books, 1982.

Nakaya, Andrea C. *Marijuana.* San Diego: Reference Point Press, 2007.

Noriega, Manuel, with Peter Eisner. *America's Prisoner.* New York: Random House, 1997.

Nuwer, Hank. *Sports Scandals.* New York: Franklin Watts, 1994.

Roszak, Theodore. *The Cult of Information: A Neo-Luddite Treatise on High-Tech, Artificial Intelligence, and the True Art of Thinking.* Berkeley: University of California Press, 1994.

Sabljak, Mark, and Martin H. Greenberg. *Sports Babylon: Sex, Drugs, and Other Dirty Dealings in the World of Sports.* New York: Bell Publishing Company, 1988.

Schlosser, Eric. *Reefer Madness: Sex, Drugs, and Cheap Labor in the American Black Market.* New York: Houghton Mifflin, 2003.

Swarts, Katherine, ed. *Club Drugs.* Farmington Hills, MI: Thomson-Gale, 2006.

Trudeau, Margaret. *Beyond Reason.* London: Paddington Press, 1979.

Thurman, Robert A. F., trans. *The Tibetan Book of the Dead.* New York: Bantam, 1994.

Will, George F. *Suddenly: The American Idea Abroad and at Home, 1986–1990.* New York: The Free Press, 1990.

Wolfe, Tom. *The Electric Kool-Aid Acid Test.* New York: Bantam, 1969.

Magazine and Newspaper Articles: Music

"Classic Rock Rules" (Interview Selections). *Guitar World*, October 1993: 32–56.

Berkowitz, Kenny. "Pickin' for a Fight." *Acoustic Guitar*, September 2006: 52–60.

Browne, David. "Kiss This: After 20 Years . . ." *Entertainment Weekly*, June 19, 1992: 28–33.

Budofsky, Adam. "Playback: Pink Floyd's Nick Mason—Writing Music History." *Modern Drummer*, July 2005: 112–115.

Cartwright, Gary. "Willie at 65." *Texas Monthly*, April 1998: 98–107.

Colapinto, John. "Rock & Roll: Heroin." *Rolling Stone*, May 30, 1996: 15–60.

DeCurtis, Anthony. "Don Henley & Glenn Frey" (Interview). *Rolling Stone*, September 20, 1990: 157–159.

Epstein, Dan. "Black Magic." *Guitar World*, July 2001: 62–97.

Evans, Rush. "Mood Elevator: The Long Strange Trip of Roky Erickson." *Goldmine*, September 14, 2007: 37–42.

Fricke, David. "Iggy Pop" (Interview). *Rolling Stone*, April 19, 2007: 56–57.

Fricke, David. "Life in the Slow Lane." *Rolling Stone*, June 22, 2000: 90–144.

Fricke, David. "Syd Barrett, 1946–2006." *Rolling Stone*, August 10, 2006: 29–30.

Gates, David. "Requiem for the Dead." *Newsweek*, August 21, 1995: 46–53.

Gilmore, Mikal. "The Madness and Majesty of Pink Floyd." *Rolling Stone*, April 5, 2007: 54–79.

Gliatto, Tom. "Papa's Odyssey: John Phillips' Dreamin' Became a Drug-Addled Nightmare Before a Recovery Too Quickly Cut Short." *People*, April 2, 2001: 62–64.

Graff, Gary. "Woodstock Music and Art Fair." *Guitar World*, June 1999: 78–79.

Harris, John. "Thirty Years of Darkness." *Rolling Stone*, May 15, 2003: 45–49.

Herdegaard, Erik. "Joe Walsh Rides Again." *Rolling Stone*, August 24, 2006: 70–75.

Hiatt, Brian. "Billy Preston, 1946–2006." *Rolling Stone*, June 29, 2006: 10.

Jisi, Chris. "After the Thunder: John Entwistle, 1944–2002." *Bass Player*, September 2002: 46–54.

Kot, Greg. "Jack Nitzsche, 1937–2000." *Rolling Stone*, October 12, 2000: 38.

Newman, Melinda. "Aerosmith" (Interview). *Billboard*, August 15, 1998: A-3.

Nugent, Ted. "The Importance of Nuge-itality." *Men's Health*, July 1999: 132.

Paul, Alan. "Miller Lite." *Guitar World*, October 1993: 21–27, 168.

Rotondi, James. "Sunshine Supermen: Britain's Psychedelic Guitar Wizards." *Guitar Player*, February 1997: 86–102.

Schruers, Fred. "Back on the Chain Gang." *Rolling Stone*, October 30,
    1997: 32–41.

Sheffield, Rob. "Aerosmith." *Rolling Stone*, April 26, 2001: 40–44.

Sischy, Ingrid. "Focus, Thy Name is Lou." *Interview*, May 1998: 90–95.

Teeman, Tim. "I Couldn't Bear to See Freddie Wasting Away." The
    (London) *Times*, September 7, 2006: 8.

Thompson, Art. "Call of the Wild: Ted Nugent Shoots to Kill on
    'Craveman.'" *Guitar Player*, December 2002: 68–78.

Tolinski, Brad. "Flying High Again." *Guitar World*, January 2008:
    70–106.

Tolinski, Brad. "Now That's Entertainment!" *Guitar World*, January
    2008: 80.

Uhelszki, Jaan. "Lynyrd Skynyrd: A Southern Ghost Story." *Guitar
    Legends # 106*, 22–30.

Uhelszki, Jaan. "The Making of 'I Wanna Be Your Dog' by the
    Stooges." *Uncut*, September 2008: 48–50.

Waddell, Ray. "25 Years Later, Skynryd Tragedy Haunts Survivors."
    Billboard, October 19, 2002: 1, 82.

Waddell, Ray. "Skynryd's Wryte Stuff." *Billboard*, December 5, 1998:
    LS 8–27.

Waddell, Ray. "Waters Revisits the 'Dark Side.'" *Billboard*, May 13,
    2006: 12.

Wenner, Jann S. "Jagger Remembers." *Rolling Stone*, December 14,
    1995: 49–72.

Wild, D. "The Soul of a New Machine." *Rolling Stone*, October 31,
    1991: 74–79.

Magazine and Newspaper Articles: Culture and Drugs

"Victor Maymudes" (Obituary). *The New York Times*, February 1,
    2001: 7.

The Best of High Times, Volume One, 1982: passim.

Buckley, William F. "The War on Drugs Is Lost" (Forum). *National Review*, February 12, 1996.

Glaister, Dan. "Marijuana Law Goes Up in Smoke." *The Guardian*, August 11, 2008: 17.

Goldberg, Jonah. "Ozzy Without Harriet: What *The Osbournes* Tells Us About Drugs." *National Review*, June 17, 2002.

Knopper, Steve. "Al Aronowitz." *Rolling Stone*, September 8, 2005: 40.

Leibovitz, Annie. "Annie Gets Her Shot." *Vanity Fair*, October 2008: 350–402.

Samuels, David. "Dr. Kush." *The New Yorker*, July 28, 2008: 48–61.

Schoemer, Karen. "Rockers, Models, and the New Allure of Heroin." *Newsweek*, August 26, 1996: 50–55.

Videos/DVDs

The Beatles Anthology. Apple, 1995.

Black Sabbath: The Last Supper. Epic, 1997.

Bob Dylan—Don't Look Back. New Video Group, 2007 (originally 1965).

The Decline of Western Civilization II: The Metal Years. Sony Pictures, 1987.

Gimme Shelter. Criterion, 2000 (originally 1970).

Grass. Home Vision Entertainment, 2000.

Help! United Artists, 1965.

The Kids Are Alright. Pioneer, 2003 (originally 1979).

The Last Waltz. MGM, 1978.

Led Zeppelin: The Song Remains the Same. Warner Home Video, 2008 (originally 1976).

Monterey Pop. Criterion, 2006 (originally 1967).

No Direction Home: Bob Dylan. Apple, 2005.

Pink Floyd Live at Pompeii. Hip-O Records, 2003 (originally 1972).

Reefer Madness. Motion Picture Ventures, 2002 (originally 1936).

Woodstock: 3 Days of Peace & Music. Warner Home Video, 1997 (originally 1970).

Internet

www.blacklistedjournalist.com

www.hightimes.com

www.norml.org

Blown Speakers, Blown Minds: A Druggy Discography

Because the experience of taking psychotropic drugs is so subjective, depending on both the taker and the drug, there neither is nor should be a firm definition of "drug music." A performance or recording by any artist of any song from any genre can assume a greater potency to a chemically enhanced listener; likewise, the mental state of the composer or player, whether cold sober or blissfully delirious, will not always be obviously reflected in the final work.

Nonetheless, there are many records from the 1960s and '70s whose continued influence has made them inextricable from the drug culture, either due to their popularity as accessories to the enjoyment of cannabis or acid, or the public reputation (and legal convictions) of the musicians who created them, or both. The list offered here is therefore not "The Greatest Rock Records of All Time," though some of these would certainly meet any critical standard as such, nor does it consist of "The Most Psychedelic Records Ever Made," though again, many of the following would qualify. Instead the albums cited are those with the strongest historical links to the expanding drug scene of the period 1964 to 1980 and most linked with recreational and addictive substance of all kinds. The author and publisher assume no responsibility for any results that may occur while playing selections from this catalogue, and advise them to be heard only in consultation with experienced advisers or cool friends.

Aerosmith

Toys In the Attic

Rocks

Whiplash hard rock courtesy of the Toxic Twins, Steve Tyler and Joe Perry. You can almost hear the lines being chopped on "Nobody's Fault" and "Round and Round."

The Beach Boys

Smiley Smile

Lots of great singles came from the California harmonists, but this album, Brian Wilson's last, self-destructive bid to top Lennon and Mc-Cartney, reflects his and the group's evolution from surf and sun to pot and pills. Contains the luminous "Good Vibrations."

The Beatles

Rubber Soul

Revolver

Sgt. Pepper's Lonely Hearts Club Band

The Fabs rising to their drug-abetted peak. Certified masterpieces in any condition, but virtual revelations for tokers and trippers in '65, '66, and '67 and still packing a head-twist today.

Big Brother and the Holding Company

Cheap Thrills

Southern Comfort psychedelia from the tortured mistress of white girls' blues. Highlights: "Piece of My Heart," the cover of Gershwin's "Summertime," and the Monterey showstopper "Ball and Chain."

Black Sabbath

Master of Reality

Vol. 4

Most Sabbath discs are distinctly "drug records," but these two, from 1971 and 1972, respectively, are among their most explicit. "Sweet Leaf" and "Snowblind" remain anthems of cannabis and cocaine.

David Bowie

Diamond Dogs

Young Americans

Ziggy with Zig-Zags and the Thin White Duke getting thinner and whiter.

The Byrds

Mr. Tambourine Man

Electrified Dylan covers from Crosby, McGuinn, and Co. defined folk-rock, and the fish-eyed cover shot was an early glimpse of acid imagery.

Cheech & Chong

Cheech & Chong's Greatest Hit

Collection of the duo's best-known routines, like "Dave" and "Let's Make a New Dope Deal." Amusing enough when straight, comic genius when stoned. Go figure.

Eric Clapton

Layla and Other Assorted Love Songs (as Derek and the Dominos)

461 Ocean Boulevard

Slowhand

Not so much drug albums as albums by a man descending into and then emerging from devastating drug addiction, though "Bell Bottom Blues," "I Shot the Sheriff," and "Cocaine" are unmistakable songs of indulgence and dependence.

Cream
Disraeli Gears
"Strange Brew" and "Tales of Brave Ulysses" are wah-wah-what psychedelic guitar and lyrics were all about.

Crosby, Stills, and Nash
Crosby, Stills, and Nash
From the group originally called the Frozen Noses, these three superstars set the standards for record industry wealth and hedonism; this debut is also a fine record of idyllic vocals, delicate acoustic guitar, and sensitive lyrics.

Donovan
Sunshine Superman
Heavy mellow from the original wizard of English hippie whimsy.

The Doobie Brothers
The Captain and Me
The name of the band says it all.

The Doors
The Doors
Strange Days
Waiting for the Sun

All the Doors' records could stand as artifacts of the rock-and-drugs epoch, but their first three, with "Light My Fire," "People Are Strange," and "Not to Touch the Earth," are quintessential psychedelia as well as the living legacy of the late great Mr. Mojo Risin'.

Bob Dylan
Bringing It All Back Home
Highway 61 Revisited
Blonde on Blonde
The former Robert Zimmerman wired on speed, chilling on weed, and making history. Everybody must get stoned.

The Eagles
The Eagles
Hotel California
Blue-jeaned longhairs hit the big time, trading mushrooms and a lid of homegrown for premium flake—the rise and fall of the West Coast counterculture is told herein.

Emerson, Lake and Palmer
Brain Salad Surgery
Impenetrable progressive rock for university dorms well past curfew. The cover by H. R. Giger complements the classical-surreal dimensions of the music.

Fleetwood Mac
Rumours
The Big One. A landmark, multiplatinum document of relationships, self-awareness, and coke-boosted sophistication. Smooth as a mirror and gleaming like a silver spoon.

Funkadelic

Funkadelic

Deadly stoner R&B, like Jimi Hendrix in slow motion. What is soul? Soul is a joint rolled in toilet paper. Mommy, what's a Funkadelic? Eddie Hazel's guitar.

The Grateful Dead

Workingman's Dead

American Beauty

Live Dead

The ex-Warlocks were synonymous with drugged-out rock music and musicians throughout their history, and their long strange trip is perhaps best depicted by these discs, although many will contend the band's real impact was made not in the studio but on stage. Marin County bluegrass that's vibrant like a new batch of Owsley, and sweeter than Cherry Garcia. *Live Dead* was mixed with the players taking hits of nitrous oxide at the studio console.

Merle Haggard

Greatest Hits

The poet of the workingman has numerous compilations to choose from, but anything containing "Okie from Muskogee," "The Fightin' Side of Me," and "Silver Wings" will do. Wise and ironic correctives to San Franciscan self-satisfaction from a man who's been there and back; would bring out the redneck in Gore Vidal.

Jimi Hendrix

Are You Experienced

Axis: Bold as Love

Electric Ladyland

The three "official" albums of Jimi's career are required listening for musicians and highly recommended for heads—the catalogue offered in this trio, including "Purple Haze," "Are You Experienced," "If Six Was Nine," "One Rainy Wish," and "Voodoo Chile (Slight Return)," are as trippy and as good as it gets.

Iron Butterfly
In-a-Gadda-da-Vida
Hypnotic and soporific precursor to heavy metal can still render immobility in the vulnerable.

The Jefferson Airplane
Surrealistic Pillow
After Bathing at Baxter's
Volunteers
The Airplane at maximum altitude, taking its audience along for the ride. Radio classics like "Somebody to Love" and "White Rabbit," plus deeper agitprop cuts like "We Can Be Together."

Led Zeppelin
Led Zeppelin IV
Presence
No strangers to hard partying over their entire career, Zeppelin is at their most positive on these discs ("Misty Mountain Hop," "Going to California") and negative ("For Your Life," "Nobody's Fault But Mine") in their doped-up and coked-out outlook. Awesome albums by any measure, even more so considering their backstory.

Love
Forever Changes

1967 cult gem from Arthur Lee's influential LA act, with numbers like "You Set the Scene" and "Bummer in the Summer," is today regarded as a high point of psychedelia.

Lynyrd Skynyrd
Second Helping
Southern-fried rock by fried Southern rockers boasts "The Needle and the Spoon," "Workin' for MCA," and the deathless Neil Young rejoinder "Sweet Home Alabama."

The MC5
Back in the USA
Committed freaks' and Detroit druggies' charged proto-punk.

The Mamas and the Papas
Greatest Hits
John Phillips's coed choir of Laurel Canyon beautiful people made some of the loveliest and most subtly subversive pop of the mid-'60s; any anthology with "California Dreamin'," "Monday, Monday," and "Dream a Little Dream of Me" will light up a hazy afternoon.

Bob Marley/the Wailers
Live!
Burnin'
Exodus
There's a Caribbean boatload of material to choose from, but this trio presents a choice sample of Bob's most potent strains. The amount of marijuana consumed worldwide while listening to "Get Up, Stand Up," "No Woman No Cry," "Three Little Birds," et al, is incalculable—so is the amount of marijuana consumed while making them.

Moby Grape

Moby Grape

Nineteen sixty-seven debut by one of the seminal San Francisco acts; overshadowed by bigger names and bigger sellers, but a fitting companion to the Dead and the Airplane.

The Moody Blues

In Search of the Lost Chord

Days of Future Passed

Original prog rockers scored big with "Nights in White Satin," "Ride My See-Saw," and other brain blasts—Salvador Dalî in stereo.

Willie Nelson

Red Headed Stranger

The chief outlaw's first concept album reflected his newly open affinity for the styles of the hippie movement, sprinkled with his own Texan individualism and taste for loco weed. Features "Blue Eyes Crying in the Rain" and the beautiful instrumental "Bandera."

Pink Floyd

The Piper at the Gates of Dawn

A Saucerful of Secrets

Meddle

Dark Side of the Moon

Wish You Were Here

With the Grateful Dead, the rock band most associated with drug use on the part of members (especially founder Syd Barrett) and fans. Hard to find anything spacier than "Echoes," "Astronomy Domine," "Interstellar Overdrive," "Set the Controls For the Heart of the Sun," or any comedowns more languorous than "Breathe," "Time," or "Wish You Were Here." Essential.

Lou Reed

Transformer

Take a walk on the wild side. A sleazy and strung-out travelogue of the dank urban undergrounds where the other sex-and-drug revolution went down.

The Rolling Stones

Let It Bleed

Sticky Fingers

Exile on Main Street

Goats Head Soup

The Stones at their most stoned, during a near-lethal run of inspiration, fornication, and intoxication from 1969 to 1973. They were never this bad or this good before or since; no one has who's lived to tell the tale. Listen to all these in one sitting and you'll need a blood change yourself.

Rush

2112

Sui generis progressive hard rock from the long-lived Canadian power trio; many a leaf besides maples were unfurled on the sleeve of this one.

Santana

Abraxas

Latin blues acid rock guitar enters the sublime realms of "Oye Como Va," "Samba Ta Pi," and "Black Magic Woman."

Sly and the Family Stone

Stand!

There's a Riot Goin' On

Back-to-back peaks of the Family's run, showing off sunny psychedelic soul on the former and trance-inducing funk on the latter. Sly Stone has never recovered from these.

Soundtracks

Easy Rider

The Harder They Come

Woodstock

Don't Bogart That Joint, my friend—You Can Make It If You Really Want, so Draw Your Brakes, The Pusher and I Want to Take You Higher before we hear The Star-Spangled Banner.

Peter Tosh

Legalize It

Enough said.

Various

Nuggets: Original Artyfacts from the First Psychedelic Era

Celebrated compilation of garage and DIY acid rock has strobe light faves like "Psychotic Reaction" and "I Had Too Much to Dream (Last Night)."

The Velvet Underground and Nico

The Velvet Underground

An avant-garde obscurity upon its release in 1967, this has since been lauded as one of the most influential rock records ever made. Graphic tracks like "Waiting for the Man," "Run Run Run," and "Heroin" put it at the forefront of the drug music canon.

The Who
Meaty Beaty Big and Bouncy
Remains the best collection of 1960s Who singles; "My Generation," "I Can See for Miles," "The Seeker," and "Magic Bus" were some of the boldest portrayals of drug sensations laid down from the era.

Yes
Fragile
A close rival to Pink Floyd in the art rock sphere, Yes were at their most commercial and most ornate with "Roundabout," "Heart of the Sunrise," and Steve Howe's guitar instrumental "Mood for a Day." Pretentious in retrospect, but a cosmic revelation in the black-lighted rec rooms of 1972.

Neil Young
Everybody Knows This Is Nowhere
Harvest
After the Gold Rush
Tonight's the Night
Almost the personification of the philosophical dope smoker, Bernard Shakey made candid and authentic music that is some of the most emblematic texts of the drug culture: "Down by the River," "Don't Let It Bring You Down," "The Needle and the Damage Done, "Tired Eyes," "Roll Another Number (for the Road)." These are the serene, pastoral highs and despairing interior lows of tuning in, turning on, and dropping out.

Pot get you high (Wheee)
Cop bring you down (Oooh)
Pot love your chick (Mmmm)
Cop scare your dick (Owww)
Pot do no harm (!)
Judge break your arm (!)
Pot should be free (Yeah)
Sun shine on me (Yeah)

ABBIE HOFFMAN

"THE ACTUAL EXPERIENCE OF THE SMOKED HERB HAS BEEN CLOUDED BY A FOG OF UNRESPECTABILITY BY THE UNTHINKING, UNKNOLEGABLE FEW WHO HAVE NOT SMOKED THEM- SELVES AND YET INSIST UPON SETTING THEMSELVES UP AS CENTR- ES OF PROPAGANDA ABOUT THE SAID EXPERIENCE."

ALLEN GINSBERG.